DEC 0 9 2013

The Curve

NICHOLAS LOVELL

THE CURVE

How Smart Companies Find

High-Value Customers

PORTFOLIO/PENGUIN

PORTFOLIO / PENGUIN
Published by the Penguin Group
Penguin Group (USA) LLC
375 Hudson Street
New York, New York 10014

USA I Canada I UK I Ireland I Australia I New Zealand I India I South Africa I China
penguin.com
A Penguin Random House Company

First published by Portfolio / Penguin, a member of Penguin Group (USA) LLC, 2013

ISBN: 978-1-59184-663-5
Printed in the United States of America

1   3   5   7   9   10   8   6   4   2

To Catherine, Alasdair and Lucy

Contents

Preface   ix

1. The Curve   1
2. Scarcity and Abundance   26
3. Competition, Economics and a Man Called Bertrand   38
4. Everything, Just for You   51
5. The Tyranny of the Physical   65
6. What's it Worth?   87
7. Freeloaders   104
8. Gawkers   113
9. Superfans   128
10. The Power of the Crowd   137
11. Make-it-Yourself   151
12. We're All Retailers Now   166
13. Harnessing the Curve   189
Epilogue: The Curve Redux   218

Acknowledgements   220
Notes   223
Bibliography   233
Index   235

Preface

'Steal it. Steal away. Steal, steal and steal some more and give it to all your friends and keep on stealing, because one way or another these mother fuckers will get it through their head that they're ripping people off and that's not right.'[1]

The words of an anarchist? A member of the Pirate Party? No, those are the words of Trent Reznor, the front man of Nine Inch Nails, an industrial rock band that released its first album, *Pretty Hate Machine*, in 1989. By 2007, at a gig in Sydney, here was Reznor exhorting his fans to steal his music and calling his record label 'greedy fucking assholes'.

How did it come to this, and how did Reznor expect to make money if his fans were all downloading his music for free?

Reznor grew up in rural Pennsylvania, a place where 'there was nothing going on but the cornfields'.[2] Music was his outlet and he started playing the piano at the age of five. At high school, he played tenor saxophone and tuba in the jazz and marching bands. Reznor's musical accomplishments are not limited to piano and brass: the instruments he plays include guitar, piano, synthesizer, Mellotron, keyboards, bass guitar, saxophone, cello, double bass, drums, tuba, sousaphone, harmonium, marimba, pan flute, harpsichord and vibraphone.[3]

Despite his musical abilities, Reznor chose to study computer engineering at Allegheny College, but dropped out after a year to move to Cleveland with the intention of becoming a full-time musician.[4] His break came when he got a job at Cleveland's Right Track Studio as an assistant engineer and janitor. Studio owner Bart Koster was impressed by Reznor's work ethic and intensity: 'He is so focused in everything he does. When that guy waxed the floor, it looked great.'[5] Reznor asked if he could use the studio to record demo tracks himself. 'How could I possibly stand in this guy's way?' said Koster, interviewed in 1995. 'It wasn't costing me anything, just a little wear on my tape heads.'

Reznor had found a recording studio. The trouble was that he couldn't find musicians willing to work between 3 a.m. and 8 a.m., without pay. So he did what any self-respecting, driven perfectionist would do. He decided to play all of the instruments himself.[6] After all, he reasoned, it had worked for Prince.

It worked for Reznor, too. He soon signed with TVT Records and released the Nine Inch Nails' debut album, *Pretty Hate Machine*.[7] It sold a million copies, and TVT put pressure on Reznor to create another commercial success. In a pattern that was to be repeated throughout Reznor's career, and would ultimately lead to his split from the traditional record-label system, Reznor resisted this interference in the creative direction of Nine Inch Nails, leading to a vicious court battle.

Eventually, Reznor broke with TVT and signed to the Interscope label, releasing the EP *Broken* in 1992. Over the next decade, Reznor's music career followed an almost clichéd path: huge success with *The Downward Spiral*, a long period of drug-fuelled writer's block and successful collaborations with, amongst others, singer Marilyn Manson, film director Oliver Stone on *Natural Born Killers* and game developer id Software on *Quake*.

Reznor's relationships with record labels had been fractious in his early days, and they came to a head over the prices that Interscope's parent company, Universal Music, charged for his albums in Australia. In an interview with Music 2.0, Reznor said:

Year Zero is selling for $34.99 Australian dollars ($29.10 US). No wonder people steal music. Avril Lavigne's record in the same store was $21.99 ($18.21 US). By the way, when I asked a label rep about this, his response was: 'It's because we know you have a real core audience that will pay whatever it costs when you put something out – you know, true fans. It's the pop stuff we have to discount to get people to buy.' So, I guess as a reward for being a 'true fan' you get ripped off.[8]

That's when Reznor exhorted his astonished fans to steal his music. It was also when he started to look for an alternative way to make money from recorded music.

Reznor was very familiar with digital technology. Not only had he studied computer engineering before dropping out, he was an avid gamer with a love of technology. Nine Inch Nails had experimented with a technology-heavy viral marketing campaign for his *Year Zero* album in 2007. Fans attending his concerts found USB keys in the toilets. They contained new songs but also a noisy audio file that, when run through a spectrum analyser, drew an audio wave in the shape of a phone number.*

The phone numbers led to answering machines offering conspiracy theories. Fans found other fake websites strewn across the internet. Before long, internet forums and wikis emerged to debate the messages and theories, culminating in the release of *Year Zero* in April.

Reznor's technology know-how, his dislike of the label system and the emergence of the internet as a viable distribution channel all culminated, in 2008, in a perhaps inevitable outcome. Reznor split with Interscope Records and formed his own label. His next musical release was a perfect example of how an artist could harness the power of the internet to make a financial success of an album that he gave away for free.

Ghosts I–IV is a thirty-six-track instrumental industrial rock album. In fact, it's more like four nine-track albums released as one. Reznor decided from the beginning to offer his album at a variety of price points.

Ghosts I he released for free as a digital download. Anyone could download it from his website in return for an email address. Reznor went one step further. He wanted to maximize his potential audience and to do so, he chose to upload *Ghosts I* to filesharing sites such as BitTorrent and The Pirate Bay.

The full version, *Ghosts I–IV*, was released as a digital album for $5. Of course, many fans already knew how to get this for free from

---

* I am in awe of the fans who decided to run this file through a spectrum analyser to see what they could find.

filesharing sites, where the content would appear as soon as the album was released, but Reznor offered his fans an 'honesty box' where they could give him money if they wanted to. There was also a traditional physical CD for $10 and a Deluxe Edition for $75, but Reznor's brilliance lay in his $300 Ultra-Deluxe edition.

The Ultra-Deluxe Edition contained a four-LP set of *Ghosts I–IV* on 180-gram vinyl and three embossed, fabric-bound hardcover books in a large fabric slipcase. Each Ultra-Deluxe Edition was numbered and signed by Trent personally. Only 2,500 were produced. They were limited to one per customer.

Reznor sold every single Ultra-Deluxe Edition in less than thirty hours, grossing $750,000. In the first week, his record sales were worth $1.6 million.[9] Yet he gave his content away for free and showed his fans how to find it on filesharing networks that would inevitably carry his entire album within hours of it being released.

Reznor is a trailblazer who has shown us how the transition from analogue to digital has destroyed our preconceptions about the mass market, pricing and the dangers of free.

Businesses of all kinds are under threat from digital and the trend towards a price of zero. The real threat is not piracy; it is competition. When people like Reznor figure out how to give their product or creation away for free and still make more than enough money to keep them in business, it becomes much harder to keep existing price points and ways of trading.

The challenge of the twenty-first century is this: sharing is easy but finding an audience is hard. Consumers expect more and more for free, yet the creation of the products they want is expensive. How can we afford to make the stuff that our audience and customers crave?

The solution is to flip your thinking. To focus not on finding the biggest possible audience but to seek out the superfans who love what you do. To use the cheap distribution of the internet to start the process of connecting with fans – and then craft products, services and artistic creations for which they will pay lots of money.

The twenty-first century will be about relationships, about variable pricing, and about the ending of the tyranny of the physical.

Welcome to the Curve.

1
THE CURVE

The Curve is a new way of doing business, making art or running a not-for-profit organization. It focuses on building connections with real people and finding ways to encourage or let them spend money on products, services and experiences they value. It encompasses musicians trying to make a living in an era of widespread casual piracy, charities trying to find new ways to attract donations from a technology-savvy population and a miller trying to sell premium flour to a discerning audience of at-home bakers. The Curve connects the disciplines of marketing and sales with a sprinkling of technology to offer a better way of doing business in a connected world.

The Curve comes in three parts: 1) find your audience; 2) use all the tools at your disposal to figure out what is important to them; 3) let them spend anything from a little to lots (and I do mean lots) of money on things they truly value.

Finding an audience or customer base has always been an important part of any business. The discipline of marketing has evolved over the past two centuries to address that challenge. In the last thirty years, a new tool has emerged to change the rules. The internet has made it possible to share information and ideas globally in a way that was previously unfathomable. On the one hand, this has led to a wave of casual piracy and filesharing that has reduced the revenues of the recorded music industry from $14.6 billion in 1999 to $6.3 billion in 2009, a drop of $8.3 billion in annual revenue.[1] On the other, it has seen an explosion of new content reaching new audiences, whether that is the 100 million views that independent musician Alex Day has garnered on YouTube, the 80 million registered users of free online game *DarkOrbit* or the 25,000 users who subscribe to Home Depot's series of practical do-it-yourself videos.

This book posits the theory that free stuff – whether pirated, part of a marketing budget or given away by businesses or creators – is the starting point in a relationship with customers or audiences. It doesn't even have to be free: Nespresso coffee machines, Canon inkjet printers, Sony PlayStations and Gillette razors are all sold at low or negative margins and make their money from the ongoing relationship they have built with their customers. While the razor-and-razor-blades model is long established, this book argues that most companies don't go far enough in understanding their audience and focusing on moving low-spending customers along the demand curve – while also identifying the superfans who will be the backbone of their business.

The long battle to fight free content will prove to be pointless, although there is logic in not jumping to a free price point faster than necessary. It will be pointless not because the pirates will win but because the competition will start to discover how to use free more effectively. It will figure out how to use the Curve to give something away to attract an audience and make money from that audience somewhere else in the value chain. The real disruptive threat comes from competition, not piracy.

In the short term, not going free may well be very successful. Artists like the Eagles, the Rolling Stones, the Beatles and Pink Floyd can keep their music away from streaming services like Spotify or Pandora and away from YouTube in order to protect their value. They can continue to sell albums, memorabilia and, in some cases, live tours, to an audience of baby boomers who discovered their music on the radio, through word of mouth or by copying music to cassette tape.

What they won't be doing is finding new generations of fans. The audiences who will grow up, get jobs, earn money and start spending that money on experiences and physical artefacts they truly value. A record label pursuing this strategy is like a hidebound oil exploitation business that owns an oilfield and is pumping out the oil using techniques developed in a different era. It is not an exploration business, seeking out new reserves, and neither is it embracing new techniques to extend the life cycle of its existing resources.

The Curve says that most people in the world want to pay nothing or very little for what you offer. Statistically, amongst the 7 billion humans on the planet, demand for your offering is a rounding error. Fixating on the challenges and opportunities at the low price points is a mistake anchored in twentieth-century thinking, focused on the wrong scarcities and held in place by the tyranny of the physical.

In this book, I will argue that the era of the mass market is ending and the tyranny of the physical is eroding. That the web has enabled businesses and creators to make one-to-one connections with their customers and audiences. That smart businesses and creators will focus on allowing their biggest fans and best customers to spend lots of money on things they truly value. I will describe games businesses where players spend tens of thousands of dollars on a single game and Kickstarter campaigns where 15 per cent of the supporters generate half the income.

Many people are trapped in a world view that sees price as being fixed, and where the only way to make more money is to increase the volume of products or services sold. But things have changed. We now live in a world where it is cost effective to offer customers products at very different price points. Successful businesses, creators and non-profits will stop thinking in terms of units sold or number of donors and instead start thinking about average revenue per user. Artists and creators will learn how to connect with their fans, to provide them with context for their spending and to allow those fans to become part of the journey of creation. They will still be able to finance their art, even as they give it away for free.

We will see how the concept of value is changing. In the developed world where consumer goods are as accessible and as cheap as they have ever been, companies need to compete on something other than price. I will show how value is rooted in evolutionary psychology as a means of self-expression within a social context. I will show where value lies and how you can create it through a careful application of the Curve.

Finally, I will explain how technology is the glue that holds this together. The web has enabled customers and fans to have one-to-one connections with the companies and artists they patronize. A smart organization will use this connection to allow their customers and fans to spend as much as they want – a figure that is probably much higher than you think. Customer Relationship Management (CRM), analytics, behavioural modelling and other technologies are a key part of being a successful Curve organization.

Many companies, creators and charities are already using many of the ideas and concepts outlined in this book. Yet many of them are not connecting the disparate elements of the Curve into a single philosophy that finds users, understands them, and lets them spend wildly varying amounts of money. The Curve joins the dots, and offers a hopeful message: the downward pressure of free competition is inevitable and nothing to fear. Smart organizations will use free to lay a solid foundation on which to build, making money and delighting their biggest fans in the process. They will harness the Curve.

To show how the Curve can work, let's go back to Trent Reznor's experiment and consider how he could have released *Ghosts I–IV* in a pre-digital age. Downloads didn't exist, but he could still have offered the standard CD at $10, the Deluxe Edition for $75 and the Ultra-Deluxe for $300.

The big problem would have been distribution. Every music store in the world might stock the standard CD, but where to send the 2,500 Ultra-Deluxe Editions. Would Londoners buy fifty copies? How many should record stores in San Francisco get? Were there significantly more fans in Cleveland, where Reznor first got his big break?

Reznor, or his label, would have had to judge where to send the premium items. In some cases, they would guess right, and the Ultra-Deluxe Edition would fly off the shelves, but in others the fabric slipcases would moulder in the stockroom, gathering dust and falling in value until a manager put them in a bargain bin to make way for new stock.

With the emergence of the internet, such problems have been eliminated. Reznor was able to sell his Ultra-Deluxe Editions directly to fans from the Nine Inch Nails' website with no intermediaries. It didn't matter whether his fans were in Tulsa, Tonbridge or Toulouse, they could find the Nine Inch Nails website and pay their $300.

The challenge was to make sure that these fans knew about the music. The free download of *Ghosts I* and the inevitable piracy of *Ghosts I–IV* were a marketing channel that enabled Reznor to find and communicate with the 2,500 fans who were prepared to spend $300 on his Ultra-Deluxe Edition and the thousands more who liked his music enough to buy the physical or digital versions he offered from his site.

It did more than that, though. Reznor was trying to persuade his biggest fans to spend $300. He needed to make sure that they felt they had received value for their money. Some of that value appeared in the extra content: the books, the artwork and so on. Some of it was in the production values: glossy printing and fancy covers. Some of it was in the scarcity value: only 2,500 copies, each autographed by Reznor. All of these additional elements of value, however, make most sense in a social context. Reznor created value by widening the awareness of his music as much as possible, such that when a friend visited the house of a true Nine Inch Nails fan, he would say something like, 'Wow, you've got one of the limited editions of *Ghosts I–IV*. That's so cool.' The value of the scarce and expensive Ultra-Deluxe Edition was enhanced by the awareness of the music that Reznor's approach to sharing his work for free created. Far from treating free as an enemy, Reznor harnessed it to spread the word and then worked to move his fans along the Curve to becoming high-end, extremely valuable, customers.

To many companies, the emergence of free is a terrifying prospect. Trapped in an analogue world view, they are transfixed by the spectre that digital distribution is a race to the bottom, an inevitable slide to a price of zero that will destroy entire industries unless it can be stemmed by legislation and technological restrictions. They fail to see the converse of zero. When something, anything, becomes digital, it can be shared freely *at no extra cost to the creator*. This is an extraordinary opportunity to share; to reach new audiences; to, in the parlance of internet businesses the world over, widen the funnel.

At the same time, it erodes the notion of the mass market. The mass market – where all consumers pay the same price for the same item – is a created concept. It was created by factory owners who found cost-effective ways to make thousands or millions of identical copies of a particular product. The factory owners then worked with marketing agencies and the mass media to build consumer desire. The mass market was not driven by the desires of the consumer. What consumers thought of as their own desires were manufactured by marketing and advertising processes that were every bit as efficient as the processes in the factories that made the goods. The mass market was driven by the cost efficiencies of the producers.

Henry Ford explained the creation of the mass market in his autobiography:

> Making 'to order' instead of making in volume is, I suppose, a habit, a tradition, that has descended from the old handicraft days. Ask a hundred people how they want a particular article made. About eighty will not know; they will leave it to you. Fifteen will think that they must say something, while five will really have preferences and reasons. The ninety-five, made up of those who do not know and admit it and the fifteen who do not know and won't admit it, constitute the real market for any product . . . If, therefore, you discover what will give this 95 per cent of people the best all-round service and then arrange to manufacture at the very highest quality and sell at the very lowest price, you will be meeting a demand which is so large that it may be called universal.[2]

What the Nine Inch Nails experience showed was that this is no longer necessary. The amount of money a consumer is prepared to spend varies from individual to individual. Some people valued *Ghosts I–IV* at zero; others at $300. Reznor could reach millions of people for almost no cost and find the 2,500 who loved his music so much that they would pay a hefty premium for the Ultra-Deluxe Edition.

Reznor intuitively understood that consumer demand is variable, not uniform, and the internet has enabled companies to find and satisfy that demand. Whether in entertainment, retailing or manufacturing, digital transition allows us to respond directly to the curve of consumer demand.

The core argument of the Curve has three strands. The first is that people value products at different amounts. Historically, without the rapid communication and distribution enabled by the internet, the job of a business was to find the average price that satisfied the most demand. In the twenty-first century, it has become possible, perhaps even necessary, to be much more discriminatory in your pricing and to find ways to offer customers products and services at wildly differing price points, ranging from free to extremely expensive. We are moving away from an era in which the only way to increase revenue was to sell more units. Now it is possible to vary the price such that the biggest fans of a content creator might pay thousands of times as much as a casual passer-by. It is a totally different way of thinking about pricing, customers and customer relationships.

The second strand is that value is a very complex concept. The value of a product or service is driven as much by how it makes us feel as by its utility. Drawing on the work of biologists and evolutionary psychologists, I will show that the value of something is divorced from its cost, especially at a time when the costs of distribution are plummeting. We will explore ideas of value through the lenses of status, self-expression, mate selection and a range of other intangible factors which all affect our perceptions of value, and our preparedness to pay.

The third element is both liberating and terrifying to large businesses. I will argue that there is no point in fighting free, even though the Curve is much more focused on those customers who do want to give you money than on those who don't. Businesses are currently trying to fight rapidly falling prices for mass-market products, particularly in the entertainment sector, with legislation, litigation and technological solutions such as Digital Rights Management. As 3D printing becomes a reality, casual piracy will hit Alessi lemon squeezers and Tiffany jewellery in the same way that it has decimated the music industry and threatens books, movies and TV.

The real risk is not that consumers will stop paying for things they value; it is that rival companies will learn how to use the unprecedented power of the internet to reach enormous audiences, potentially by giving away for free what you are trying to sell. They will then make money in different places by allowing those customers or fans who love what they do to spend lots and lots of money on things they truly value.

So you should stop worrying about free. The iron laws of economics, competition and technology mean that it is here to stay. Smart companies will instead look at how they can build upwards, embracing or accepting free, and figure out how to build close, direct, consumer relationships with customers for whom the pirated cheap version doesn't fulfil their needs. The Curve will show you how to adapt to this new reality.

Let's start by imagining that every single person on the planet is a potential customer or fan for whatever it is you do. All 7 billion of them. Now let's pretend that we can peer inside their heads and pinpoint how much each individual is prepared to spend on your product, creation or service, whether that is a bag of flour, a live concert or the installation of a luxury swimming pool. Now we sort them by how much they would be happy to spend and arrange them all into a very long line. Those who would be happy to spend the most stand towards the left and those who are prepared to spend the least stand on the right.

Next, we superimpose a bar chart on top of them. Above their heads, floating in space, is a solid bar representing the amount they are prepared to spend, what we might call their individual 'demand'. The more they are prepared to pay, the taller the bar. If they would not pay for your service, there is no bar. If they are the Sultan of Brunei, one of the richest men in the world, the bar might be very tall indeed. Drawing a line through the tops of those bars would result in a curve that looked a little bit like Figure 1.

To the right are the customers who don't value what you do. In a world of 7 billion people, that includes nearly everyone. Close to where the curve begins to rise away from zero is the current price point for most products: $10 for a CD, $15 for a DVD, $300 for a silver pendant from Tiffany. Further to the left, as the amount each individual is prepared to pay starts rising more steeply, is where the superfans live. Those are the customers and fans who will happily spend tens, hundreds or thousands of dollars on things you create that they truly value.

Figure 1 is a representation of how much money each of your potential customers is prepared to spend with you, increasing as you move from the right to the left. The total area under the curve is the total amount of money that you might be able to generate from your buyers.

In a world bounded by physical limits, producers had to pick a

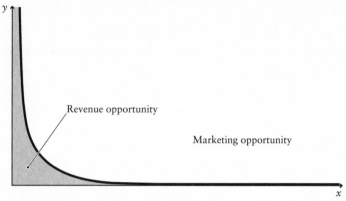

x-axis: Every person in the world, ranked by the amount they are prepared to spend with you
y-axis: Amount a person is prepared to spend with you

Figure 1: The Curve

single price for their products. So when albums used to be sold for around $10 in retail stores, there were fans who would have been prepared to pay much more for an album from their favourite band. That was money left on the table. Other people would have thought that the album was not worth $10. They would not buy it, wait for it to be discounted or pirate it from a friend. That was money left on the table too. With only one price point available for producers, they had to make their best guess of how much someone would pay for a product and hope that they got it right.

As this book will explain, that strategy has become both less effective and no longer necessary. The emergence of the internet as a communications medium and as a distribution channel has made it possible to offer many different price points to your customers. The Curve says that if you can build relationships with your customers and your fans, often by giving away stuff that they value, you can, over time, enable them to spend lots more money on things they value even more.

Many people and businesses fixate on the part of the curve to the right, where the downward pressure of piracy and increasing reluctance to pay is, in the phrase beloved of the media industry, turning physical dollars into digital dimes. I see the rightmost section of the Curve as an opportunity. An opportunity to talk to more customers than ever before at a very low cost. An opportunity to spread your net wide, to widen your funnel, to draw more people into your orbit than was possible when physical costs limited your ability to expand. With that opportunity comes a challenge: it is harder to persuade customers to pay for that which they are becoming accustomed to getting for free. So don't try. Instead try to find the 10 per cent or so of your audience who are prepared not only to pay, but to pay handsomely. Don't limit how much they can spend, but allow them to spend ten, fifty or a hundred times the previous fixed price. That way you are not only widening your audience reach at the lower price points but replacing much of the lost revenue by nothing more complex than enabling those who love what you do to pay more for things that are valuable to them.

An economist or hard-headed capitalist might rub their hands with glee at the prospect of squeezing every last cent of revenue out of these customers and fans. That is not the point of the Curve. It is also unlikely to work. The Curve is about allowing customers to spend differing amounts depending on their connection with the creator, their circumstances and their own personal sense of value. It enables producers to stop focusing on one-size-fits-all products and gives them the opportunity to satisfy or delight everyone from the casual user to the most ardent superfan. The Curve is about flexibility and choice, and heralds a new era of creative and business freedom.

The Curve will come to dominate how everyone who does business over the internet views their customers. Entertainment businesses will feel it first. Music, books, movies and games are all trending towards free, yet companies who understand how to use the Curve are already making tens, hundreds, even thousands of dollars from individual fans who love what they do and are willing to pay.

As 3D printing and digital manufacturing become first a commercial reality and eventually a presence at least in every village, and possibly in every home, they will influence manufacturing industries that previously thought themselves immune to the disruption of the internet and piracy.

This book explores how a fixation with free is only half the story. How the end of the dominance of the mass market is a massive opportunity. How physical artefacts will increase in value even as the price of anything that can be shared as bytes over the internet will collapse.

It is a book that answers the burning question of the internet age: how can we sustain a global economy when the price of everything digital falls to zero?

Perhaps the best place to start is to ask the question: what is value? We all understand that value and price are not the same thing. I value my collection of Lego from when I was a small child not because it would be expensive to replace it – I could afford to do so – but because it transports me back thirty years to a time when I was happy, contented and relaxed. Other people might get the same emotional response from eating a homecooked meal made with fresh, high-quality ingredients, watching a football game on a large flatscreen television with friends or driving an open-topped Maserati through the French countryside.

Such emotional responses are more important than the amount of money we spend on the experience. Perhaps the simplest example of this is a daily ritual undertaken by millions of people every day: drinking a cup of coffee.[3]

To understand the value of a cup of coffee to a twenty-first-century city dweller, we need to go back far in time to our roots as an agricultural society. For millennia, when we lived in an agrarian world, our economy was based on commodities: the animals we could hunt or farm; the vegetables we could forage or grow; and the minerals we could dig out of the ground. The key question that concerned us was *availability*. If we wanted coffee, was it available at all?

As mankind became better at harnessing technology through the Industrial Revolution and beyond, commodities ceased to be the staple of our economy. As entrepreneurs and businessmen constructed factories and mills, they were able to harness economies of scale: the more product they made, the cheaper each unit of that product became to make. By manufacturing a large number of identical items, businesses could spread the cost of the factory over many units, and employ lower-skilled labour to work on the production lines. Successful businesses processed large quantities of commodities, turning them into large quantities of goods. Availability improved and consumers started to focus on *price*.

In the post-war period, goods began to be commoditized themselves. Manufacturing advances and then globalization pushed costs down until price no longer became the primary differentiator. The first phase was a transition from price towards a focus on *quality*. We found quality in the product itself, but we also found quality in the services that surrounded it: home delivery, customized products such as cars or computers, better after-sales service and so on. We moved from being a goods economy to a service economy.

Today, services are being commoditized. Availability, price and quality are becoming assumed as given. We assume we can get great quality consumer goods, great quality food and great quality service whenever we want, for a good price. Which brings me back to coffee.

Coffee is a tradable commodity with prices published on financial websites and in the financial press for investors and speculators to track. When it is roasted and ground, it turns into a good: a pound of premium blend ground coffee at my local supermarket costs just under £5 ($8), and on average that will make around thirty cups for a price of 17p per unit. When sold in a cheap café, its price might rise to £1, or £1.50. When sold in a specialist outlet such as Starbucks, that figure will probably double. Why are people prepared to pay Starbucks as much as £3 for something they could have at home for 17p? Starbucks isn't selling the commodity of coffee, or the good, or even the service. It makes its margin by selling the experience. In fact, Starbucks is so confident in its ability to keep selling the experience that it no longer worries about telling its customers how much mark-up they are paying on the commodity of coffee.

I used to think that the reason that Starbucks charged such a lot for its coffee was because coffee was expensive. It must be, I thought, given the prices that Starbucks charged. My local Starbucks has made it clear to me that this is not true. They now have a sign up that says 'Add an extra espresso shot to your coffee for 15p.' That's 15p to double the amount of coffee in my £3 cappuccino, which is about what it would cost me if I made it at home. Starbucks is so confident in its value – in the brand, in the environment, in the habits and expectations of its customers – that it is prepared to showcase the disconnect between the price of the commodity it is selling and the cost of the experience it offers on its pricing board.

In the commodity era of limited availability, we asked 'Can I get it?' In the goods era of manufactured product, we asked 'How much does it cost?' In the service era of quality, we asked 'Is it any good?' Now that we can get great products cheaply whenever we want, we have started asking a new question: 'How will it make me feel?'

We can take this discussion of value further. The film industry may object that if it does not receive fair value for its product it will no longer be able to spend $220 million making movies like *The Avengers*.[4] The problem with that argument is that the amount a movie costs to make has no effect on how much a consumer pays. We pay the same for a cinema ticket or for a DVD whether it's a $200 million summer blockbuster or a $20 million art-house film. Price has become divorced from the cost of production.

This is playing out again and again now that distribution via the internet has become easy. Consumers are establishing their own sense of how much something is worth. A cup of coffee in a Starbucks environment is worth many times the cost of the underlying commodity. A digital download is worth less to a consumer than a DVD, or a trip to the cinema. The downward pressure of competition and consumer expectations mean that it is irrelevant how much something cost to make; what matters is how much customers value it.

The key to understanding value lies in an understanding of evolutionary theory. In 1859 Charles Darwin published *On the Origin of Species*, a world-changing book that posited two complementary theories for how life evolved to create its most complex example: humanity. Natural selection whereby organisms adapt in response to their environment or threats from other species is well known. His other theory, sexual selection, has long been relegated to secondary status. Sexual selection posits that evolution does indeed have intelligent design at its heart: the intelligent design of choosy females selecting the males with which they wish to mate. The two theories complement each other because for a species to survive and evolve, two things need to happen: the species needs to adapt to the threats and opportunities of the environment and competing species (natural selection) and individual males and females need to pass their genetic material to the next generation (sexual selection). Sexual selection explains why peacocks have evolved huge tails, why nightingales sing so beautifully and why the human mind evolved the capacity for altruism, art, religion and politics.

Evolutionary psychologists such as Amotz Zahavi and Geoffrey Miller have used Darwin's sexual selection theory to explain many human traits that are hard to reconcile with an evolutionary path fixated on 'survival of the fittest'. Zahavi's Handicap Principle suggests that certain physical traits have evolved to demonstrate conspicuous consumption of energy. The mere existence of a handicapping trait such as a peacock's tail is a proxy for the strength and vitality of the peacock itself because only a strong, healthy peacock can afford to squander the energy needed to produce and maintain a beautiful tail. For humans, handicapping traits include our predilection for art, for humour, for gaining economic status and for conspicuous consumption. Our sense of value, evolved over millennia, is rooted in a social context, which has been amplified by the ease of sharing in a digital environment. It has become internalized and socialized. Our behaviours are no longer driven purely by sexual selection but by the habits, traits and cultural expectations that have evolved alongside them.

As a result, value is not in the realm of the bean counter or the bill of materials. Value lies in the way something makes us feel. Every time you choose to buy a branded product in a grocery store instead of the own-brand version, you are paying additional money because of how it makes you feel. When you buy organic or premium or an expensive microbrew beer, you are making a statement about who you are, to yourself or to others, with your choices.

There may be other reasons why you may be prepared to pay more. That microbrew beer might cost more because the small brewery does not have the economies of scale of a global brewing giant like Anheuser Busch. It might attract a premium due to its scarcity. It might claim to be made with organic or premium ingredients. Many of these may, however, be part of the rationalization that you make to yourself for *why* you believe this beer is worth the extra money. In the end, the beer may taste better simply because it is more expensive.

The theme of value will crop up time and again throughout this book. Some people value self-expression. Some value status. Some want to be the first to get something and will pay a premium for that. Other people will happily trade money for time. Many of these motivations are deeply embedded in human psychology and evolution. Understanding where, why, and what consumers value will be the key to building or maintaining a successful business in the twenty-first century.

Focusing on how much it cost you to make something, especially if that thing can be distributed electronically at almost no outlay via the internet, will blind you to the opportunities that this new era of distribution can bring you.

My understanding of the Curve emerged from a close involvement with media businesses since 1994, first as an investment banker covering media and technology through the dotcom boom and then as an entrepreneur working in the online and video game sectors. Throughout that period I have come to believe that many industries, particularly in the media, have misunderstood the areas of their business where they add true, sustainable economic value and where they have been able to extract value simply by the happy accident of the historic – and disappearing – limitations of physical products.

In the days before the internet, the challenges facing a newspaper business were enormous. Every day, they had to discover what the news was, decide what was worth printing, copy- and sub-edit the text, lay it out, print it and distribute millions of copies to retailers or subscribers up and down the country. Having solved that problem, it made sense for the newspaper business to bundle up all sorts of other businesses – classified advertising, weather reports, financial analysis, crossword puzzles and so on – into the same distribution channel.

Today, we are living in a period of great unbundling. I write a blog on the business of games. It has a niche audience who care very much about how the games industry is changing and how they can make money from it. I have 20,000 readers every month, an audience that is far too small for most newspaper businesses to care about. Most importantly, and unlike the newspaper businesses, I don't need an expensive infrastructure to deliver this news and analysis. I can reach the audience interested in my blog on the business of games sitting at my computer. In my living room. In my underpants.*

Many of the elements that make up the newspaper business remain

* I don't. But I could.

the same: the gathering of the news, the filtering and the editing. But the distribution element is going away. It's still expensive to do that distribution. What has changed is that too few people now value that aspect of the business enough to pay for it, and since the fixed costs of printing and distribution, and the commercial and managerial infrastructure that supports it, is not getting rapidly cheaper, traditional media businesses are in trouble.

This is not a problem of piracy, or one of customers refusing to pay for high quality. It is a technological shift driving a process first described by economist Joseph Schumpeter, one that is crucial to the operation of a thriving capitalist economy: creative destruction.

Schumpeter was an Austrian-American economist writing in the 1950s. To him, the engine of growth of the capitalist system was the disruption caused by entrepreneurs innovating with new products or services at the expense of the existing companies and workers who had carved out for themselves a position of power. That power might derive from market dominance, from political support, from logistical and distribution excellence or from technological advances. Flexible, adaptable entrepreneurs attempt to find better, cheaper or faster products that fulfil a market need while incumbents struggle to adapt. Schumpeter's work has been built on by other economists, notably Clay Christensen, who coined the phrase 'The Innovator's Dilemma' to exemplify how successful companies focus on their customers' existing needs and struggle to change business practices to meet future or unstated ones. Entrepreneurs, looking for ways to offer new products and services, bring what Christensen calls 'disruptive innovation' to the market.

Creative destruction and disruptive innovation are vital to the health and dynamism of a capitalist society. They are part of the reason capitalism has proven to be such a powerful force for business, technological and arguably social innovation compared with other rival ideologies. They show why it is so difficult for companies to adapt to rapid technological change and that, in the long run, their failure to adapt doesn't matter to society at large. More accurately, it is a good thing for society. Old businesses fail and fade away. New businesses arise to take their place. The world adapts to the new behemoth until it, in turn, faces its own disruptive interruption. Think of how IBM, a manufacturer of mainframes, was disrupted by Microsoft who wanted to put a PC on every desk. How Microsoft was disrupted by Google in turn, moving the centre of computing away from the desktop and towards the cloud. And now Google must adapt to a world where search – its core business – is being disrupted by the rise of the social web and Google's dominance of our experience of the internet via the browser is threatened by Apple's success with smartphones and tablets.

The technology world has long been used to the pace of creative destruction. Other industries are only just beginning to feel it.

In 1989, a middle-aged woman suddenly imagined a book that she would write.

'I wrote the early chapters in about an hour – as though they were being dictated to me. I wrote in longhand, on a lined copy book and I believe, though the originals are now in Boston, that few changes were made to these opening chapters when the novel was published in early 1991. Then, I stopped. I did nothing at all with them.'[5]

Her busy life meant that she did not carry on writing her first draft of her debut novel despite pressure from her husband to do so. Then something changed.

The woman was producing a play. After the play, she and her husband went to dinner at Scott's restaurant, an expensive eatery in London's exclusive Mayfair, with two friends, a couple who had been to see the play with them. Her husband said, 'Josephine is writing a novel.'[6] Josephine said, 'Hush.' Her friend said, 'May I see it?'

The woman was Josephine Hart. The husband was advertising entrepreneur Maurice Saatchi. The friend was Ed Victor, one of the highest profile literary agents in the world. The book was *Damage*. It sold over a million copies worldwide, was translated into twenty-six languages and made into a 1992 film by Louis Malle, starring Juliette Binoche and Jeremy Irons.

That story illustrates how many people view the process of getting a book published. Be connected. It's not about your talent, it's about who you know. Approaching the slush pile never works.

They are not entirely wrong.

Ed Victor is a literary agent who moves in socialite circles. Not only are he and his wife Carol invited to every literary party going, but they also attend fashion, film and society soirées. As the *Guardian* puts it, 'anywhere the beautiful, famous and talented are gathered, Victor is certain to be in their midst, his gentle New Yorker charm and affability concealing the fabled steely core'.[7] Aspiring writers have wondered how they are going to get representation from Ed Victor. At the Hay Literary Festival, an annual jamboree of literature and the arts held in the small Welsh town of Hay-on-Wye, one audience member had a question for Victor.

'How do I get my manuscript to you if I don't go to that kind of party?'

'You don't,' Victor replied.

Ed Victor is not a believer in the 'slush pile', the book publishing industry's term for the collections of unsolicited manuscripts that sit around the office of a literary agent or, more rarely, a publisher's office waiting to be read and evaluated, usually by a junior employee. To many writers, the slush pile seems like their only hope of discovery. They send manuscript after manuscript, printed double-spaced, single-sided on A4 paper, following specific and often contradictory instructions on whether to staple or to bind, how much biographical detail to put on each page or more. They read terrifying statistics such as 'only 1 per cent of books from the slush pile get published' and despair of ever bring able to find a publisher for their work.[8] In Ed Victor's world, and the world that many aspiring writers imagine to exist, getting published is not an issue of raw talent, hard work or dogged persistence; it is a matter of who you know.

There is another way.

In April 2010, a young writer in Austin, Minnesota was trying to work out if she could afford to make the trip to Chicago to see an exhibition of Jim Henson's Muppets. A huge Muppets fan, she was happy to make the eight-hour drive, but she couldn't afford the fuel, let alone pay for a hotel.

The woman wasn't a stranger to hard work. She had a full-time job caring for disabled people that earned her $18,000 a year. In her spare time she wrote. Prolifically. By the time she was seventeen, she had written fifty short stories and finished her first novel (although by her own admission it wasn't very good). Ten years later, she had seventeen completed manuscripts, mainly in the genre of young adult paranormal romantic fiction. She had also collected dozens, perhaps hundreds, of rejection letters.

Unlike Josephine Hart, this young writer didn't hobnob with the rich and famous. Instead, she was lucky to have been born several decades later. The writer decided that if she wanted to make the trip to see the Muppets, she needed to do something radical. She offered one of her books as an ebook in Amazon's Kindle store.

In the first six months that she self-published her books, Amanda Hocking made $20,000 selling 150,000 copies.[9] By January 2012 she had sold 1.5 million copies and earned $2.5 million. As with Josephine Hart, Hollywood came knocking. In February, 2011, Canadian screenwriter Terri Tatchell optioned one of Hocking's trilogies. Not bad for an author who had been turned down time and again by respected literary agents and publishing houses.

The stories of Josephine Hart and Amanda Hocking each represent extremes: the one of the old, privileged Establishment of publishing, the other of a new, electronic, free-for-all where talent that lies unrecognized by traditional channels can reach its audience in new, unfettered ways, freed from the tyranny of the slush pile, the agent and the marketing-led editor. They are not representative of the experience of the majority of aspiring writers, but they do highlight some persistent myths about the publishing process as well as the pace of rapid change.

Defenders of the traditional process point out that the quality of submissions is generally terrible. Blogs such as Slushpile Hell highlight howlers from covering letters including risible grammar, awful prose and a level of high-handed arrogance that would make even a literary agent blush: 'Look, I have two international bestsellers on my hands, you can trust me and make lots of money or not trust me and miss out on making your career, either way, I've got the bestseller.'[10]

Against this background, the literary agent and the publisher are all that stands between the public and a tide of effluent, say proponents of the value of publishing. This is arrant nonsense.

There is no doubt that there is huge value in the role of the editor. Few books spring from an author's mind perfectly formed and ready to be published, and the same is true for screenplays, for television scripts, for graphic novels, for music tracks or for video games. A seasoned and professional editor or producer can make an enormous difference to the quality and commercial success of a product. The danger is when the commercial role of the editor as gatekeeper gets mixed up with the creative role of the editor as creative adviser. The role of the gatekeeper is a function of the pre-internet world, and has a much diminished value against a backdrop of abundant digital distribution. An understanding of the Curve shows the rapid change from the era of Josephine Hart to that of Amanda Hocking. At its heart is the changing nature of what is scarce and what is abundant.

In 1989, when Hart first put pen to paper, the internet barely existed. In 1992, the year that *Damage*, the movie based on Hart's novel, was released, I was at Oxford University, editing a paper called *The Oxford Student*. One of the reasons I remember *Damage* so clearly is that we had only very basic technology. We had advanced from literally cutting and pasting stories to typesetting using a desktop publishing program called QuarkXPress, but getting access to pictures was enormously difficult. If we were lucky, we could persuade the press departments of movie distributors to send us, by post, high-quality 8″ × 12″ black-and-white stills from the movie. I can still remember the glossy image from *Damage*, Jeremy Irons and Juliette Binoche in a (tastefully) naked embrace, not least because it was one of the few pictures we had. We reused it on every possible occasion.

In that era, easy access to digital content was scarce. Photographs had to be taken, developed, scanned and cropped. Film was expensive. Storing pictures was expensive. A photographer with the key to a darkroom was a huge asset to a student newspaper, reducing our reliance on publicity shots. We only had one such photographer. The distribution and sharing of content was difficult. The formats were overwhelmingly analogue.

When the ability to make copies of content is scarce, it also tends to be expensive. As an editor, I was aware of the enormous cost of printing 13,000 copies of a paper every week. (Enormous by the standards of a student union, anyway.) In the same way, a commissioning editor reviewing content from the slush pile would have been aware of the enormous cost of accepting a book into the publishing process. Not only did the book need to be professionally edited, typeset and designed, it had to be printed, sold into retail channels, and distributed. The amount of money required to bring a physical book to market was colossal, and there was no alternative.

Fast forward twenty years and almost every aspect of the process has been rendered vastly cheaper by the advance of technology. Modern word processors can do much of the typesetting of the book as the author writes. (My self-published book, *How to Publish a Game*, was entirely typeset in a default theme from Microsoft Word.) Design is still expensive, but designers are easier to find than ever before using websites or social media. Retail is no longer the only way to reach an audience and physical books are no longer even necessary. What was previously scarce has become abundant.

The one element that still remains incredibly valuable is the role of a good editor. Almost every piece of creation can be improved by a strong partnership between creator and editor. The creative value of the editorial role remains strong. The gatekeeping aspect is the element that is dwindling in value.

In the Amanda Hocking case there was no editor to perform either role. Hocking put her novel up on Amazon as it stood, rejected by professionals in the publishing world. There it found an audience. That audience spread and multiplied by that oldest of marketing techniques, word of mouth, multiplied by the power of social media. Naysayers will rightly point out that Hocking's books would have been better if they had had a professional publishing organization behind them. They might have been tighter. More grammatically sound. More closely plotted. They also would not have been published.

This distinction between the creative role of the editorial function and the gatekeeping role is at the heart of the changes to the business landscape driven by the internet. A gatekeeper used to have scarce resources to allocate to publish a book. Now a self-published author can reach millions of potential readers just by uploading her content to a blog, to an eReader or to a new distribution channel.

There are those who bemoan this change. Who fear the tide of dross that will emerge when anyone, not just the privileged few, can publish and when a tight-knit cabal of English Literature graduates no longer have control over what can and cannot be turned into a book. A quick glance at the bestseller list at Christmas, packed with ghost-written celebrity memoirs and sure-fire hits from established novelists, suggests that the cabal does not always put great quality or original content first.

The demise of the gatekeeping role will lead to an explosion in creativity across all entertainment businesses, and then across all businesses. Good ideas can spread faster than ever before, fanned by the winds of social media and effortless sharing, untrammelled by the costs of distribution and finding new users, whether niche or global, at a speed and scale unimaginable when *Damage* was released.

With this abundance comes a new scarcity: that of attention. The problem is no longer how to get published; it is to get noticed when you have been published. That is the challenge facing twenty-first-century businesses: how to attract attention in a world of almost limitless information.

It is said that Samuel Taylor Coleridge was the last man to have read everything. Or at least everything that mattered. Thomas Young, born in 1773, was also said to be 'the last man who knew everything'.[11] Imagine if they lived today. When Google is busy digitizing every out-of-copyright book, and many that are in copyright, too. When a hundred hours of video are uploaded to YouTube every single minute.[12] When armies of professionals, amateurs, bloggers and bystanders are creating content at every second of every day. Surely they would have cried out for a gatekeeper?

Perhaps. Or maybe they would have preferred to see ideas shared, spread and discussed widely. To see communities springing up around topics that were deemed too niche to be successful for mainstream audiences. To see topics which were dumbed down when produced for a mainstream audience reach their full potential for a niche audience that can be reached in the cheap distribution environment enabled by the internet.

(I used to use as an illustration of this emergence of niches that could not thrive under the traditional music publishing business the idea of a jazz-bluegrass-fusion band. When I first pitched this book to my agent, he immediately named a jazz-bluegrass-fusion band called

Phish that he really liked. They play jazz, bluegrass and pretty well anything else you can imagine improvised into one unique whole. The niches are thriving.)*

In the world before the web, the only viable option was *curation*, where we as consumers let paid professionals choose which works we would get to see and which ones were destined never to be released. We had no choice: the commercial realities of distribution meant that curation was necessary to persuade companies to invest the meaning-ful sums of money necessary to bring a product to market. Now, in the twenty-first century, we have an alternative: *filtering*. The filtering model takes advantage of the fact that we can now distribute and share digital content at almost no cost and puts the quality control filter in place after publication, not before.

Traditional gatekeepers bemoan the lack of curation in today's markets. There is no doubt that the internet is flooded with poor-quality content, mainly because of the low barriers to entry. On the other hand, quality, like beauty, is largely in the eye of the beholder. Is opera inherently more important than grime? Does *Perry Mason* trump *Vampire Diaries*? Is a blog on the business of games more or less valuable than one on the ins and outs of commercial bread making?

It no longer matters. It is so cheap to publish that anyone who cre-ates can put their content out to be judged by the only group that matters: their audience. The gatekeepers are losing their grip on the content world. There are many challenges to the digital world, and many of the tools that we will need to make sense of the abun-dance of content in the twenty-first century have yet to be written. The reality is, though, that gatekeepers are losing their power. As the role of the gatekeeper diminishes, so the opportunities for the creator grow.

The Curve doesn't apply only to art and content, although it is easiest to grasp through that lens, since the world of entertainment is the world that is being affected by the digital transition more

---

* Note that Phish were formed in 1983. They instinctively understood the Curve even in the days before the internet.

rapidly than any other. It can apply to any business that deals with consumers.

Marcus Sheridan had a problem.

It was 2009 and his business was in trouble. River Pools and Spas was a twenty-employee installer of in-ground fibreglass pools in Virginia and Maryland. Before the financial crisis hit, the firm averaged six orders per month. Now they were down to two. That winter, four customers who had planned to install pools costing more than $50,000 asked for their deposits back. The company was consistently overdrawn and heading for bankruptcy. Four years later, River Pools and Spas is thriving. The company is making more revenue than it did before the financial crisis while its advertising costs have plummeted. Why? Marcus Sheridan was an early adopter of the Curve.

Fibreglass swimming pools are expensive. It's hard to say just how expensive, because there are so many options and variables, but the cost can range from $20,000 to $200,000. Most of River Pools' customers pay between $40,000 and $80,000. Sheridan's business already had the top end of the Curve covered: it offered expensive, bespoke solutions to its customers' needs. His challenge was at the low end of the Curve.

Sheridan's response to his troubles in 2009 was unconventional. He was spending $250,000 a year on advertising on radio, television and via pay-per-click on the web. He slashed the budget by 90 per cent. At the same time, he started talking directly to his customers:

> I just started thinking more about the way I use the internet. Most of the time when I type in a search, I'm looking for an answer to a specific question. The problem in my industry, and a lot of industries, is you don't get a lot of great search results because most businesses don't want to give answers; they want to talk about their company. So I realized that if I was willing to answer all these questions that people have about fiberglass pools, we might have a chance to pull this out.[13]

Sheridan started to try to answer the questions that his customers had about pools. He wrote articles about the problems and issues that affect fibreglass pools. He listed all his competitors in Virginia and Maryland in a single post. He wrote blog posts about how much they cost. Within twenty-four hours of posting about the cost, his article was the top search result for every fibreglass pool, cost-related phrase you can think of. Sheridan has generated $1.7 million in business that originated just from that single post that he wrote four years ago.

River Pools is one of the first websites that many people find when searching for the costs or problems of fibreglass pools. The company's website acts as a resource for anyone trying to find out about pools as much as it acts as a sales mouthpiece. Sheridan is honest about the shortcomings of fibreglass pools and that gains him the respect and trust of his customers. A customer who has read a lot of Sheridan's online material, thirty pages or more, and then books an appointment, converts to a purchaser 80 per cent of the time, compared with an industry average of 10 per cent.

What Sheridan started doing in 2009 is now known as content marketing. He is building a relationship with his audience by offering high-quality, useful information for free. He uses analytics and data tools to help him understand what his audience wants. Then he allows his customers to spend lots of money on, in his case, a swimming pool.

Different businesses, organizations or creators will adapt to the Curve in different ways. Some will find that what they do is already available for free, and will have to seek out ways to let their biggest fans spend large amounts of money on things they value. Some will have products that are naturally personalized or expensive and use the free distribution of the web to pursue a content marketing strategy. Charities will use the web to reach new potential donors and offer them a range of donation points, all in a social, connected context. Retailers will stop focusing on shifting products and focus on the average revenue per customer. All will use technology to share stuff with their customers and to track and analyse their preferences.

The Curve shows artists, retailers, manufacturers and service providers how it is still possible to make money in a world where the price of so many things is heading towards zero. It is a time filled with possibilities. To make the most of it, we need to look at what has changed to make the Curve a possibility. We will start by examining how what was once scarce has now become abundant and what was once abundant is now scarce.

2
SCARCITY AND ABUNDANCE

Lady Gaga is a twenty-first-century star.

It's not that she doesn't work with a record label. Her first album, *The Fame* (2009), was released by Interscope Records, as was *Born this Way* (2011) and *ARTPOP* (due in 2013). Lady Gaga has chosen to work with the traditional record industry to release records in the traditional way. It's just that record sales represent less than a quarter of her income. More than that, Lady Gaga has direct connections with her fans. A lot of fans.

Lady Gaga is the most followed person on Twitter. In May 2013 she had 37,520,337 Twitter followers. Her Twitter stream includes political statements such as:

> I JUST GOT OFF STAGE IN COLUMBIA!! CONGRATULA-TIONS MR. PRESIDENT @BarackObama We are so proud to be American tonight! YES!!! YES! YES!![1]

and talking to and about her fans:

> OI GALERA! In Rio + My beautiful fans are wearing leather & bandanas in the sun, bad asses, gorgeous smiles & fists in the air! I HEAR U![2]

These tweets are more than just marketing. They are about allowing fans to have a glimpse inside the life of a superstar. They allow the fans to feel that they have a one-to-one relationship with Lady Gaga, even though they know they are only one of 38 million followers. They allow Lady Gaga to speak directly to fans without having to go through the filter of a TV interview, a newspaper article or a magazine spread. They allow Lady Gaga to appear genuine.

Lady Gaga doesn't stop at Twitter. The music video for 'Bad Romance' is one of the top ten most popular videos on YouTube with 495 million views by November 2012.[3] It is freely available to watch on YouTube and Lady Gaga has said that she is fine with her fans getting her music for free, whether legally or illegally. In an interview with *The Times*, she said, 'big artists can make anywhere from $40 million for one cycle of two years' touring. Giant artists make upwards of $100 million. Make music – then tour. It's just the way it is today.'[4]

'Bad Romance' is available for free on YouTube, but this doesn't seem to have hurt its sales. 'Bad Romance' sold over 9.7 million copies in 2010, making it the second most purchased single in the world that year, behind Ke$ha's 'TiK ToK'.[5] This isn't a one off event either. Lady Gaga has five songs in the top fifty best-selling singles of all time (see Table 1).[6]

We must be careful how much we read into Table 1. There are issues with the underlying data, the implications and the conclusions that we might be tempted to draw. The sales data is incomplete because it includes only the number of downloads in the year of release, sourced from the International Federation of the Phonographic Industry, and there are claims that 'Poker Face' has in fact sold over 12 million copies. The YouTube video views can't be directly compared to the sales figures, because they were taken from YouTube on 9 November 2012 and represent aggregate views, not just those in the year of release. We also need to be cautious of causality: did Lady

Table 1: Lady Gaga's most popular tracks

Track	Release year	Downloads in release year	YouTube views (November 2012)
'Poker Face'	2008	9.8 million	141 million
'Bad Romance'	2010	9.7 million	495 million
'Just Dance'	2008	9.6 million	155 million
'Born This Way'	2011	8.2 million	102 million
'Telephone'	2010	7.4 million	153 million

Gaga sell so many digital downloads because her songs and music videos have been so popular on YouTube, or did each of these songs fail to reach their potential and hence sold fewer copies because so many fans were able to watch and listen to them without paying a dime? If the latter is the case, it is possible that Lady Gaga has suffered enormous financial loss from all the customers who have experienced her music on YouTube and as a result chosen not to bother spending money on buying her singles and albums.

What we do know is that Lady Gaga has sold a phenomenal number of singles while also having a phenomenal number of YouTube views. She is an artist who has put a great deal of effort into using social media and modern distribution channels to disseminate her music and videos. She has a clear and stated strategy of making sure that her music gets in front of her fans, wherever they are and whether they have paid or not. She also has five of the best-selling singles of all time. The correlation is strong.

There is an important question, though: has all this success made Lady Gaga any money? Boy, has it. *Forbes* magazine estimated Lady Gaga's earnings in 2011 at over $100 million, and perhaps as high as $130 million.[7] However, of that revenue, only 24 per cent came from record sales. Even with some of the best-selling singles of all time, Lady Gaga made only around $25 million from record sales. Seven per cent of her income came from endorsements and sponsorship. The lion's share of her income, 69 per cent, came from touring and merchandise.

Lady Gaga has chosen to accept that many people won't pay for that which costs her nothing to distribute – her videos, her albums, her singles – and instead has concentrated on selling that which is expensive or scarce – her time, the live experiences of her shows, her reputation.

She doesn't always make zero from giving away her music. Some people are still happy to pay for digital music via services like iTunes and Spotify. Even on YouTube, where Lady Gaga doesn't make money directly from end users, there is a revenue stream for artists. YouTube is a commercial platform owned by Google and has (finally) started to build a viable advertising business around its video content. Before I could watch a video of 'Poker Face', I was shown a pre-roll video for a new Girls Aloud album. The record label is likely to have bought that advertising slot, and the average cost of 1,000 views of an online video in early 2012 was around $10.[8] If Lady Gaga had an ad at that rate for every one of the video plays of her five most popular songs, she would have made $10 million in advertising revenue alone. That doesn't include those ugly banners that appear over her video while it is playing either, just the pre-rolls. After Google takes its share of the revenue, Gaga would have netted somewhere over $5 million. In practice, I suspect that the figure is far lower. Google didn't really get its act together for video advertising before 2010, and some of the ads will be at a much lower CPM. The revenue is probably significantly lower than $5 million, possibly as low as one-tenth of that.

You know what? It doesn't matter. Lady Gaga is not building her financial success on the strength of the advertising income she makes from her music videos. She is not building it on the paltry $167 she was alleged to have made from a million plays on Spotify in 2010.[9] She is not going to get rich by selling sponsored tweets to advertisers.

This is just icing on the cake. When Lady Gaga started spreading her music on YouTube, she wasn't expecting to get any money at all. The purpose was to start building a one-to-one relationship with her fans. The 54 million Facebook likes that Lady Gaga has garnered is just the start. As her business manager Troy Carter says, 'A "like" [on Facebook] doesn't necessarily translate as a fan. It's a very passive relationship. It's more important to have the one million diehard fans, than to have 54 million people who aren't necessarily fans or they might have liked one thing you said, or one video. It's being able to segregate those audiences and knowing who the super-fans are.'[10]

The next step for Troy Carter and Lady Gaga is to start strengthening and deepening their relationships with their biggest fans. Lady Gaga's *ARTPOP* album will be an app. She has launched her own social network, littlemonsters.com, which by November 2012 had a million dedicated fans on board. They are moving the casual listeners of Lady Gaga who first discovered her through YouTube, through Spotify, through the radio and elsewhere along the demand curve, converting them from casual listeners to people who like her music to true fans.

Lady Gaga is moving her fans along the Curve. She knows that her time is scarce, but her recordings are now abundant. They can be shared at a trivial cost. She has adapted her thinking to a strategy that gives away freely that which is now abundant (digital recordings) and makes money from that which is scarce (her time at live gigs, the self-expression and social context of belonging to her fan club, her reputation). While other musicians bemoan the rise of iTunes, YouTube and Spotify as destroyers of value, Lady Gaga and her team see those services as harbingers of change. Instead of fighting the inevitability of what was once scarce becoming abundant, she is embracing it. To understand how and why, we need to dig deeper into the themes of scarcity and abundance.

I started my career as an investment banker in 1994. The internet as we know it had not yet been invented. I had had no email at university and never once used a computer while I was there. I wrote my essays longhand with a fountain pen, perhaps part of the last generation to do so. It's not that I was a Luddite. Back at home, I was a PC gamer. I tracked down shareware copies of *Doom* and finished it. I played role-playing games like *Ultima V* and *Darklands*. I took control of a Star Wars starfighter in *X-Wing*.

When I joined Morgan Grenfell, a subsidiary of the German giant Deutsche Bank, in September 1994, I was looking forward to the high technology I would get access to. I was an investment banker, a specialist in helping companies buy and sell other companies and in raising money from the stock market or private equity companies. I wasn't a trader, with their high-tech trading screens bringing up-to-the-minute alerts on market-moving information. I worked in a more sedate world where deals took months to complete, not seconds. We had the luxury of time. We still needed information, though.

I joined the Acquisitions Research Team, which housed Deutsche Bank's experts in particular industries. I focused on media and telecoms. As a junior executive, I was expected to know a lot about my sector. I had to prepare presentations summarizing the operations of different companies that might be acquisition targets for others. This is where I hoped to encounter some technological wizardry.

Not a bit of it.

Our basic source of intelligence was the library, hidden in the basement with little natural light. The librarians presided over our stock of physical, hardcopy information on every company we could think of. We had the annual reports that public companies are required to produce for their shareholders, detailing their financial results but also full of marketing and public relations material. We had what were called 'broker's notes', reports from stock market analysts on the company's prospects and valuation. For private companies, the files were often very thin.

One of our best sources of information on what a company did was brochures. If anyone from Morgan Grenfell, senior or junior, visited a company they kept their eyes open for those glossy leaflets that companies leave in reception for visitors to browse. If you were lucky, this brochure would list all the departments of the company. It might give their turnover or number of employees. It might tell you which countries they operated in, what products they made and so on.

Our competitive advantage was our ability to file brochures stolen from the receptions of major companies better than our competitors.

We did have some technology. DataStream was a sophisticated tool for showing share price performance against any number of benchmarks, marred by an impossibly complex user interface. While I was there, Reuters and Extel and Bloomberg continually improved their electronic services. There is no doubt, however, that even in 1994, I joined an organization overwhelmingly dependent on paper files and in which information was scarce. We added value to our clients simply by providing them with publicly available information on their competitors that they were unable to source themselves.

Fast forward twenty years and the world has changed. (To be fair, it had changed by 2003, when I left the City.) There is internet access on every desktop. We have huge amounts of information on every business. Public companies have whole sections of their websites devoted to investor relations, full of legal filings, glossy PDFs and pages of information on their activities. Private companies have 'About Us' pages and describe what they do in detail for all to see. Instead of laborious 'press searches', a junior investment banker in 2013 uses Google. The competitive advantage for an investment bank is not to have information: it is to filter out the noise and find the important nuggets, whether public or proprietary, that will be useful for their clients. In less than twenty years, information has gone from being scarce to being abundant, changing the way bankers and clients value it.

My professional experiences are not the only change. When I was a child in the United Kingdom in the 1970s, there were just three television channels. The launch of a fourth channel in 1982 was an amazing moment. I grew up without a video recorder. If we wanted to watch a television programme, we had to watch it when it was broadcast or it was gone for ever. Every year at Christmas, my mother would buy a copy of two rival magazines. *Radio Times* gave the television schedule for BBC1 and BBC2, *TV Times* for ITV, and later Channel 4. My brother and I would pore over the listings, circling the shows, particularly the movies, that we wanted to watch. We would have to negotiate with other family members so that we could watch the programme on the single television in our house.

My five-year-old son would find that concept incredible. He has a hundred channels to choose from. If he doesn't want to watch anything on those, he has a shelf full of DVDs. He has catch-up TV that lets him watch pretty well anything that has been broadcast in the last seven days or longer. He has our subscription to Lovefilm to order DVDs through the post or to stream movies onto our PlayStation 3.

My scarcity was of programming. I watched whatever was on because I had so few choices, and because if I missed it, it was gone. My son, even as a five-year-old, has a scarcity of time. He could not watch all the children's programming that is available to him in a single day. There is too much of it. For him, programming is abundant. He has choice.

Even the internet, the engine of change, is itself changing. The file-hosting site Dropbox figured out that storing digital files in the cloud was becoming so cheap that it could offer the service for free. Today you can sign up for their free service and store 2GB of files with them at no cost. You can 'earn' more free storage every time you refer a friend, up to a maximum of 18GB. If you want more storage you can pay $99 a year for 100GB or $499 for 500GB. If you are a business, Dropbox has a useful slider showing you exactly how much you will pay to have Dropbox available for multiple users ranging from $795 for five users up to $31,420 for 250 users. (Beyond that, you are in the realm of negotiated prices.) Dropbox is estimated by *Forbes* to have made $500 million in revenue in 2012 and to be profitable, even though only about 4 per cent of users pay it any money at all.[11]

Similarly Aweber, a provider of email services to marketers, lets customers build a mailing list of up to 500 contacts entirely for free. Their blog is full of specific, practical advice on how to build an email list, how to make your emails more effective and how to make more money from your email marketing. As customers grow their email lists, Aweber charges an increasing amount based on the number of subscribers each client is emailing. Dropbox and Aweber have harnessed a new abundance, used the power of free to acquire customers and developed a variable pricing model to avoid the biggest dangers of the freemium model – that the paying users don't pay enough to subsidize the free users.

Although advances in technology can make what was once scarce now abundant, our perceptions sometimes take a while to catch up. In the 1960s plastic became cheap and accessible. The disposable culture of plastic bags, polystyrene cups and shrink-wrapped, pre-packaged food took hold, because plastic was so cheap to produce. It took two decades before we realized that the abundance of cheap plastic had created a new problem in the form of waste and landfill and rubbish. For example, bottled water consumption in the US has risen from 5.7 litres per capita in 1976 to 132 litres in 2011.[12] An estimated 50 billion plastic bottles are produced in the US each year for drinking water alone. The recycling drive is a response to the realization that plastic is not as cheap as we once thought. It is cheap for those directly involved – the producers who make the water and the consumers who drink it – but it has a cost to all of us in pollution, in waste of natural resources and in the difficulty and expense of disposing of all those empty bottles. Plastic is now abundant. The corresponding scarcity is of waterways uncluttered by Evian bottles and landfill sites unfilled with Dasani.*

---

* The impact of the bottled water craze on our environment and waste management needs is an externality. Externalities are an important economic concept. They are consequences of an economic transaction that are not reflected in the price, or that do not affect the buyer or the seller. For example, the costs to society as a whole of air pollution are rarely reflected in the price we pay for products except via government intervention. The banks that were 'too big to fail' successfully externalized their risk onto the taxpayer, allowing the participants in financial transactions to benefit handsomely, while society at large ended up on the hook when things went wrong.

I recently promised to take a 6lb salmon, cold and poached, to a family christening on a Sunday. On Saturday morning, I walked down to my local fishmonger to pick up the fish I'd ordered. When he saw me, he blanched. 'I'm terribly sorry,' he said, 'I forgot. Billingsgate will be closed by now. There's nothing I can do.'

After a few minutes of blind panic, I did what any self-respecting Londoner would do in such an emergency. I called Harrods.*

The Harrods fishmonger asked me if I wanted line-caught or farmed. I wasn't thinking straight, so I said, 'How much for the line-caught salmon?' 'Three hundred and thirty pounds,' he said. I gulped. My fishmonger's mistake looked as if it was going to cost me dearly. With a strangled voice, I asked, '. . . And for farmed?' 'Thirty-eight pounds,' which was only a slight premium over my fishmonger's price. The christening was saved.

The difference in price is staggering. Salmon fishing for me conjures up mental images of men in tweed jackets and hats stuck full of hand-tied lures standing in a flowing river in thigh-high waders. Of course, salmon caught that way was expensive. Even if my mental image is wrong, salmon used to be an expensive fish to buy. All that changed when commercial salmon farming began in the 1970s. During the 1980s and 1990s, commercial salmon farming became well established in many temperate countries around the world, particularly Norway, Chile and Scotland. By 1996, farmed salmon exceeded all commercial harvests of wild salmon, and farmed salmon now accounts for more than two-thirds of the world harvest.[13]

There has been a crash in the prices of wild salmon as consumers have become able to buy cheaper, more reliable farmed salmon. The commercial price of some wild salmon species has fallen by over 70 per cent since 1988. Even as the price has fallen, though, our expectations remain that salmon is a premium foodstuff. As I was preparing the salmon for the christening, someone walked past my kitchen window along the street outside. I heard him say, 'Crikey, they must be rich, they have a whole salmon.' I was tempted to yell after him that it was cheaper, pound for pound, than a joint of beef.

---

* I have only been to Harrods four times in my life. You should go there at least once, if only to visit the ice cream parlour.

The facts have changed, but our perceptions or prejudices or expectations have not. Humans just aren't very good at accepting that something that was once scarce is now abundant. We are wired as a species to understand scarcity better than abundance. Just as we've evolved to overreact to threats and dangers, one of our survival tactics is to focus on the risk that supplies are going to run out. Abundance, from an evolutionary perspective, resolves itself, while scarcity needs to be fought over.[14] The cheeky passer-by commenting on the price of my food was wrong, because the world has changed around him without him noticing. In the same way that the value of information has changed and that scarcity of programming became scarcity of time to watch the almost limitless amount of televisual content. In the same way that it is now more sensible to throw a toaster away when it breaks than to try to repair it, despite the waste. There just isn't anyone in the UK who can cost-effectively repair a toaster when the price of a new one is under £20.

Containerization made it possible to shift products cheaply and efficiently around the world, destroying the livelihoods of stevedores and longshoremen but ushering in an era of globalization, of cheap manufacturing and of falling costs of living in the West. The single television of my childhood was replaced by a set in every room, with a games console and a DVD player and more. The Green Revolution of the 1960s dramatically increased food production such that, in the US, the cost of food fell from one-third of the average US household income in 1955 to less than 15 per cent in 2008.[15] This change is so remarkable that for the first time in history, poor people are not starving to death in the US. The biggest food-related problem affecting poor people in the US is obesity.

Think about that for a moment. Poor people's health is at risk because they are too fat. Our perceptions take time to change. Food is plentiful. We no longer worry about whether we will have enough food to eat: we worry about whether the food is good enough, healthy enough, nutritious enough. The poor people of the West may have enough food, but they may still be malnourished because a diet based on the cheap, available food is high in fats and sugars, and low on fresh produce with all the vitamins, fibre and minerals and so on that the body needs.

We are about to face new changes in scarcity. For a century, we have assumed that personalization was expensive because tycoons like Henry Ford optimized their manufacturing processes to make identical products. Creating a bespoke product in a mass-production factory was expensive. As 3D printing becomes a reality, that presumption becomes incorrect. It makes little difference to a 3D printer if it prints a hundred identical widgets or a hundred similarly sized different widgets. While economies of scale will keep the traditional manufacturing processes viable for some time, the 3D printing revolution will enable new businesses to emerge that harness the new abundance and make money from the new scarcities, ranging from personalized dolls to laser-scanned replacement parts for classic cars and into new business ideas that have not yet been contemplated.

In order to thrive in the world of digital, we need to make sure that we are not like the man walking past my kitchen window. We need to make sure that we adapt to the end of scarcity and its replacement by abundance by seeking the *new* scarcity. When something collapses in value, something else rises in value alongside it. We need to adapt to abundance thinking, where we not only discover what will become cheaper, but also look for what will become more valuable as the result of the shift. That is where the opportunities will lie.

'In an information-rich world, the wealth of information means a dearth of something else: a scarcity of whatever it is that information consumes. What information consumes is rather obvious: it consumes the attention of its recipients. Hence a wealth of information creates a poverty of attention.'[16]

Those were the words of social scientist Herbert Simon, writing in 1971. Forty years later, it is clear that his prognosis that we would have a poverty of attention have come true. We live in an always-on, permanently connected world.

Few of us are ever more than a few feet from a powerful communications device: our mobile phone. Media consumption of teenagers and young adults is on the rise, particularly given the increase in multimedia consumption: listening to the radio while playing a game, interrupted by texts, Twitter and Facebook messages. At the same time, our living standards have risen such that consumer goods which would have seemed like extravagances to our grandparents – televisions, personal phones, games consoles, central heating, dishwashers, one car per adult family member – are becoming the norm. Food is abundant, not scarce. Yet many businesses are still struggling to adapt to these changes.

The issues are most pressing in those businesses whose core product is easily shared in digital form. Scarcity is becoming abundance in many areas of our lives, but it is happening fastest in the world of bits and bytes, where making a duplicate copy of something that already exists is trivially easy. There are those who believe that the downward pressures on price are being driven by a combination of technology and the preparedness of vast swathes of previously law-abiding citizens to suddenly embrace illegal activities.

I don't agree. The downward pressure is being driven by more powerful laws than those of computing or copyright. It is being driven down by the laws of economics.

3
COMPETITION, ECONOMICS AND A MAN CALLED BERTRAND

On 9 January 2007, Steve Jobs took to the stage at the Macworld Conference and Expo at the Moscone Center in San Francisco. Dressed in a black turtleneck, blue jeans and sneakers, Jobs addressed a crowd of business partners, journalists and Apple enthusiasts, many of whom whooped and cheered as he delivered his keynote address.[1]

> This is a day I've been looking forward to for two and a half years. Every once in a while, a revolutionary product comes along that changes everything. One is very fortunate if you get to work on just one of these in your career. Apple has been very fortunate. It has been able to introduce a few of these into the world. In 1984, we introduced the Macintosh. It didn't just change Apple, it changed the whole computer industry. In 2001, we introduced the first iPod, and it didn't just change the way we all listened to music, it changed the entire music industry. Today, we're introducing three revolutionary products of this class. The first one is a widescreen iPod with touch controls. The second is a revolutionary mobile phone. And the third is a breakthrough internet communications device.

In amongst the whooping and cheering, Jobs clicked and clicked on his Keynote controller, cycling through the logos of the widescreen iPod, the revolutionary mobile phone and the internet device.

'So three things. An iPod, a phone and an internet communicator.'

As Jobs spoke, the three logos moved and joined at the corners to form a single element, a spinning cube that revolved in time with his words.

'An iPod. A phone. Are you getting it? These are not three separate devices. This is one device. And we are calling it iPhone. Today, Apple is going to reinvent the phone.'

The iPhone has been a phenomenal success. Directly, Apple has sold over 300 million iPhones in the five years since Jobs announced the reinvention of the mobile phone.[2] Indirectly, the company spurred competitors away from building phones with tiny keyboards towards building hand-held computing devices that combined a touchscreen, the ability to make phone calls, and internet access over both the cellular and Wi-Fi networks. In the fourth quarter of 2012, there were an estimated 1.1 billion smartphone subscribers in the world. That's a huge number of people with a powerful personal computer in their pocket. That number looks likely to grow, too: smartphones represent only 17 per cent of global mobile subscribers, which means that another 4 billion mobile users are yet to move on from featurephones to smartphones.*

The biggest rival to the iPhone is the ecosystem built around Google's Android operating system. Google opened its operating system to third parties, unlike Apple, and as a result, it is growing like crazy. Android shipments, measured by the cumulative number of units shipped since launch, have been six times that of iPhone, and Android has a larger market share than the Apple operating system (known as iOS).

Not content with reinventing the phone, Apple went on to reinvent the personal computer for a second time. The iPad, unveiled in January 2010, created a new form of computer – the tablet. The form factor has proved so successful that it has destroyed one of technology's most successful monopolies: the Windows operating system.

If you define a 'personal computer' to include smartphones and tablets (and you probably should), then the days of Microsoft's dominance of personal computing are well and truly over. Research from Mary Meeker, a doyenne of technology research who led Morgan

---

* I suspect 'subscribers' is a legacy catch-all term, and includes users on pay-as-you-go schemes.

Stanley's technology equity research team through the dotcom boom and who now works at legendary venture capital firm Kleiner Perkins Caufield Byers, shows that Microsoft's share of personal computing operating systems declined from 96 per cent, which it maintained from 1998 to 2005, to around 35 per cent in 2012.[3] The change is due almost entirely to the growth of iOS and Android, which between them now have a 45 per cent market share.

In fact, the transition is more startling than that. Researchers Katy Huberty and Ehud Gelblum at Mary Meeker's old firm, Morgan Stanley, estimate that there will shortly be an inflection point. We have already passed the point where the total *shipments* of smartphones and tablets combined exceeds that of PCs (including desktop, notebook and netbook). That happened in Q4 2010. At the time of writing, Huberty and Gelblum's estimate was that the *installed base* of smartphones/tablets would overtake that of PCs sometime during the second quarter of 2013. Apple is disrupting the very market it helped to create back in 1984. That's a very smart way of dealing with the Innovator's Dilemma.

From the point of view of content creators, though, Apple's invention of the iPhone or the iPad is not the biggest change to their way of doing business, important as they were. That distinction belongs to the App Store.

The App Store was announced – again by Steve Jobs, again at Macworld, again in January – in 2008, a year after the announcement of the iPhone and six months after its release. The App Store was positioned as a way for developers, both large corporations and one-person shops, to get their apps in front of every single iPhone user in the world.

Apple had long followed an 'integrated' strategy seeking to control both the hardware and the software. Now it added a third leg: a service layer. The App Store was in many ways a logical extension of the thinking behind iTunes. Apple had already shown how the integration between hardware (the iPod), software (the operating system the iPod used, admittedly something much simpler than the operating system in the iPhone) and a service (iTunes), could transform how users listened to and purchased music. Perhaps the same could be done for application software for smartphones.

The App Store approach to software distribution was very different from that of most traditional ways of getting software onto your phone. Typically controlled by the operators, the carrier 'deck', as it was known on a feature phone, was a gatekept, curated experience. Developers needed to invest an enormous amount of time schmoozing the handful of executives at each major carrier who decided which games would appear on the deck. If they were unable to do that, they could try to find a publisher or aggregator who would get their game on the deck, typically for a hefty fee. After the carrier share and the aggregator share, the application developer had only a small percentage cut.

Apple was offering to eliminate the gatekeeper. It was going to allow anyone to upload anything, subject to some basic rules around obscenity, malware and privacy violations. It was going to let developers set the price at which they wanted to sell the product. It was going to offer discovery features through the App Store. It was going to do all of this and give the developer a 70 per cent share of the revenue that their app generated. No additional fees for credit-card processing. No additional fees for distribution. No additional fees for marketing. As Steve Jobs said, 'this is the best deal going, to deliver applications for mobile platforms'.

The real heart of the App Store announcement was not the revenue share, though. It was how Apple was going to handle a price point that was to change the way consumers viewed content on their phones:

> We talk about the 70/30 revenue split, but the developer gets to pick the price, and you know what price a lot of developers will pick? Free. So when a developer wants to distribute an app for free, there is no charge for free apps. There is no charge to the user and there's no charge to the developer. We're going to pay for everything to get those apps out there for free. The developer and us have the exact same interest which is to get as many apps out in front of as many iPhone users as possible.[4]

The App Store has proven to be a boon for some developers, particularly those of video games. By January 2012, Apple had paid out $4 billion to developers of apps on the App Store.[5] Given the 70/30 split, that means that those apps had grossed $5.7 billion, leaving Apple with $1.7 billion as its share. By January 2013, that figure had risen to $8 billion, having added $1 billion in the previous month alone. App Store revenue appears to be accelerating. It looks as if Steve Jobs was correct in the last sentence quoted above, where he said that developers and Apple have the exact same objective, no?

Well, no. His statement is complete nonsense.

Apple is currently the most valuable company in the world. It has a market capitalization of half a trillion dollars. At the end of September 2012, it was sitting on $121 billion of net cash. In the financial year that ended on 29 September 2012, the company reported revenues of $156 billion, of which $80 billion (51 per cent) came from iPhone, $32 billion from iPad (21 per cent) and $23 billion (14.8 per cent) from Macs. Apple's share of the revenues generated from downloads of apps from the App Store was a little over 1 per cent of its total revenue.

Typically, software income is seen as 'better quality' than hardware income by financial analysts and investors because there are very few costs associated with it. When Apple sells an iPhone, it has to pay for the physical components, their manufacture and their distribution. That eats into the profit margin. In contrast, an app's direct costs are just the cost of processing the credit card and the bandwidth to deliver it. (In both cases, there are other fixed costs, such as the cost of running the retail infrastructure for the iPhone or the App Store for the apps.)

Apple, however, is so successful right now that it is making a gross profit of $68 billion, a margin of 43.9 per cent. Even after all the fixed costs are taken into account, it has a margin of 35.3 per cent. In short, if Apple stopped making any money at all from the App Store, it would barely dent its bottom line. Apple doesn't care about making money from the App Store.

What it does care about – deeply, passionately – is making the family of iProducts the most desirable products in their class in the world. It does that through design. It does that through marketing. And it does that through making sure that there is a vast library of applications available at very low prices or for free so that anyone considering buying one of their products knows that they have all the software they might ever need for a very cheap price just a couple of finger taps away.

Apple is interested in selling hardware. That developers can make lots of money from the App Store is not in question nor, as we will shortly discover, is it in doubt that they can make lots of money by giving their apps, particularly games, away for free. But Apple's interests are not aligned with those of its developers. This disconnect – between the needs of Apple and the needs of its developer ecosystem – is as good an illustration of how the price of a digital good tends to free as any we can find in the world today.

To understand it, we need to dive into some basic economics, starting with Bertrand competition.

Joseph Bertrand (1822–1900) was a distinguished French mathematician. So distinguished in fact that he has two paradoxes, one postulate* and a form of economic competition named after him.

Bertrand's explanation of one model of competition came when he critiqued the work of another nineteenth-century French economist, Antoine Cournot. Cournot was interested in understanding how companies compete and in 1838 published *Recherches sur les principes mathématiques de la théorie des richesses*.†

The heart of Cournot competition is that the key factor driving the profits that two companies competing in a similar market will make is predicated on the quantity that they produce. If one company is producing shoes from a factory and a second company wishes to compete, it will be careful not to flood the market with too many shoes, driving down the profits for both businesses. Even without active collusion, both companies would keep production low enough to make profits for both parties.

Recherches, which is now widely respected, was ignored at the time. Cournot died in 1877, and after his death a group of young economists thought his work deserved wider recognition and called for his models to be re-examined. Bertrand studied *Recherches* and

* A conjecture, subsequently proven, that there is at least one prime between n and $2n - 2$ for every $n > 3$, if you must know.
† Researches into the mathematical principles of the theory of wealth.

thought it was ridiculous. In particular, he thought that Cournot's decision to assume that production volume was the key unit of competition was so arbitrary that he set out to reconstruct Cournot's model using a different variable. Bertrand picked price, not volume, as his variable, and in the process he found a new theory of competition.

Bertrand's logic works like this: Imagine that two companies are making identical products. If the products are identical, buyers will choose to purchase the one that is cheaper. Note that there are some substantial assumptions here. It is assumed that distribution costs are negligible or identical. It assumes that the cost of making the goods is identical for each firm. It assumes that customers don't factor in the cost of research to find the best price. It excludes the value of branding or marketing.

Sticking with our footwear example, let us imagine that the shoes cost $1 per pair to make, what is known as the marginal cost. (The marginal cost excludes the fixed cost of the factory that makes the shoes, and can be defined as 'the change in total cost that arises when the quantity produced changes by one unit'.) Firm A decides to sell its shoes for $5, making a handsome profit of $4. Firm B, making an identical pair of shoes, sells them for $4. Buyers flock to Firm B, and it has 100 per cent of the market. 'Hang on a minute,' says Firm A. 'I've got this expensive factory and workforce sitting here and I need to sell something. I don't need that huge profit, and two can play at the pricing game. I'll cut my price to $3.'

And so it goes, with each firm undercutting the other until the price stops at $1. Why $1? Because that is the marginal cost. If either firm prices below that level, they will be making a loss at the per unit level on each pair of shoes they sell. So Bertrand competition has only one stable state, the state where both firms are selling their products for the cost of production. If one of them tries to push the price higher, all of its customers will immediately flock to its competitor. In a competitive market, price falls to the marginal cost.

The problem with Bertrand's model is that it has long been viewed as theoretical. It assumes that there are few switching or research costs for customers. It assumes perfect competition, and there were few perfectly competitive markets in late-nineteenth-century France. As a result, economists have spent more than a century trying to figure out which industries are better understood by using the Cournot competition model and which are better suited to using the Bertrand competition model. Cournot competition fits best when capacity or production cannot be easily changed by the firm. Bertrand competition is best suited to markets where the quantity of products being produced can be increased rapidly and efficiently. Chris Anderson, the former editor-in-chief of *Wired* and author of *Free*, says, 'In abundant markets, where it is easy to make more stuff, Bertrand tends to win; price often does fall to the marginal cost.'[6]

When Steve Jobs announced the App Store, he announced that it would cost developers nothing to distribute their apps if they were free. Apple would swallow the hosting and distribution costs of the software. They would take care of making sure that the developer could get its product in front of the consumer at absolutely zero cost to both developer and consumer. It is Bertrand competition in its cleanest form. Many of the assumptions that are flaws of the theoretical model – that there are no capacity constraints, that distribution costs are negligible – turn out to be true in practice when the product is digital bits and bytes that can be replicated perfectly and where the costs of the replication and subsequent distribution are fully borne by the late Uncle Steve and his team in Cupertino, California.

So what happened? I'm going to focus on games. We can expect that smart business people, well versed in economics, would understand that Bertrand competition was inevitable, that the inevitable price point would be the marginal cost of production – that is to say zero, and set their price to free. Can't we?

Can we heck. At launch in 2008, the going price for a game on the App Store was $9.99, although you'll be hard pushed to find a game anywhere near that price today. The reasons were clear enough. Games on featurephones cost anywhere from $3 for simple puzzle games to $7 for branded tie-ins like *Assassin's Creed* or the game of the latest blockbuster movie. Charging a premium for games on the iPhone seemed sensible, especially when those games compared favourably with titles on platforms like the Nintendo DS, whose customers were used to spending $20 or more on a single game. Companies like Sega and Electronic Arts released games such as *Super Monkey Ball*, *Bejeweled 2* and *Tetris* at very high prices.[7]

It wasn't just premium games that were asking for premium prices either. Many developers and publishers of mobile games had got used to the cosy relationship they had with the carriers, who acted as gate-keepers to content. Because the carrier decks were curated, if you had an 'in' with the carrier team, you could get your product in front of consumers and get them to buy it. It didn't have to be the best possible product, it just had to be the one in front of the consumer. With less competition, since the carriers didn't want to be bothered with hundreds of different developers, the publishers had a comfortable position.

All this changed when Steve Jobs opened up the store and let anyone reach the entire audience of iPhone users. No longer could publishers rely on their clout with carriers to ensure that their products were published while small independent studios were unable to find a route to market. As Justin Davis, editor of *IGN Wireless*, put it:

> When the App Store launched, companies like Gameloft thought they could get away with charging $3.99 or more for simple solitaire, chess and Sudoku apps. The companies didn't even consider the free competition that would result in these categories. Either from budding programmers cutting their teeth on these uncomplicated genres or from companies releasing a free product to advertise their other paid titles.[8]

It wasn't just competition from every Tom, Dick and Henrietta who could now pay $99 for an iOS software development kit and become an iPhone developer. Companies trying to maintain premium prices started to discover that they didn't just have competition from young startups with nothing to lose. Established competitors were beginning to play the same game. All in the name of discovery.

We've seen that every abundance comes with an accompanying scarcity. It used to be that it was hard to get hold of games. When I was a core PC gamer, about a decade ago, I could tell you something – not much, but something – about pretty well every game that was released in an entire year, gleaned from regular reading of PC gaming magazines. Now, several hundred games are released for iOS *every single day*. For developers, getting their games seen is truly a make-or-break issue. For consumers, finding the games that will appeal to them can be hard.

The most effective gauge, at the moment, is the charts on the App Store. Apple is beginning to tweak and adjust the algorithms, in much the same way that Google tweaks its search algorithms, to make it easier for users to find good games, but in the early days of the App Store, the algorithm was fairly simple: number of downloads.

It didn't matter if your product sold at 99 cents or $9.99, Apple counted only the number of downloads. If you wanted to chart, you needed to get a lot of people to download your game. As Justin Davis said:

> It became a painful choice for studios. Although in the end it ended up not being much of a choice at all. You could sell your title for $4.99, the price it likely deserved, and never sell enough copies to chart. Your game would be invisible to most iPhone owners. Or you could sell it for $0.99 and hope to sell five times as many copies by cracking the top twenty-five. The race to the bottom had begun.[9]

Electronic Arts accelerated the process in 2009. Figuring that being at the top of the charts on Christmas Day as consumers opened their brand-new iPhones and iPod Touches would lead to a massive spike in sales, they slashed the prices of many of their top branded games to 99 cents. They did it again in 2010, dropping prices of such household names as *Need For Speed*, *SimCity*, *Madden NFL* and *Scrabble*. It seemed to have worked, since at one point, all the top twelve iPad apps and six of the top ten iPhone apps were from Electronic Arts.[10]

Bertrand competition was, and remains, in full force.

The same process is likely to play out in ebooks. The marginal cost of distributing an ebook is very low, as close to zero as makes no odds. Michael R. Hicks is a science-fiction author who has written the Harvest trilogy and three further trilogies that go under the 'In Her Name' banner. He first self-published his books on the Amazon Kindle in 2008. He now has twelve books available to buy. Three of them are available for free as ebooks on Kindle, Nook, Smashwords, Kobo, iTunes and Google Play. Hicks explains his reasoning: 'The reason I'm doing this is very simple: *I want you to get hooked on my books.* I want you to try these freebies, because if you like them, you're going to want to get the rest (and if you don't, you haven't lost anything but a bit of time). So download away, and tell your family, friends, and co-workers to come here and get their own copies, too!'[11]

In 2012, Hicks estimates that he gave away 250,000 ebooks for free. He also sold 90,000 books at prices ranging from $4 to $25. A person stuck in pre-digital thinking might look at those numbers as representing a quarter of a million units of lost sales, costing Hicks somewhere between $1 million and $6.25 million. A web business person would think that Hicks had a conversion rate of 36 per cent, which looks pretty good.

In late 2012, a price war broke out between Amazon and Sony over ebooks in the UK. Sony was offering books from certain publishers for as little as 20p. Amazon matched it. The publishers and authors received their normal royalties, but consumers paid a heavily discounted price, and the discounted books rocketed up the bestseller charts. I bought two ebooks at that price in late 2012. I have yet to open either of them, but I contributed to their chart rankings.

We may not see Bertrand competition coming to ebooks as fast as it came to iOS games for two reasons. Firstly, Amazon has a more sophisticated recommendation algorithm than Apple. It makes book suggestions based on detailed personal information about your reading habits. Apple relies more on raw data, such as number of downloads or gross revenue. Secondly, Amazon is a retailer, not a hardware manufacturer. Apple created the App Store to sell more iPhones; Amazon wants to sell more books (and other things). If the day comes when Amazon decides it could make more money from selling Kindle Fires than from selling books, the book industry will be in even more trouble than it already is.

A lot of the argument around the issue of prices trending towards free has focused on copyright. Nothing about the Curve argues that copyright should not exist. Copyright needs to be reformed, and many people are discussing how best to do it. I am not a 'free-tard', the disparaging term used by those who wish to preserve the status quo for those who believe that everyone should give their content away for free. The Curve is all about harnessing the power of free to make money. It also doesn't involve a requirement to be free, although I believe being so is often valuable. Remember, the secret of the Curve is about building upwards from whatever base you have, finding and satisfying customers who love what you do and allowing them to spend lots of money on things they value. Starting by offering them something for free, so that you can begin a relationship, is great. If you choose to start by making them pay, you will increase the barrier to entry, probably necessitating higher marketing spend and a slower path to the higher end of the Curve. That is your choice, and it is a valid choice, particularly if you already have a well-known brand, significant marketing expertise and deep pockets. I just think when all of your competitors are trying to find ways to give their customers a great experience for free, you are in a difficult place if your starting point is paid.

Content has long been charged for but, on the App Store at least, those heady days when you can charge almost a dollar for a game are long gone for many developers. The prevailing price point on the App Store is currently free. The good news is that in 2011, at least nine games grossed more than $30 million. One Finnish company, Supercell, is generating over $2.4 million in revenue per day from two free games, *Clash of Clans* and *Hay Day*, through the sale of virtual goods to a subset of its audience. In 2013, the company sold shares worth $130 million to investors at a valuation of $770 million.[12] British publisher NaturalMotion has stated that its hit game *CSR Racing* made $12 million in the first month.

The heart of the issue for anyone facing Bertrand competition is this: no matter what you would like to do, if there is a viable alternative for your product, your competitors will reduce the price of their offering to the marginal cost of production. In a world where anything that can be distributed digitally – books, games, films, television shows and, when 3D printing becomes a reality, physical goods – has a marginal cost of zero, or so close to zero as makes no odds, competitors will force the price down to zero.

The pace of change varies by market. Music and ebooks are small files so the cost and time to download is tiny. Console games and HD movies are huge files, so the cost and time is more significant. Physical objects can't yet be easily distributed as digital files and printed on demand because the technology to do so is not as ubiquitous as PCs and smartphones. These are temporary issues, though. Bandwidth is ever-improving and 3D printing is decreasing in price every year.

You can argue that your product is better. That there is only one Led Zeppelin or Snoop Doggy Dogg or Ke$ha or Adele. That you set the price.

But in the long run, that argument does not hold. The price is set by your competitors and by consumer expectations. And to understand that, we need to look at the approaching end of the mass market.

4
EVERYTHING, JUST FOR YOU

In 231 BC, Zhao Zing, king of the Chinese state of Qin, set out to conquer the six remaining independent kingdoms of China. Within ten years his armies had conquered them all, unifying China and ushering in more than two millennia of imperial rule. He took the name Qin Shi Huang, First Emperor.

All because of mass production.

Qin Shi Huang's conquests were the culmination of 250 years of warfare and struggle in China known as the Warring States Period. During that time, warfare changed as armies developed a stronger focus on infantry and cavalry than chariots. The widespread use of crossbows made it easy to field large armies of relatively ill-trained soldiers. The size of these armies was immense. Different sources report armies of over 1 million men for at least two of the warring kingdoms, with death tolls at the battles of Maling (100,000) and Yique (240,000) implying slaughter at an industrial scale.

These numbers need to be taken with a pinch of salt. Not only were soldiers paid by the number of enemies killed, which created a significant incentive for exaggeration, but the dynasty that Qin Shi Huang founded had a strong interest in emphasizing the stability of their imperial rule compared to the warfare, destruction and death of the Warring States Period.

There is no doubt, though, that there were hundreds of thousands of soldiers in the field. Those soldiers needed to be armed. Historian David Williams has made convincing arguments that this was achieved through one of the first known examples of mass production.[1]

Crossbows were originally manufactured by individual craftsmen. Each craftsman was responsible for every component of the bow: the trigger, the stock and so on. Williams argues that during these wars, Qin Shi Huang's armies commissioned what was perhaps the first example of mass production, line assembly and a modular approach to mechanized weapons in history. The wooden stocks were easy enough to produce, but trigger mechanisms demanded accurately machined bronze components that could be manufactured in vast numbers.[2] Qin Shi Huang's solution was to use moulds to produce self-contained trigger and release mechanisms which could be secured to the stock using just two bolts. The practical impact of Qin's innovation was that crossbows became readily available, and, since their use required less training than other weapons, so did crossbow-armed infantry. The impact of mass production on history was established.

Mass production as we currently understand it developed during the late nineteenth century. The prerequisites of mass production – interchangeable parts, machine tools and power – all reached a tipping point as the nineteenth century gave way to the twentieth and one of the most famous pioneers of mass production, Henry Ford, took the stage. Ford's great achievement was to develop and put into practice mass production via the assembly line. He started by focusing on how to reduce the cost of manufacturing:

> In a little dark shop on a side street an old man had laboured for years making axe handles. Out of seasoned hickory he fashioned them with the help of a draw shave, a chisel and a supply of sandpaper. Carefully was each handle weighed and balanced. No two of them were alike. The curve must exactly fit the hand and must conform to the grain of the wood. From dawn until dark the old man laboured. His average product was eight handles a week, for which he received a dollar and a half each. And often some of these were unsaleable – because the balance was not true.
>
> To-day you can buy a better axe handle, made by machinery, for a few cents. And you need not worry about the balance. They are all alike – and every one is perfect. Modern methods applied in a big way have not only brought the cost of axe handles down to a fraction of their former cost – but they have immensely improved the product.

It was the application of these same methods to the making of the Ford car that at the very start lowered the price and heightened the quality. We just developed an idea.[3]

Ford, however, wanted to do more than make the price a bit lower and the quality a bit higher.

> I will build a motor car for the great multitude. It will be large enough for the family but small enough for the individual to run and care for. It will be constructed of the best materials by the best men to be hired, after the simplest designs that modern engineering can devise. But it will be so low in price that no man making a good salary will be unable to own one – and enjoy with his family the blessing of hours of pleasure in God's great open spaces.

So in 1909 he announced one morning that in the future Ford was going to build only one model, that the model was going to be Model T, and the chassis would be exactly the same for all cars. He added: 'Any customer can have a car painted any colour that he wants so long as it is black.'

The sales people were not happy. They wanted more models, to satisfy a wider range of customers. They wanted to satisfy what Henry Ford called the 5 per cent, that vocal minority who had the ear of the salesmen, not the 95 per cent who just bought what they were offered without any fuss:

> The selling people could not of course see the advantages that a single model would bring about in production. More than that, they did not particularly care. They thought that our production was good enough as it was and there was a very decided opinion that lowering the sales price would hurt sales, that the people who wanted quality would be driven away and that there would be none to replace them.

As we all know now, the sales people were wrong. Ford pushed through his unrelenting focus on reducing the production costs of his vehicles.*

---

* Ford's focus on reducing production costs did not come at the expense of his workforce. He paid $5 a day, more than twice the going rate. As a result, the best and most highly motivated mechanics flocked to work for him.

Ford's low cost car and aggressive marketing worked. The company had sold 250,000 Model Ts by 1914. By 1918, half of all the cars in America were Model Ts. The line was eventually discontinued in 1927, by which time Ford had sold over 15 million of them.

Ford benefited from, and focused on, a declining cost curve. The more he made, the cheaper each unit was to produce. He wasn't just benefiting from economies of scale. He worked hard to refine the assembly process to improve costs. He took inspiration from the meat packers of Chicago. 'The idea came in a general way from the overhead trolley that the Chicago packers use in dressing beef,' Ford said.[4] At the stockyards, butchers removed certain cuts as each carcass passed by, until nothing was left. Ford turned the process on its head, giving each mechanic a particular task to do, standing at a single work location, with all the parts and tools within arm's reach. The result: in 1914, 13,000 workers at Ford made 260,720 cars, while the rest of the industry combined made roughly the same number of cars (286,770) with over five times as many workers (66,350).

By manufacturing large numbers of identical items, Ford had shown that a firm could spread the cost of the factory over many units and reduce the overall labour cost. Professor John M. McCann of the Fuqua School of Business at Duke University says, 'Thus it became economically feasible, perhaps even imperative, to manufacture large quantities of a good at increasingly lower costs.'[5]

There is a clear consequence of the development of mass production. Ford is often believed to have declared that customers would have to have black Model Ts because it would make his cars cheaper to have just one colour. (In fact, only 12 million of the 15 million Model Ts were black.)[6] All manufacturers wanted their customers to desire exactly the same products, because that would reduce the cost per unit. It was no longer a case of 'Is it available?' Ford made it all about affordability and price. To make money, companies needed to produce lots of the same product. Instead of changing their products to match what customers wanted, companies started to change what customers wanted to match what the companies produced. The era of mass marketing was born, although it wasn't until the end of the Second World War that the mass market in its current form was established, particularly in the United States.

During the war, over 16 million Americans served in the armed forces. Factories were converted from producing consumer goods to producing planes, tanks, ammunition, weapons and all the equipment a military fighting a global war needed. With so many working age men in uniform, vast numbers of women were employed in the factories, leading to an economy that had full employment and a reduced supply of consumer goods. There was little to buy, so there was a high savings rate, encouraged by the US government as a means of financing the war. Professor McCann argues, 'When the war was over and the men returned home, there was high pent-up demand due to the large accumulated wealth.'

Throw in the massive investment in the Interstate Highway System, inspired by the German Autobahns, supported by the automobile and oil industries, and suddenly cities were connected to each other, and outlying areas were connected to their nearby cities, with high-quality roads. The needs of the military during the war had improved electronics, in particular the standards of radio and television. Now add extra demand from a reunited population that rushed to the altar and soon produced a large crop of babies – the baby boomers – and you have all the requirements for a mass market: mass demand; mass transport and the ability to get to malls and large stores; and mass communications in the form of affordable radio and television.

In many ways, the nature of marketing that we are familiar with today – the soap operas sponsored by Procter & Gamble in the 1950s, the familiar television format of hour-long shows interrupted by frequent advertising breaks, the full-page ads that subsidize magazines and newspapers – are all predicated on the idea that the product is fixed and the objective of marketing is to make us all want the same thing, because that is the most efficient way of us all getting high-quality products at a low price.

The mass media was created by the needs of advertisers, not the wants of consumers. Mass marketing supported the business world when consumers still worried about whether products were available, affordable and of acceptable quality. But we have moved on from 'Is it available?' and we have moved on from 'How much does it cost?' We assume that good-quality products are available at a low price. What matters now is how it makes us feel.

Management theorists James Gilmore and Joseph Pine have written about this phenomenon in their books *The Experience Economy* and *Authenticity*. They argue that the web has enabled a new era, an era of mass customization. Dell offers us computers with customization options for every single component. Starbucks offers 87,000 different drink combinations.[7] It enables us to have exactly what we want, in any of their coffee shops around the world, while also providing a cost-effective experience that is both individualized and standardized at the same time. Our holidays are becoming less about the package and more about the 'experience', as we increasingly find that how something makes us *feel* is a core part of our purchasing decision. The very process of customization creates value for consumers who are no longer looking for the same product as everyone else at a good price.

Customization comes at a price. Psychologist Sheena Iyengar has demonstrated, using jam, that when presented with too much choice, people consistently choose not to choose. She ran an experiment where customers to Draeger's, a large grocery store in San Francisco, were offered the chance to sample jams made by the British jam manufacturer Wilkin & Sons. Everyone who sampled the jam was given a coupon worth $1 off a jar of Wilkin & Sons jam. One group sampled from a table that held twenty-four different varieties of jam. The second group sampled from a table that contained only six varieties. Iyengar was testing the presumption that more choice was a good thing: that the table with more varieties on offer would attract more customers and make more sales. The initial results supported the presumption. Of all the customers who entered the store while the small assortment was on display, 40 per cent stopped to sample the jam. When the large assortment was on display, that figure jumped to 60 per cent of all customers walking through the door, a 50 per cent increase.

The results were reversed when Iyengar checked with the store tills to see how many customers had bought jam with a coupon. Of those who had tried the large assortment, only 3 per cent went on to make a purchase. With the small sample, that figure jumped tenfold to 30 per cent. Combining the two figures, customers were six times more likely to make a purchase when they had less choice. Iyengar's research assistant noted that customers who had experienced a wide range of options appeared to struggle to make a decision:

> [P]eople who had sampled the large assortment were quite puzzled. They kept examining different jars, and if they were with other people, they discussed the relative merits of the flavours. This went on for up to ten minutes, at which point many of them left empty handed. By contrast, those who had seen only six jams seemed to know exactly which one was right for them. They strode down the aisle, grabbed a jar in a quick minute – lemon curd was the favourite – and continued with the rest of the shopping.[8]

It appears as if more choice, the logical outcome of a market environment where there are fewer gatekeepers, might result in fewer sales. Luckily, Iyengar's recommendations for how to offer a vast range of products and services while making it easier for customers to make purchase decisions employ the kind of technology solutions that are widely used in the online world. She recommends employing 'the well-organized' choice. Grouping products into categories helps people make choices. For example, Iyengar found that shoppers felt as if they had more choices if there were fewer options overall, but more categories. Arranging a smaller selection of magazines under a wide range of subheadings like 'Health and Fitness' or 'Home & Garden' created a structure that made choosing more efficient and enjoyable.[9]

The categorization doesn't have to be structured by the retailer. Crowd-sourced tags can help customers find products in an online store. Amazon's recommendation engine provides a list of products tailored to your recent store-browsing history and offers suggestions of 'things that other people who viewed this product also bought'. Meanwhile, we rely on word of mouth as we have always done, multiplied by social media and the ease with which we can go from a recommendation on Facebook, Twitter, LinkedIn or a web page to the purchase of a product in just a few clicks. The challenges that Iyengar raises are real, but her solutions are often technological, and the technology industry is experimenting with ways to make it easier for customers to choose while also offering almost limitless choice.

There is a paradox here. The dominance of mass-market products is coming to an end. Technology is enabling cost-effective personalization in everything ranging from $30,000 cars to $100 dolls and $10 cuff-links. The long tail of unlimited shelf space means that if a product can be conceived of, it can be marketed online. T-shirt manufacturer Solid Gold Bomb boasts over 500,000 clothing lines available on Amazon, most available for around $20 plus shipping.[10] Many of them are T-shirts with randomized variants on the 'Keep Calm and Carry On' meme. None of these products exist. When a customer orders a T-shirt it is automatically printed and shipped. There is unlimited shelf space and zero working capital for these T-shirts because they do not exist until they are ordered.[11]

Kevin Kelly, the founding editor of *Wired*, pointed out that in the world of the long tail, where shelf space is unlimited and a vast array of products can be 'stocked' cost-effectively, there are two winners: a few lucky aggregators such as Amazon and Netflix and 7 billion potential consumers. 'The long tail is a decidedly mixed blessing for creators. Individual artists, producers, inventors and makers are over-looked in the equation. The long tail does not raise the sales of creators much, but it does add massive competition and endless downward pressure on prices.'[12]

There is a solution to this problem. It involves shifting our perspec-tive. Those at the end of the long tail need to avoid selling products purely on a volume basis. They need to find ways to add value through personalization, self-expression, scarcity and by thinking about how what they are doing makes their customers feel. That is where and how the niche will thrive. We are seeing the emergence of the niche. Of the personalized. Of the 'authentic' and of the 'experience'. The para-dox is that the internet has enabled this fragmentation. It has enabled Dell to cost-effectively manufacture each PC individually and Solid Gold Bomb to offer a range of half a million T-shirts. It has made the era of the niche and the era of the customized viable.

It has also made the big get bigger.

On 25 December 1977, 28 million Britons ate turkey, opened presents, watched the Queen's Speech and, later that evening, settled into arm-chairs and sofas to watch *The Morecambe and Wise Show*.[13] Eric Morecambe and Ernie Wise were Britain's best-loved double act. The tall funny one and the short straight man, their programmes were part sketch-show, part sitcom, with a hefty dose of music hall and variety thrown in.

The pair first met in 1941 when they were both working on the variety circuit. *The Morecambe and Wise Show* started on the BBC in 1968 and rapidly established itself as one of the nation's favourite television programmes. Indeed, its popularity continues to this day. In 2000, the members of the British Film Institute were polled to determine the best British television shows ever to have been made.[14] *The Morecambe and Wise Show* came fourteenth, ahead of such offerings as *Blackadder*, *Absolutely Fabulous*, *Only Fools and Horses* and *Father Ted*. (*Fawlty Towers* took the top spot.) In 2006, a television show broadcast to celebrate fifty years since the launch of Britain's first commercial broadcaster, ITV, ranked Morecambe and Wise as the second most popular television stars in Britain (behind David Jason), as voted for by the viewing public.

Yet 1977 appears to have marked the high point of not just their popularity, but of a single television programme's popularity. While the exact ratings figure is disputed, there is no doubt that somewhere between 21 million and 28 million people watched *the same programme at the same time* that Christmas evening in 1977. Given that the British population in 1977 was approximately 56 million, perhaps as much as half of the entire population watched that single show.

By 2012, the British population had risen to 63 million. Yet the most popular show of the year, the closing ceremony of the Olympics, garnered 24.5 million.[15] If you strip out one-off events (the Olympic opening and closing ceremonies, the two most popular finals, the Queen's Diamond Jubilee and three Euro 2012 football games), the first 'proper' television programme in the list is the final of *Britain's Got Talent*, which peaked at 13.1 million, not quite half of Morecambe and Wise's record and only approximately a quarter of the UK population. To many this is a clear example of how the market is fragmenting. Of how choice (in the form of new terrestrial channels, then paid-for cable and satellite, then more free terrestrial channels, not to mention non-televisual entertainment options) has splintered audiences, made the niche viable and created a challenging environment for broadcasters and programme makers to make money in and survive.

In fact, the fragmentation is more substantial than that. We are seeing fragmentation in channels. We are seeing fragmentation in time-shifting, initially via VHS recorders, now by Personal Video Recorders, catch-up TV and streaming services such as Netflix. We are seeing fragmentation in business models, such as the increasing trend for customers to watch entire series at a time, either purchased as physical boxed sets, downloaded from services like iTunes or streamed either on a pay-per-view basis or as part of a subscription service like Netflix.

Yet this fragmentation is creating new opportunities. *Los Angeles Times* television critic Roger Lloyd sees the changes to television as creating new opportunities:

> [Television] caters now to myriad smaller but often more intensely dedicated audiences, inspiring a sense of ownership and of community reminiscent of the way pop music works ... to be seriously into *Breaking Bad* or *Pretty Little Liars*, *Doctor Who* or *Fringe*, *Bob's Burgers* or *Adventure Time*, Rachel Maddow or Jimmy Fallon, *The Voice* or the *Real Housewives* of here and there, now confers status – and the basis for an identity – in the same way that liking the Velvet Underground, Skrillex or the Alabama Shakes might ... Like pop music, television today is multifarious and factional, and with the expansion of cable and cable's leap into original production, it has acquired something like an 'indie' or alt-TV component to complement its still substantial mainstream.[16]

Our relationship with television is changing. We are no longer tied to a single screen in the living room, a shared space where we once chose what we viewed from a few options and watched it with family or friends. It's no longer even tied to any particular room. As music changed when it moved from record player to the transistor radio, the Walkman and the iPod, so television is becoming portable, personal and shifted to a time and place of our choosing. The BBC iPlayer service which allows catch-up viewing of broadcast programmes now sees around 30 per cent of viewing on smartphones and tablets, and that percentage is climbing.[17]

'The life of any television series – or the hooky television moment, for that matter, in this age of viral replication – may be extended indefinitely,' says Lloyd. 'This is similar to, but fundamentally different from, the traditional syndicated rerun model, which caters to mass tastes and depends on them.' Even television, the ultimate mass medium, is becoming niche.

The end of the mass market and the rise of social media have changed the way we view many things. Our musical tastes still define us. In my student days, if you were invited back to someone's room you would surreptitiously check out the CDs arranged on their shelves to see if there was any basis for long-term compatibility. Today's students have MP3 players and access to almost unlimited amounts of music, whether legally or illegally. It is not cool to have music. Everyone has that. It is cool to *discover* music. Similarly, television used to be all about the shared experience. Everyone watching that episode of *Dallas*, *The Morecambe and Wise Christmas Special*, *Doctor Who*. Now it is about that, but it is also about time-shifting, about boxed sets, about watching what you want when you want to watch it, rather than being at the whim of the broadcast scheduler.

The niche is thriving, yet the mass market is thriving too. As we saw earlier, large events such as the Olympics and the Queen's Diamond Jubilee are still massive winners along with major sporting events. Even the most popular studio programme in the UK, *Britain's Got Talent*, has adapted to the times: it is a reality TV show which is significantly less entertaining once the results are widely known. Excluding reality TV shows, sports and unique events, only two programmes (single episodes of soap opera *Coronation Street* and period drama *Downton Abbey*) remain in the top twenty.

Of course, we can't exclude all of those events. Broadcast television gets the biggest audiences when it does what it does best: create event programming that is at its most powerful when enjoyed either live or as a shared cultural experience. The prevalence of events and reality television is not a weakness of broadcasting, it is a strength, showing how it is keeping control of the prime-time viewing that gives us all something to talk about around the water cooler or, increasingly, via Facebook, Twitter and the second screen.

We can see these examples – of how the big are getting bigger – again and again. The biggest pop sensation of 2012 was Psy, a thirty-four-year-old South Korean pop star whose video for 'Gangnam Style' has been viewed over 1 billion times on YouTube. It has 6 million

Facebook Likes.[18] It has been shared on Facebook over 25 million times and on Twitter 1.2 million times. Psy has been on a world tour, teaching people like Britney Spears, Madonna and UN Secretary General Ban Ki-Moon the signature moves of his dance, a sort of horse-riding hop. My two-year-old loves it. So do I.

Psy, who has made five previous albums which failed to make much of an impact on his global audience, is sanguine about his success: 'I don't call this success. This is a phenomenon. I didn't do anything. It was by people, not by me. So on the next one, what if people don't do it again?'[19]

The speed at which 'Gangnam Style' became a global phenomenon is amazing. A great product that happened to hit our need for cheesy entertainment at just the right moment, its spark met the accelerant of social media and the resulting inferno has swept the word. The big get bigger.

In May 2008, Take-Two Interactive released *Grand Theft Auto IV*, its latest incarnation in a highly successful video game franchise. Within a week, the company announced that it had broken all entertainment launch records, measured by dollar value.[20] *Grand Theft Auto IV* sold 3.6 million units globally in its first day on sale, generating $310 million of sales at retail. In the first week, it sold approximately 6 million units with an estimated retail value of $500 million.

In November 2009, it was Activision's turn, announcing a record launch for its blockbuster title *Call of Duty: Modern Warfare 2*. The first five days' sales were $550 million, beating every other entertainment launch in history. *Modern Warfare 2*'s launch beat all previous first- and five-day entertainment industry box office, book and video game sell-through records. That includes the five-day worldwide and domestic box office records, held by *Harry Potter and the Half-Blood Prince* ($394 million) and *The Dark Knight* ($203.8 million), respectively, and the largest reported first-day book sales in dollars, held by *Harry Potter and the Deathly Hallows* ($220 million).[21]

In 2010, Activision did it again. Its follow up to *Modern Warfare 2*, called *Call of Duty: Black Ops*, had five-day sales of $650 million.[22] And in 2011, *Call of Duty: Modern Warfare 3* generated $775 million in retail sales, smashing the series' own record a second time.[23]

You would think that this kind of success would mean that the games industry was in rude health. You would be wrong. More accurately, you would be wrong about the traditional games industry, as represented by these huge budget, blockbuster titles played on powerful PCs or home consoles like the Xbox 360 or PlayStation 3 and, typically, sold in boxes on the high street.

In November 2010, just as Activision was about to smash its own sales record with *Call of Duty: Black Ops*, Disney CEO Bob Iger stated that his company 'probably will end up investing less on the console side than we have because of the shift we're seeing in consumption'.[24] They shut down several acquired studios with strong expertise in console development and refocused their activities towards mobile, tablet and online games, many of which are free to play, but allow players the choice of spending money on a variety of upgrades and virtual goods as they play. In March 2012, the UK's largest specialist retailer of video games, GAME, ran into trouble and was restructured. Hundreds of stores were closed and thousands of employees lost their jobs.[25] Publisher THQ, once generating revenues of $1 billion a year, albeit with only $68 million in profit,[26] collapsed into bankruptcy in late 2012.[27]

Data from NPD, the market research firm that tracks retail sales of games, suggests that 2008 was a high-water mark, and that every year since has seen fewer games sold at retail.[28] While Activision and Take-Two were breaking sales records with predictable regularity, the market was changing. As with television, and as with book hits such as *Fifty Shades of Grey*, the big are getting bigger and taking an increasing slice of the market.

At the same time, those who don't just want the mainstream fare served up to everyone else, or who do want it but also want more, have more routes to discover games than ever before. Indie games thrive on platforms like Steam and Kongregate. Mobile games are improving in quality all the time, and most of us now routinely carry a high-quality gaming device in our pockets. Facebook introduced a whole swathe of people who had never played games before to the likes of *Farmville* and *Mafia Wars*. Companies like Jagex, Bigpoint and Gameforge create sophisticated games with enormous fan followings that can be played by anyone who has a web browser.

What we are seeing is a polarization of the market. The big is getting bigger. The niche is getting more viable. The middle is getting squeezed. Squeezed so hard that it seems likely to pop out of existence.

The mass market as we understand it is going away. There will still be global hits, shared frames of reference that we all understand, cultural touch points like major sporting events, the final of *The X Factor* and blockbuster movies and games. Increasingly, though, we will be able to seek out niche products which appeal to us as individuals. Not that these niches need to be very small. *Doctor Who* is a niche. So is *Grey's Anatomy*. So is most music. Most games. Most books. Most television shows.

What has changed is that you no longer have to shoot for the lucky chance of getting a hit. You can build a business on many fewer people loving what you do. This changes many of the assumptions that underpin the way business has been done for hundreds of years. The new opportunities arise because we have overthrown what I call the tyranny of the physical.

5
THE TYRANNY OF THE PHYSICAL

Robert Pershing Wadlow is the tallest man who ever lived. Born in 1918 in Alton, Illinois, by the time he was eight years old, he stood 6′2″ tall. Wadlow suffered from a defective pituitary gland which led to an abnormally high level of growth hormones. Throughout his adult life, he just kept getting taller. The average height of a human male in the UK is 5′9″, in America 5′9½″. When Wadlow died of an infection in 1940 at the age of twenty-two, he was 8′11″, 55 per cent taller than average.*

The shortest man who has ever lived is Chandra Bahadur Dangi, a Nepali born in 1939 who lives in a remote village 400 miles from the capital Kathmandu. He measures just 1′9″. Dangi is just 30 per cent of the average height of a British male.

Nassim Nicholas Taleb, author of *Fooled by Randomness* and a leading thinker on how our inability to properly evaluate risk and probability affects the world, calls the realm governed by physical constraints 'Mediocristan'. Mediocristan is the world of heights and weights and other physical properties. It is a world that follows the bell curve, the Gaussian distribution familiar to many from school mathematics classes. If you were to weigh all the adult African elephants in the world and plot their weights on a graph, nearly all the measurements would cluster around a central number – the mean, or what we would unscientifically call the

---

* It is a little known fact that if you are above the average height for a man, you will be able to respond with your exact height if you are asked. If you are shorter than average height, you are never quite sure of how tall you are. I guess I'm about 5′8″, there or thereabouts.

average. The shape of the graph would resemble a bell, hence the name, with most of the elephant weights clustered around the centre of the graph and a rapid decline towards the outliers, those elephants who were either much heavier than average or much lighter. You would expect to find many elephants of around average height and few very big or very little ones. The central premise of the Gaussian distribution is that most observations hover around the mediocre, the average. The further away from the average you get, the less likely you are to find an example. In technical terms, 'the odds of a deviation decline faster and faster (exponentially) as you move away from the average'.[1] Taleb uses the example of the average height of a person to illustrate this effect. He assumes that the average height of an American (man or woman) is 1.67 metres or 5'7". The odds of being 10cm taller (more than 5'10") are 1 in 6.3. Yet the odds of being 60cm taller (7'5") are 1 in 1 billion.

In other words, when you live in Mediocristan, and someone tells you that the average of something is 1.67, you can generally be confident that most observations of such a thing will be close to 1.67, there or thereabouts. Wadlow and Dangi represent massive extremes. Just a glimpse of either of them emphasizes their very 'differentness'. In Mediocristan, small differences seem very different very quickly: a man of 6'9" is considered very tall, a man of 4'9" is considered very short. We are all clustered tightly around the average.

Ah, the average. A very misleading word, and one that will cause no end of difficulty to people trying to understand how the world works as physical characteristics become less important than digital ones. With apologies to anyone who hated maths at school, I think we need to take a brief detour into the three types of average: the mean, the median and the mode.

The mode is the largest class of observations. Let's start by gathering every man in Britain and making them all stand in groups. Each man would join the group for his height in inches. All the men who were 5'9" would stand together in a group. All the men who were 5'8" would stand in a group. All the men who were 5'10" would stand together, and so on. Whichever group was the largest would be the mode.*

---

* My bet is that the modal average, or mode, would be close to 5'9", although the only statistics I have are for mean height.

The median is found in a different way. We would stand all 30 million or so British men in a line, ranked by height from the shortest to the tallest. The man who stood exactly in the middle of the line would have the median height.*

The mean is the average that we are all familiar with: we would add up the heights of every man in Britain and divide it by the number of men in the sample. In this case, we already know the answer is 5'9".

It's hard to get data on the mode, the median and the mean for the height of the average British man. The mean is the most widely quoted statistic. I have hazarded a guess that the mode, the median and the mean are the same. I am absolutely confident that the height of the average British male, on all three measures, is between five and six feet tall. The averages are clustered together. This is a property of a Gaussian distribution, and much of the way we view the world is filtered through this easy-to-understand lens. Unfortunately, the lens only works in Mediocristan. To understand how dangerous that property is, we need to turn to an example of a measurement that exists in Extremistan.

Extremistan is the realm not governed by physical constraints. Wealth, for example, is not determined by physical laws like those of gravity or human biology. The distribution can be widely spread. The median wealth of a household in the UK is £232,000 ($357,000),[2] including property, cash, investments and pension wealth.† I am not sure how much the poorest person in Britain is worth, but I imagine that for the purposes of this illustration, we can call their wealth zero.

The richest man in Britain is Lakshmi Mittal, chairman and CEO of ArcelorMittal, the world's largest steelmaking company. The *Sunday Times* estimates his wealth at £12.7 billion ($19.5 billion).[3] Lakshmi Mittal is over 6 million per cent (62,254 times) richer than the average Briton. Meanwhile the US Census puts the median wealth of a household at $68,828 in 2011.[4] The richest man in the US, according

---

* Again, I would hazard a guess that he would be 5'9".

† Note that most people don't count their pension wealth in their net assets, since it is locked away until they retire. It can be a surprisingly large sum, yet yield a disappointingly low annual income, a fact worth bearing in mind if you think that £232,000 sounds like a lot of money.

to *Forbes*, is Microsoft's founder Bill Gates with a net worth in 2012 of $66 billion. Bill Gates is nearly a million times richer than the median household (958,912 times), or nearly 96 million per cent.*

So the tallest man who ever lived was 50 per cent taller than the average Briton, while the richest man in Britain (who is not even the richest man in the world) is over 6 million per cent richer than the average Briton. That is the difference between Mediocristan and Extremistan.

The key thing to grasp is that any business whose products can be digitized is moving from Mediocristan to Extremistan. In Mediocristan, if I were to say that the average amount a user spends on a game is $20, you would have a reasonable guess that most users actually spend $20. A few spend up to $30 and a few spend as little as $10 and hardly anyone spends any other amount. You might also guess that the mean, the median and the mode would all be roughly in line. And you would be right.

In Extremistan, however, you would be completely wrong. Let's take as an example Bigpoint, a German company that is a market leader in browser-based games, games that can be played in Internet Explorer, Chrome, Safari or Firefox with no dedicated technology and no lengthy downloads. They have three particularly successful games, the spacefaring *DarkOrbit*, the piratey *Seafight* and farming sim *Farmerama*. In 2009, the company made revenues of €60 million ($85 million) from 130 million registered users.[5] Many media industry participants would instantly conclude that the company was making on average about fifty cents per user.

This is true, but misleading. The truth is that 80 per cent of Bigpoint's revenue, approximately €48 million ($68 million), came from just 23,000 users, spending an average of over €2,000 ($2,800) each. Bigpoint's users do not inhabit the Gaussian distribution of Mediocristan. A few outliers can massively affect the average, and the mode, median and mean are widely separated.

To understand that, let's dig a little bit deeper. Let's imagine that a player can spend any amount of money in a game. Most spend the

* Note that the US median wealth figures exclude pension and life insurance wealth as well as home furnishings and jewellery, so cannot be compared directly to the UK.

minimum amount (say €1) as they dip their toes in the water of playing the game. The modal average, or the amount spent by the largest single group of users would be €1. If you lined all the players up, ranked by the amount of money they had spent in the game, some would have spent more than €1, so you would expect the median – the player who appeared exactly in the middle of this ordered list – to have spent more than €1, but the very large number of players in the modal group would keep the median down.

On the other hand, we know that *DarkOrbit* has a small number of players spending very large sums of money indeed. These players have barely any impact on the median or modal averages as these averages only count the number of people in each group, not how much they spend. They have a disproportionately large impact on the mean. A single player who spent €20,000 would raise the mean massively compared to 20,000 players each spending €1.

In the old model, if you were told that a games company had 10,000 customers and the average spend was €20, you would be making a reasonable assumption if you said that most people spent €20. In the new model, you are almost certainly wrong. It is much more likely that 90 per cent spent nothing at all while the remaining 10 per cent spend an average of €200. Remember, of course, that even *that* average is misleading, hiding its own curve of distribution.

In economic speak, Extremistan is the land of the power law. The Pareto principle. The 80:20 rule where 80 per cent of the reward comes from 20 per cent of the effort. The power law, or an approximation of it, is the heart of the Curve.

The Curve has only come about because of the end of the tyranny of the physical.

Bits and atoms are different. Fundamentally different in a way that many find hard to grasp. It always costs money to make something using physical atoms and to move them around in the physical world. For something made of bits and bytes, the costs of producing a perfect copy and distributing it anywhere in the world are falling, trending towards a cost that is so small that it becomes possible to treat it as being free. Chris Anderson argues that the three components of costs in a digital world – processing power, storage and bandwidth – are becoming so cheap that it is viable to imagine them becoming 'too cheap to meter'. That has already happened for apps, because Apple is prepared to swallow the costs. As these three costs continue to fall, it will become easier and easier for digital products to be shared for free. The marginal cost is trending towards zero and Bertrand competition drives the price of a product to its marginal cost. That is to say, zero. The consequences of these costs falling are not just about eliminating the costs of distribution. They are much more wide-reaching. They are about eliminating the tyranny of the physical.

When people like me talk about how the ending of the physical product frees up new distribution models, critics often respond by saying that it shows that I misunderstand the cost model of the industry: when the physical cost of creating and distributing a physical product is such a small part of the cost structure of the organization, eliminating that small element of cost makes little difference to the financials of the company.

To say that the physical costs of manufacture are small is true, but completely misses the point. The tyranny of the physical is not about the physical costs of manufacture; it is about the consequences for the entire organization of making big bets.

The costs of having a physical product are enormous, and dwarf the costs of the actual manufacture. They include the costs of shipping and warehousing physical stock together with the IT systems necessary to track and manage the inventory. Substantial working capital is tied up as companies pay for products to be created which then have long periods of time sitting around before they are sold at retail, followed by a longer wait for the retailer to pay them. Costs might also include money spent managing and absorbing returns. There are the challenges of determining how many copies of the product to make, where to sell them, and in what quantity. There is almost always a substantial, expensive managerial overhead designed to mitigate the risks of getting this wrong.

That is the tyranny of the physical. The paradox is that in order to decrease risk, companies increase risk. More accurately, in order to decrease *operational risk*, the risk that a product won't sell, most companies increase *financial risk*, the amount of money that will be lost if the product sinks without trace. Sometimes this can be a sensible investment. Other times, the spending of extra money is just a backside-covering exercise by senior executives who need to be able to demonstrate that they spent lots of money, in all the traditional ways, to ensure that a product worked. Either way, the risk is increased.

It's easy to see how this process happens. Consider the process of publishing a book. In this world of digital publishing, all it takes to publish is an author to write the words and an internet connection to upload the book to a site such as Amazon or Smashwords. An author might conclude that her manuscript would be better if it was reviewed by a professional editor. She reaches into her own pocket to pay an editor. Her operational risk – that her book sucks – is decreased but her financial risk has increased because she is now hundreds or even thousands of dollars out of pocket. She might conclude that knocking up a cover in Photoshop isn't enough and hire a graphic designer to make a professional jacket. Her operational risk – that the marketing of her book sucks or that potential buyers take one look at the cover and conclude that it is too amateur to justify the risk of buying the book – is decreased a little more but she is further out of pocket. She might consider advertising her book somewhere, or paying a marketing agency. Each time, she would be decreasing the risk that the book sinks without trace but increasing the amount of capital she is risking.

Now imagine that same scenario at a large publisher. Here it is the publisher who has to consider how much to spend on marketing and how hard to push a book to retailers. Each book has an opportunity cost too: by choosing to publish this author's particular book, what other books will the publisher have to reject due to financial or capacity constraints? So the publisher creates processes and committees and authorization procedures to maximize the chance that only good books will get through the system. But those processes and procedures do not come for free. Once again, each decrease in operational risk increases the financial risk.

In games publishing, the sums involved are even larger. *Modern Warfare 2* cost $50 million to develop, but the total budget including marketing, distribution, manufacturing and the royalties due to PlayStation and Xbox for the right to publish on their platforms pushed the total up to over $200 million.[6] Small wonder that the games world, like the movie world, is so full of sequels and copycat ideas.

The tyranny of the physical is coming to an end. This brings new opportunities for experimentation. It is also terrifying for existing organizations whose processes and expertise have evolved to mitigate the operational risks of operating in Mediocristan. Those organizations have been accustomed to being the gatekeepers and that function is rapidly coming to an end.

Alex Day is an unusual pop star. He does not have a record label. He does not have a manager. You won't hear his songs on the radio. He does have 640,000 subscribers to his YouTube channel. His videos have been watched over 100 million times. He also holds the record for the highest chart position for an unsigned artist in the UK.

On 11 November 2011, Day released 'Forever Yours', which he describes as 'a simple great dance pop song that a lot of people can get behind'.[7] He also launched an active campaign to get his legions of YouTube fans to download, share and spread the word not just about the song – which they could watch for free on YouTube – but about his attempt to get a Christmas number 1 as an unsigned artist, something that no one had ever achieved before.

Day had one trick up his sleeve. Due to a loophole in the way the Official Charts Company counts sales, multiple versions of the same song all count towards the chart position. If he released multiple versions – acoustic, live, the demo and so on – and his fans bought, say five of them, it looks to the chart compilers as if they have bought 'Forever Yours' five times. The fans get five different tracks and Day gets one combined chart credit.[8] To avoid criticisms of cashing in, Day promised that all money from the sales of alternative versions would go to charity, mainly World Vision, a charitable organization working in Third World countries to fight child poverty.

On Sunday 18 December 2011, as Day's campaign to become a Christmas number 1 peaked, he sold 10,000 copies of 'Forever Yours' on iTunes. In the Official Charts for the week before Christmas, 'Forever Yours' reached number 4 on the UK singles chart, behind Military Wives, a choral tie-in to a television programme, which sold over half a million copies, X Factor winners Little Mix (116,000) and Dominick the Donkey (92,731). 'Forever Yours' charted higher than Coldplay, whose single 'Paradise' achieved just over 50,000 sales in the week, earning it fifth place. Globally, Day sold over 100,000 copies in a single week.

Day had not become number 1, but he had broken chart history with the highest chart position for an unsigned artist. (He also broke a second record, that of fastest fall out of the charts in the whole of their fifty-nine year history, the following week when 'Forever Yours' fell to number 112, selling just 4,938 copies.)[9] Martin Talbot of the Official Charts Company, said,

> The week before Christmas is always an incredibly competitive sales week, so for Alex to make such a big impact in the Top 10 without the support of a traditional record label – big or small – is truly impressive. 'Forever Yours' is certainly one of the most successful self-released tracks we have ever seen. The Official Charts are based on sales, and sales alone, so Alex's achievements this week are a genuine reflection of the passion of his army of fans, and of course, the power of social media.[10]

Day is not against record labels. He'd love to work with them but feels as if they don't know how to work with an artist who is already making a decent living from his music. 'I think they expect you to be a bit in awe of being in a record label building having a meeting with someone at a real record label that might change your dreams. So when I started asking, "What is it that you can do for me?" they didn't really know what to say.'

Day says he would really like a record label to be upfront about what they can offer. 'If they just said, "Look, just keep doing what you're doing and we'll get you on the radio and we'll take 20 per cent," that would be fine. The ideal would be if they were happy to do what they excelled at and happy to just let me carry on. "You've built up this network, just get on with it." Then I can just plug in to the machine whenever I have a new song.'

Day is perhaps not your typical young star. His initial success came from a YouTube channel. Day's father bought him a hand-held video camera and he started making videos by editing together the best bits of a popular movie and adding little jokes over the top of it. Day describes them as 'like *Harry Hill's TV Burp*, but with a movie'. Friends and family liked them but he wanted to test them in front of a brutal audience, so he uploaded them to YouTube. YouTubers loved them.

Day started making short video diaries that took about an hour to produce, compared to the weeks it took him to compile a movie commentary. The diaries got the same number of views as the movie commentary, and Day also learned about copyright. So he took down his movie commentaries and just uploaded his video diaries. He also wrote songs, and every time he wrote one, he uploaded that as well.

Day left school at eighteen, and had a choice to make. His parents had split up, and if he didn't stay in full-time education, his mother would no longer receive benefits for him. He had to keep studying or find a way to contribute to the family finances. Day tried university, where he studied philosophy. ('I didn't enjoy it.') He got a job at the Apple store on Regent Street, where he worked for six months. ('I got fired.')

'I sat down with Mum and said "You've seen how I didn't enjoy either of these things, can I try my way now?"' She gave Day twelve months to prove that he could make a living from his YouTube activities. The target was set in August 2008. Day released his first album in July 2009. At the same time, the partnership programme started on YouTube, allowing popular YouTubers to take a share of the advertising revenue that their videos generated.

'I started getting enough money to buy my own food and not have my mum paying for me.' The initial money was mainly from YouTube, and wasn't very much, just £100 every now and then. By 2012, things had changed for the better for Day. That year, he earned approximately £100,000 from music downloads alone. 'I'm making about £6,000 – £7,000 a month at the moment. When "Forever Yours" happened, I sold 100,000 copies in a week, and you get about 50p for each sale.' Although a meaningful proportion of the 'Forever Yours' sales went to charity, that is easily a living wage. Day can't disclose his YouTube revenue – it's against Google Terms and Conditions to do so – but says that music sales make up 75 per cent of his income. 'It was 50/50 before "Forever Yours", but now it is more in favour of music sales.' He partners with Channelflip, a subsidiary of Shine Group, to help generate advertising revenue on YouTube, which makes up much of the rest of his income.

Day has not followed the traditional musician route that involves playing pubs and bars to build a fan base. He used the global distribution platform of the internet instead. 'I've played gigs before and I think I'm good at them. I've certainly enjoyed them. I do it rarely simply because YouTube is so global. If I announce that I am doing a show in one specific city, the comments are just filled with people not in that city, saying "Why can't you play in my city?" I wouldn't want to do that until I could do a big tour and cover a lot of ground at once. So instead of going to a pub and doing gigs, I am using YouTube.'

Day has built a huge audience of 600,000 subscribers to his YouTube channel. He doesn't think of those people as superfans, though. 'I may have 600,000 subscribers, but I don't sell 600,000 copies of my records. For "Stupid, Stupid" [released in December 2012], I asked anyone who wants to help me if they would give up their time to push and promote it and get it in the charts. I asked people to email me and 2,500 people did. That's really good, but it's not half a million emails. I think I've got 2,500 superfans, because those are the people who are prepared to give up their time for me.'

Day is a new breed of musician. He does worry about the amount of time he spends on administration, not creation. 'I sometimes feel like I'm no longer a professional musician, but a professional writer of emails and music is just my hobby.' He understands how to reach a global audience from his bedroom with well-crafted pop songs, quirky videos and an entertaining online persona. At the age of twenty-three, he has a legion of fans who are not yet able to spend $100 a year on him (give it time) but are able to more than support his current lifestyle. He has managed this without a record label or a manager. He sees the benefits of their services, but has yet to be convinced that any one label or manager is right for him. Alex Day has been a beneficiary of the elimination of the gatekeeper. He found his audience, slowly and steadily, by creating content, sharing it and forming a relationship with his audience. The skills of labels and managers – administration, touring, marketing, relations with radio and the press – are all things that Day not only values, but would love to have access to. The challenge is that he wants them on his terms. The labels haven't yet adapted to the changing power relationship between creators and gatekeepers. None of the gatekeepers have. Those that thrive in the twenty-first century will have to adapt. Time is running out.

Gatekeepers are all that stand between us and a tide of effluent. That is the argument put forward by critics of the approach taken by Alex Day. Society needs book publishers and record labels and movie studios and television broadcasters to ensure that we can find the high-quality content that will inform, educate and entertain us. Without publishers, we would drown in a tide of videos of small children biting other children, of self-indulgent young adult paranormal romances with poor plots, weak characterization and terrible grammar, of the tuneless warblings of adolescents with mistaken beliefs in the extent of their musical abilities. The skills of the publisher as curator are vital to society to protect us from ourselves.

That characterization is self-serving and relies on an idealistic view of the role of the gatekeeper. Gatekeepers exist to make money. The tyranny of the physical means that they seek to minimize operational risks because the financial risk of commissioning, publishing and distributing content is so high. The biggest marketing investments of the big publishers are generally for celebrity autobiographies and sequels from some of the brand names of fiction – Grisham, Patterson, E. L. James – because they will sell. The BBC, the British, publicly funded broadcaster with a remit, established by its first general manager Lord Reith, to inform, educate and entertain, creates populist formats like *Strictly Come Dancing** and *Top Gear* alongside David Attenborough's *Life on Earth* and Professor Brian Cox's *Wonders of the Universe*. Record labels don't search out artists who move our understanding of music onto a higher plane; they look for people who will sell records and concert tickets. Movie and game businesses make sequel after sequel because they know there is an audience for that work.

My extreme characterization is untrue as well. For every Simon Cowell and Simon Fuller, manufacturing bands like One Direction

---

* The title is an amalgam of a long-running BBC TV dance competition *Come Dancing* and the film *Strictly Ballroom*. In most of the rest of the world the show is called *Dancing with the Stars*.

and the Spice Girls, there are dedicated A&R scouts looking for new talent and new sounds. For every celebrity autobiography or vapid potboiler there is a *Life of Pi* or *Bring up the Bodies*. Stuff that changes the world sits alongside lowest-common-denominator content. As it does in a world without gatekeepers.

At the end of 2012 there were nearly 130,000 apps on the App Store. Many of them were rubbish. There are millions of web pages and blogs and Tumblrs and Pinterest boards, many of which are mind-numbingly uninteresting to almost everyone. Again, it doesn't matter. The important question is whether users can somewhere find good quality, interesting content with which they can engage. It looks as if they can.

Content creators and publishers complain about the problem of 'discovery'. In a world of unlimited shelf space, how will consumers find high-quality content? How will they find good games, good books or good music without publishers? It turns out that this is not a question most consumers ask. The question is actually a plaintive lament from gatekeepers: 'How can we get people to buy our games, our books and our music when we no longer control the scarce distribution channels?'

Consumers seem to have no problem finding great games on the App Store, but traditional publishers seem to have great difficulty in shovelling games that don't entertain players quickly and keep them playing for a long time. In their previous incarnation, game publishers had a massive advantage. Sheena Iyengar's work on choice and jam experiments seems encouraging, because it appears to argue that consumers are bewildered by choice and that an increase in choice decreases people's propensity to spend. That is good for a gatekeeping organization which aims to keep the number of products small. Iyengar's work also offers another possible conclusion: the challenges consumers face when choosing from amongst a wide array of options can be addressed by an alternative mechanism to curation. Technology solutions allow consumers to choose their products or services based on filtering, not curation.

In a curated world, nothing can be brought to market without the permission of a gatekeeper. In a filtered world, almost anything can be brought to market. Instead of having no choice but to rely on the judgement of a curator, a consumer in a filtered world has a long tail of limitless shelf space filled with products. To make sense of that, they can use filtering systems – searches, recommendation algorithms, Amazon's 'the page you made', social media recommendations and so on – to limit their choice. The expansion of product available in a digitally distributed world has been matched by the range and quality of filtering tools and options to help consumers make sense of this abundance of choice. The elimination of the exclusive role of the gatekeeper has enabled new products, services and art to reach audiences in a way that was impossible in a world of purely physical distribution.

The gatekeepers have their own vested interests at heart, which may or may not be good for the consumer. Publishers liked having a curated channel to which they could manage access because they could be reasonably sure that they could recoup their money from products that went through that channel. A powerful publisher could strongarm a retailer to take weak products by promising preferential treatment or terms for strong products. It could manage the flow of information to the press to help secure favourable coverage. It could be reasonably certain that even if a product was a stinker, it would still sell just because it was one of the few releases that had made it through the gatekeeper channels that week, prominently displayed in the retail channels where consumers went to buy. All of this mattered because of the tyranny of the physical, the fact that the cost of the products is not in the cost of replication and distribution, but in the need to spend substantial working capital on them, the need to take big bets and the corresponding need to build an expensive infrastructure of risk-management, of consensus building and of accountability which goes with it.

With the elimination of this tyranny, many of the raisons d'être of the gatekeepers go away. Gatekeepers like to think they exist to bring good works to the surface, to help the public find things they will love, to improve the sum of human nature. All of that is true. But their much bigger role is financial. They exist to mitigate risk. That risk is much smaller than it used to be. The gatekeepers no longer control the channels which allowed them to mitigate risk in the past. They will have a much diminished role in the future.

Let's think about risk in different ways. In the UK, every year, even under the old gatekeeper system, around 120,000 books are published.[11] In the US, over 300,000 books were published in 2011.[12] Of those, 148,000 were self-published, leaving over 150,000 titles published by traditional routes.[13] I think you would be hard pressed to argue that all of those books were equally valuable. You could also think 'I've read some of those books and they were *terrible*. I shudder to think how bad the rejects were.' Those rejects may have been terrible. Or they may have been the next *Lord of the Flies* (rejected twenty times), *Dune* (rejected twenty times) or Harry Potter (rejected a dozen times).[14]

Now let's imagine a world without gatekeepers. We have already seen that maybe about 1 per cent of the slush pile – that writer's bogeyman of a pile of manuscripts sitting on an overworked literary agent's desk – ever gets published. That suggests that perhaps as many as 10 million manuscripts are submitted every year in the UK and the US alone (although there will be a lot of duplicate submissions to multiple agents). I suspect that there are many more manuscripts sitting unsubmitted around the world, stuffed in desk drawers, cluttering hard drives, unread and unloved. I've got novels, graphic novels and drafts of non-fiction books that are unlikely to ever see the light of day. How many are there in the world? To make a guess, let's estimate that for every submitted book there is at least one unsubmitted book. So there are perhaps 20 million books in existence as manuscripts, of which only 100,000 make it through the publishing process every year.

In a world without gatekeepers, how many of those would get published? Should all 20 million of them get the chance to be read? To my mind, the answer is an emphatic yes. I don't understand the argument that says that preventing these books from seeing the light of day is somehow enhancing for society.

Note that I am not saying that there is no role for publishers in the future. Publishers fulfil two totally different roles in the creation of content. They have a commercial role as gatekeepers and marketers and they are also part of the content creation process itself. This book has been greatly improved by the work of my editors. I am sure that Amanda Hocking's fiction and Alex Day's music could benefit from having other experts involved in their creation (although that contribution from other experts comes at the cost of creative and financial control that may seem too high to many creators). I am arguing that the pretence that curation is a necessary benefit for society, and that the benefit is sufficiently large that it justifies the incumbents actively keeping new players out of the market, is nonsense.

From a consumer point of view, curation does have benefits. How do consumers know which products they like and which ones are worth consuming? How do they know that a book is worth reading, a YouTube video worth watching or a track worth listening to, in a world without curators? The first answer is that they don't. Where much of the content is free to access (as music and many games already are and books soon will be), they can experience the content themselves to determine whether it is worthwhile for them. Of course, this abundance creates a new scarcity, that of attention, which means that consumers will seek out the forms of selection that help them filter the stuff that is high quality that they will like from the low quality and the not-for-them.

We are already seeing this play out. The charts are showing that the big are getting bigger. When something becomes a global phenomenon, it spreads faster than ever before. Consumers rely on the App Store charts when choosing what to buy, driving a relentless focus on chart position from app developers. Book buyers buy books from authors they know they like, leading, counter-intuitively, to the importance of 'owning the shelf' – having many books that a book buyer can buy with confidence – increasing in the digital age. There are TV shows we need to have watched and movies we need to have seen to fit in with our social circle or as part of the cultural zeitgeist.

Other consumers will seek out content that is recommended by people they trust. Erotica writer E. L James sold 10.6 million books in her *Fifty Shades* trilogy in 2012, generating over £47 million ($73 million) in sales and making up 3 per cent of the UK market on her own. The *Fifty Shades* phenomenon benefited from word of mouth, which led to it becoming a cultural phenomenon. Whether it's parents chatting at the school gates or hipsters sharing music recommendations on Path, teenagers sharing tracks they found on Spotify and BitTorrent sites or Facebook users clicking on a video a friend shared from

YouTube, there are more ways to find out what our friends enjoyed than ever before. More importantly, it is easier to go from the knowledge that a friend liked something to experiencing that thing for ourselves than ever before, especially if that thing is free.

Yet more will still rely on the trusted brand of a publisher, built up over many years. They will buy a book from Picador or from Usborne or from Portfolio or from Virago, and know something about the quality of the content, and its nature, from the name of the publisher. In fact, I think that it is possible that the publisher's name will become more important (although to fewer people) in the future as we, as consumers, find many different ways to filter the quality of the almost unlimited content we will find in the world around us.

Publishers can still add enormous value as organizations which improve content and drive demand; they can no longer expect to extract the value they used to have as gatekeepers. They now need to earn the right to publish. It is no longer something they graciously bestow on content creators.

In my (self-published) book *How to Publish a Game*, I argued that there were four commercial roles of the publisher. (For publisher, you could substitute record label, movie studio or, as we start talking about physical manufacturing, the organization that oversees the production, marketing and sales of physical widgets.) Publishers provide a sales function, which is part of the process of getting money from the end user into the hands of a creator. In fact, publishers typically only manage part of that process, particularly in the physical world. At the very least, the sales funnel involves an author selling to a publisher (probably via an agent). The publisher then sells to a retailer. The retailer then sells to a consumer. The money then goes back up the chain, with each link taking its cut. Specialist sales skills like translation rights, merchandising and licensing or building commercial partnerships with advertisers are also often best done by large companies that employ experts in the field.

Alongside the sales function is its partner, distribution. It's rarely good enough to persuade somebody to want to buy a product. You typically then have to deliver it. That involves, continuing with the book example, the process of printing books, taking orders, distributing them in boxes and vans and aeroplanes around the world until the beautiful hardback is in the hands of the person who paid for it. It also involves the technology and infrastructure for keeping track of all that inventory and sales reports. This is the key role of a publisher. Getting a physical product stocked in retail stores on a global basis is still a task that is beyond most self-publishers.*

I'm not arguing that the people in the sales and distribution chain don't earn their cut – although sometimes they don't. I am arguing that when using a publisher was the only route to market, authors had little choice over whether to use a publisher, how much to pay for the services of a publisher and whether that payment was good value for money. In practice, an author was offered an all-or-nothing deal: take this complete bundle of commercial and content creation services at a cost of 80 to 90 per cent of your income, or don't get your product to market. The great unbundling, initiated by the internet and continued by the evolution of consumer behaviour and new business models, is likely to change that.

Sales and distribution are logistical functions. They both need the third function, marketing, to drive demand. Marketing seeks to build demand for a product through design, copywriting, relationships with the press and good, old-fashioned, spending-money-on-advertising. The quality of marketing can vary wildly. Some publishers think that their primary role is simply to get a book on the shelves or an album in stores. Others are heavily engaged in the whole process of creating a product, which may include restyling the star, changing their name, look, dress and style and more.

The final function is providing the finance to make the whole project happen. Since professional investors are wary of taking creative as well as financial risks, publishers are often the only organizations with the scale and expertise to manage the risks across a portfolio of creative projects. The figures can be very big. While an advance for

---

* You could argue that digital distribution is similarly complex, but it doesn't have to be. A major publisher will choose to invest the time and effort to get its books into every distribution channel and every format that makes commercial sense. A self-published author just needs to start the process of finding an audience for their work. Getting onto Kindle or publishing via Smashwords is 'good enough' to get started.

a first-time author is typically in the low five figures or less, the cost of launching a book, once editorial support, copy-editing, production, marketing and sales are factored in, is much higher. That doesn't even incorporate the real cost of the tyranny of the physical: the need to reduce risk and cover corporate backsides when substantial working capital is at risk and there is a real opportunity cost involved in taking on one project over another. For a long time, it looked as if publishers were the only source of finance for creative endeavours.

That is still true if you want to get a £4.6 million advance for your memoirs, as former British Prime Minister Tony Blair did for *A Journey* (and donated to the Royal British Legion), or $4 million for your third book about risk, like Nassim Nicholas Taleb.[15] It may be true if you want to spend $200 million on a blockbuster movie like *The Avengers*, nearly $100 million on a game (RealTime Worlds' *APB*), or create a new piece of hardware like the iPhone. But it isn't true if you just want to make music, or books, or films or even physical stuff for an audience who will pay for it. You now have a choice. I am immensely grateful to Portfolio for offering me an advance. It enabled me to turn down client work and focus on the manuscript. I transferred risk from me, the author, to them, the publisher. But I could have published *The Curve* without them – it would have taken me longer, it would have been less professional, I might not have found the time – but I could have done it, as I did with my other, self-published books.

The cost of everything – production, marketing, distribution, sales, software, hardware, everything – is coming down. Advances are wonderful, but they are no longer prerequisites to getting your product to market. Getting people to want to buy your product is still difficult, but it is vastly cheaper to produce it than it has ever been. The services of a publisher are increasingly optional for a creator of content.

The erosion of the role of the gatekeeper is a good thing for consumers. There are downsides. There is a risk that too much content vying for consumers' attention means that it becomes too hard to discover the good stuff, although to date that seems like a problem for creators more than consumers. There is a risk that this discovery problem leads to a tide of lowest-common-denominator content, although as we've shown that was an equally serious problem in the era of mass-market communication. There is a risk that good stuff does not get made because there are no publishers prepared to take on the risk of new creators making amazing new content, although that can be mitigated by starting small, building an audience and a following before seeking out the funding for massive projects once you have a fan base.

I also believe that it is better, on balance, for creators, particularly those who are able to build connections with their fans. The biggest losers are those creators who were at the bottom end of the 'ability' order in the old model, but just managed to squeeze through the gate. Those who, through connections or chutzpah or luck, were able to secure a book deal or a record contract and then sold novels or albums simply because they were in the treadmill of the system. The mediocre licensed tie-in games that sold because they were one of this week's releases, sitting on a row end at GameStop, will become less viable in a digital world when the storefront is full of amazing, high-quality content. Content will get better both for the mass market and for the niche. The mediocre that existed because some publishers had access to retail channels that enabled them to force-feed content to a public with a limited choice will struggle in this new world.

Perhaps the most important downside of the absence of the gate-keeper is that it benefits creators who can hustle. Amanda Palmer, the doyenne of the new music industry, is an expert on communicating with her fans, connecting with them and letting them spend lots of money to be supportive of her creative and performance journey. She is also an outgoing performer who regularly gets naked on the web and at her gigs and who honed her performance skills performing street theatre for five years. She is an artist who embraces communicating with her audience. The skills of connecting to an audience, of selling, of self-promotion are going to become much more important in this connected world. Icelandic singer/songwriter Björk failed to raise $375,000 in a crowdfunding campaign largely because she has never made much effort to connect directly with her fans. The reclusive novelist, the anti-social songwriter and the loner screenwriter will find it harder to succeed in the world of digital connectivity and the Curve if they are not prepared to adapt the way they work.

As Benji Rogers, CEO of PledgeMusic, a website that helps musicians connect with their fans and fans to help their favourite artists make and release their records, says, 'I think it's time for artists and their managers and labels to realize that this fan experience is now part of the process and not just an add-on. When artists sell to fans and labels sell to consumers, everybody wins.'[16]

Alex Day is not against record labels. He would love to have an organization that removes the pressures of managing his commercial success from him, leaving him to focus on new material. 'My dream situation is to have a pneumatic tube in my room so that I can do a song and then just chuck it in the tube and it just goes, whoosh, and just goes off to the record label building. Then they receive it and they send it to radio and everything else. But I'm just still in my room and I just get on with it and just do the next song.' In reality, he has yet to find a record label that understands that they need to offer him services, not assume that he will take whatever he is offered and be grateful at being giving a shot at stardom. Nine Inch Nails' Trent Reznor has even returned to the label system. 'It felt like it was worth slicing the pie up monetarily to have a team that are better at marketing than I am, worldwide.'[17] Reznor's experiment gave him a new-found understanding of what he valued from a record label, and a strong position to negotiate.

I have found the need for specialist skills in my own business. GAMESbrief was founded in 2008 as a blog about the business of games. Over the past five years, it has grown to attract around 20,000 readers every month, drawn by my focus on the business of games and how to make money from giving your game away for free. During that time, I have made most of my money from consultancy.

To say that a business writer can make money from consulting is like saying a musician can make money from touring. It is true, but it ignores one of the most important challenges for any creative endeavour: how to carve out time to create. When I am consulting, I am not creating new content. I am not spending the time necessary to form new ideas, to read widely in and around my industry, to consolidate my thoughts into something which is useful for my audience. My work with clients has been incredibly useful as it has helped me understand the challenges of making the transition from a paid model to a free-to-play business model. If I consulted all the time, though, my value to my clients would rapidly diminish. I would no longer be learning and thinking (which is the heart of the creation that I do). I would just be parroting what was already known, and my value would start to decrease. Much like the musician who tours without creating any new material, I would become stale.

In a world without gatekeepers, creators now have choice. They can choose to take on the commercial roles – sales, distribution, marketing or finance – to get their creation to market themselves. They can outsource them lock, stock and barrel to a third party such as a publisher. Or they can outsource some of them and do the rest themselves. Many creators are beginning to surround themselves with experts who might previously have been employed by the publisher: web developers, community managers, marketing experts. The elimination of the requirement to have a gatekeeper does not mean that the work of a publisher no longer needs to be done. What it has done is to start the process of the unbundling of the creative roles that gatekeepers fulfil from the commercial ones.

The tyranny of the physical is what has slowed down the transition. It has also limited the ability to experiment with radically different price points and business models. Gatekeepers have evolved expertise and processes to do what they currently do really well. The digital transition means that what they currently do is less valuable than it used to be.

Exploiting the Curve involves thinking of new ways of letting the biggest fans spend lots of money on things they truly value. To many gatekeepers, what fans value is whatever it is the gatekeeper sells: a book, an album, a physical widget. In practice, value is much more complicated than that. It goes back to the early days of human evolution and forward to our present online, connected, social society. Value is hard to pin down, but pin it down we must if we are to make money in the twenty-first century.

6
WHAT'S IT WORTH?

Victoria Vox is an unsigned ukulele-playing songwriter who makes her living by making music.

Vox has a degree in song writing from the Berklee College of Music in Boston. After graduating she moved back to her hometown of Green Bay, Wisconsin and got a job in a mall. In May 2003 she quit the job to go on tour. 'That tour was a coffee-house tour in the Mid-West. No guarantees. Small audiences. Just a tip jar and the chance to sell my CDs.' By 2006 her gross income from touring and ticket sales was as much as she had earned from the mall job, but her expenses had grown too. 'Gas and clothing and equipment and instruments and microphones.' She built a network of fans, at first on MySpace, later on Facebook and Twitter. She built a list of people who wanted to be mailed a postcard about gigs or album releases and turned that into an email list with 2,000 names on it.

In 2005 she responded to fan requests to record an album using the ukulele that had become her signature instrument. She emailed the list. 'I pretty much put it up as saying, "I'm recording this record. I don't know when it's going to be done. I don't know when you'll get it, but if you pre-order it, at some point in the future, you'll get a CD."' Her list pre-ordered CDs to the value of $2,000.

Vox planned a release tour of Hawaii, the home of the ukulele. She booked travel and pressed 1,000 CDs. It cost $4,000 and she had only raised $2,000. 'I started looking at places to stay in Honolulu. I couldn't afford it. So I emailed the fans again to ask if anyone knew of somewhere I could stay for a few nights here and a few nights there.'

A German student who had seen her play in Nashville five years previously was now a graduate student in Honolulu and offered her a room. This sort of things happens to Vox all the time. She builds connections with her fans at coffee-house gigs, at larger venues and through her online presence, and they offer to help her out. During her breaks at gigs she wanders through the audience and talks to people. She puts a personal note in every CD that she mails out. Her audience care about following not just Vox's music, but her journey.

In 2008, she wanted to make another record. She again asked her fans and again they pre-ordered $2,000 worth. This album was more ambitious, so she borrowed $18,000 from her grandfather. 'I paid it all back. Every penny. It took eighteen months.' On tour in late 2009, fans kept asking about the next album. Vox worried that she couldn't afford it. The pre-order system wasn't raising enough money to create an album. She needed to try something different.

She decided to change the way she asked her fans for support. She let them spend much more than they had in the past. For $20, they got the CD; $50 got an acknowledgement in the liner notes; $100 got two copies and a T-shirt. She added more tiers: $750; $1,000. 'For $1,500, I offered to come to someone's house and play a gig for them there.'

She set a goal in her head of $4,000, double the previous pre-order total. She was flabbergasted by the response from her fans. The first sale was for a $1,500 house concert. Over the month of her campaign, she kept raising the goal in her head and the fans kept supporting her: $1,500 became $8,000 became $12,000. Eventually, the campaign raised $22,000. Five people each paid $1,500 for a house party.

Vox made sure that the fans were rewarded. She went all out on the artwork. She made limited-edition album covers that featured Vox sitting in front of a washing machine with a ukulele. The washing machine on the cover had real water in it. 'It was very expensive to do that, but it was one of the coolest things I've done.' Her fans, many of whom had been following her for a decade, wanted Vox to succeed. They had been part of her creative journey and wanted to support it. Whether it was by spending $20 or $1,500, they found value in the gigs, the limited edition, the joy of supporting an artist and the experience of being part of something.

Vox has found a way to connect with her fans. She makes a decent living as a touring artist (about $100,000 a year gross, with perhaps $60,000 in expenses.) She now makes money from touring and from selling albums and has raised more money to fund albums via crowdfunding sites such as Kickstarter and PledgeMusic. Vox has discovered how to allow her fans to experience her content for free while also letting those who love what she does spend lots of money on things they truly value.

How much is a video game worth to you?

I imagine that many readers of this book are not regular gamers. Others of you will be. What is the most you have spent on a single game? An iOS app for less than the price of a cup of coffee? A PC game for $40? A console game on the first day of release for $50?

For an American gamer called Lee, the amount is $5,000. Lee is a single, forty-two-year-old businessman whose annual income is 'in the six figures'. As *Wired* relates it:

> It was a typical weekday night after work: Lee slipped off his shoes, climbed into bed with his iPad, and booted up *Clash of Clans*. The free-to-play strategy game, in which he went by the name 'Metamorphaz', had quickly become a favourite stress-reliever for him. After the game's logo faded away, a sprawling virtual village popped into view.
>
> Uh oh. A rival player had gone aggressive, and one of Lee's fellow 'clan' members was under attack. Lee tapped a few icons, donating dozens of his troops to defend the friend from a brutal assault of archers and barbarians. Then, he pulled up *Clash of Clans*' built-in, real-money shop. While the game is free to download, its maker Supercell profits by selling virtual items to the most engaged players. Tonight, Lee's iPad questioned him with a blue pop-up window: 'Do you want to buy one Chest of Gems for $99.99?'
>
> Lee could use those gems to immediately fortify his army. He tapped 'Yes', almost without thinking. In less than a month of playing around two hours a day, he'd spent nearly a thousand dollars.
>
> Game developers have a word for players like Lee: whales.[1]

Lee is part of a new breed of customers, enabled by the internet. You can call them whales, you can call them superfans. Whatever you call them, they are key to the long-term success of any business in the digital age. Superfans are the people at the left of the demand curve, the ones who love what you do and are happy to pay lots for it. Trent Reznor made his album easily accessible on filesharing sites, very cheaply or free for digital download, and yet his biggest fans spent $300 on the Ultra-Deluxe version, buying out the whole stock of 2,500 in just thirty hours.

Sports are filled with superfans and, in the UK, none more so than soccer. In April 2012, Liverpool Football Club announced that it had 25,074 tickets for the FA Cup Final available for fans. The Cup Final is probably the most important event in the UK soccer calendar. Liverpool tried to run a fair allocation, mainly by ballot amongst supporters who had attended five of the qualifying FA Cup matches in the run up to the final. Approximately 10 per cent of the tickets were available priced at £115 ($180), 46 per cent priced at £85, 28 per cent priced at £65 and 16 per cent priced at £45.[2]

Touts were selling tickets for as much as £10,400 ($16,700).[3]

So what is the 'value' of an FA Cup Final ticket? The average of the official prices? The amount that some unnamed person reportedly paid a tout? The amount the 'average' person in the UK would pay to attend a Cup Final? I have no interest in football. You wouldn't actually have to pay me to attend, but it would be close. The value to me of a ticket to the Cup Final is essentially zero, although I guess if I could eBay it for £10,400, that's how much it's worth to me.

These stories illustrate how value is a nebulous concept. For some people, paying $1,500 for their favourite ukulele player to come to their house is worth it. I have spent far more on video games than I have on football. There are Nine Inch Nails fans who think nothing of spending $300 on a limited edition and soccer fans who would happily spend that on a weekend at an away match while thinking the Reznor fans were mad. What we value is personal, individual and unique. It can also be manufactured.

Penn and Teller are two of America's most famous illusionists. Penn Jillette is the big one. He is 6'6" with a heavy build and a stage presence which includes a fast, almost never-ending patter. His partner,

Teller, is 5'9" and doesn't speak on stage.* In 2003, they launched *Penn & Teller: Bullshit*, a television programme that aired in the US on the Showtime channel.

In Season One, they looked at the craziness of bottled water. In 2002, according to Penn & Teller, Americans spent $4 billion on bottled water. They ran a number of vox pop interviews asking people why they spent money on bottled water. The responses included, 'I like it because it's definitely got less pollutants. I like having less heavy metals in my water and generally I can find that in bottled water,' 'I think it's cleaner than our regular tap water,' and 'It's not as impure as some of the tap water can be, because some of the tap water I really don't trust.'

Data from environmental lobbying group the National Resources Defense Council suggests bottled water is often less safe than tap water. Not least because tap water is regulated by the Environment Protection Agency, which has hundreds of staff focused on the quality of the water supply. Bottled water is regulated by the Food and Drug Administration, which has less than one person to police the industry. Not only that, but 'the FDA says they don't regulate any bottled water that is bottled and sold within the same state. So many states really have no bottled water regulatory program at all,' says Eric Wilson, a drinking water expert with the Natural Resources Defense Council.

Penn & Teller carried out more vox pop interviews: 'The tap water is not always the best tasting,' 'Bottled water tastes better and it looks better, so I drink it.'

As Penn said on the show,

> Of course. The taste. Bottled water tastes better than tap water. We went to New York City to conduct one of our famous unscientific bullshit tests. No expense was spared as we filled bottle A from an ordinary New York faucet while bottle B contained a relatively expensive, store bought, bottled water. Seventy-five per cent of the people who took our test picked New York tap water over bottled water. We've now ruled out safety, purity and taste. Why would people pay such a premium for bottled water? Is it all in their minds?

---

* It is tempting to call him the short one, but as we know, he is in fact of average height.

Penn and Teller took over a fancy Californian restaurant. They created the world's first water steward.* Tim was dressed in the elegant garb of a sommelier with an easy smile and a neatly trimmed moustache.

'Good evening, folks. Welcome. My name is Tim and I will be your water steward today.'

Tim had a detailed printed menu that looked like a wine list. A sample entry read:

L'Eau du Robinet .... $4.75 per bottle.
Pure, brisk and unmistakably French, this running water is bottled directly from the source, while its natural minerals and nutrients are still at their most potent. Its aggressive flavour and brash attitude makes it a perfect complement to meat and poultry.

Tim offered the water list to a couple out for a nice dinner.

'It's like a wine list. What do you want to try? Want to try this? Sounds French,' said the woman to her date. Looking slightly unsure, she continued, 'I guess I'll get the L'Eau du Robinet.'

'The L'Eau du Robinet?' says Tim, nodding. 'Fantastic.'

Those of you who understand French will realize that she just ordered tap water. Tim then performs a deft piece of salesmanship, upselling her partner on another bottle.

'And for you, sir? Would you like to try one and maybe compare notes?'

'Yeah, do the other one,' says the woman.

'Sure, I'll do the Mount Fuji.'

Meanwhile, we lucky viewers know that every single one of the waters offered on the menu are filled from the same tap via a garden hose in the courtyard behind the restaurant. When Tim returns with the two bottles, the patrons try their different waters with all the gestures and mannerisms you might expect from a diner tasting a bottle of wine.

'It tastes clean,' she says.

'It has flavour to it,' he adds.

* It seems unlikely to me that this was the world's first water steward. I expect there are some restaurants who already had such a person. Or else they have become more commonplace since this sketch. Sometimes, you need to be careful what you parody.

'How would you compare it to tap water?' Tim asks.

The male diner is the one with the strongest opinions 'Oh yeah, definitely better than tap water. It doesn't have an aftertaste. It's got a flavour that, it almost feels like a beverage other than water but without sugar or other additives.'

Tim moves them on to tasting their second choice, holding up a bottle in the way a sommelier would present the label of a bottle of Merlot.

'It's right from the top of Mount Fuji, it's a very pure water, it's a natural diuretic and anti-toxin.'

The patrons continue their wine-tasting gestures.

'It does feel glacier . . . ,' offers the man. His partner laughs. 'It does. It feels glacier . . .'

'Glacier-oriented,' she laughs again.

'Yeah. This is good.'

Tim continues his upsell. 'I've taken the liberty of bringing you a bottle of our Agua de Culo.'

'OK,' she says.

'It's $6.50 a bottle.'

They taste it.

'Mmmm,' a high-pitched, almost squeal of delight from her.

'It's got a very fresh taste. It's crisper.'

In the voiceover, Penn asks with an incredulous tone in his voice, 'Surely this couple can't be representative.' Clips of other customers suggest that they are.

One man in his forties, dressed in a grey suit with a dark blue shirt, has three glasses in front of him in a line. 'You can definitely taste the middle one. It's a harder water, I guess, and this one, I don't taste the minerals so much.'

Tim is a master salesman. He had the props, the environment and the diners' expectations of dinner in a Los Angeles restaurant when trying to persuade people not only to spend lots of money on water they could have got for nothing, but that they could tell the difference between several different glasses of identical liquid.

Towards the end of the evening, Tim finally admits his deception.

'Now what would you think if I told you that all of these waters came from the same garden hose. I actually filled the bottles myself.'

'No, you didn't,' laughs a woman in a crisp white blouse, taking a bite of bread.

'I did.'

'You're kidding me.'

The best reaction is from the guy who said he could taste the difference between the middle one and the one where 'I don't taste the minerals so much.' He just burst out laughing, and carried on laughing. His partner laughed too. There is a couple that know not to take themselves too seriously when they have been had.

Penn and Teller are magicians. Their shows rely on misleading us, on persuading us that some things that are not real are real while others that are real are not. They are unreliable guides. Nevertheless, their light-hearted sting shows a truth about how much of the value of something is divorced from its costs or from its substance.

The water example is not the only case of consumers having their concept of the value of a product changed by external factors such as the price, the location or the way in which it is presented.

At 7.51 a.m. on a January Friday, a violinist started busking. He was nondescript, a 'youngish white man in jeans, a long-sleeved T-shirt and a Washington Nationals baseball cap'. He stood beside a rubbish bin at the entrance to L'Enfant Plaza Metro Station in Washington, DC and over the next forty-three minutes he played six classical pieces while 1,097 people passed by on their way to jobs, probably in the federal government. He made $32.17.

The busker was Joshua Bell, a world-famous violinist who can earn as much as $1,000 per minute. The pieces were some of the most technically challenging in the world, such as Bach's Chaconne, a piece that consists 'of a single, succinct musical progression repeated in dozens of variations to create a dauntingly complex architecture of sound'.[4] The violin was a Stradivarius that Bell bought for a reported $3.5 million.

Twenty-seven people gave him money. Only seven stopped. Yet Joshua Bell is one of the most sought-after classical musicians in the world, with a performance style that is described as 'athletic and passionate'. None of that mattered when Bell was stripped of the accoutrements of a grand stage, an audience with expectations and the power of his name.[5]

Behavioural economist Dan Ariely has long been fascinated with how and where we ascribe value. In *Predictably Irrational*, he looked at the powerful influence that free has on our rational perception and how we are influenced by an anchor price. He relates the business experiences of a man called James Assael, an Italian diamond dealer who fled Europe for Cuba at the onset of the Second World War.[6] There he created a new business for himself: using his contacts in Switzerland to supply waterproof watches for the American army.

Come the end of the war, Assael suddenly had a massive surplus of watches. Canny trader that he was, he found a way to make the Japanese want the watches, only they didn't have the money. He taught his son, Salvador, to barter Swiss watches for Japanese pearls so successfully that the business blossomed and Salvador became known as the Pearl King.

In 1973, the pearl king faced a new challenge. He was persuaded to go into business with a man who owned a Tahitian island that abounded with black-lipped oysters which produced black pearls. The only problem was that there was no demand for black pearls.

Initial results were unpromising. The pearls weren't even black, they were gunmetal grey, about the size of musket balls, and Assael failed to make a single sale. He considered abandoning the business or dropping the price, but he didn't. Instead he doubled down.

Assael commissioned a full-page advertisement that ran in the glossiest of magazines. He showed a string of his black pearls set amongst other precious stones that his target market was familiar with: diamonds, rubies and emeralds. He persuaded an old friend, gem dealer Harry Winston, to put the black pearls in the window of his store on Fifth Avenue, with a very high price tag. The pearls, which Assael had failed to sell at any price previously, had suddenly become very valuable. The wealthy of Manhattan lapped them up. Assael earned the nickname Pearl King a second time.

Ariely credits the success of Assael's venture to a clever use of anchoring. Essentially, very few of us know how much anything is worth. We use the concept of anchoring to help us form a view. At its most basic, anchoring is helpful: once we know the price of a single pint of milk, we have a basis from which we can figure out how much we would pay for two pints. How much should I pay for bread, for a television, for a CD?

Anchoring can also be unhelpful. Much like the baby birds who hatch from their eggs and imprint on the first moving thing they see, assuming that this is their mother, we can be misled for a very long time by the anchor. To explore this, Ariely ran an experiment to identify how easy it can be to set an anchor. He asked a group of graduate students to bid on bottles of wine. Wine is a good example because few of us know the intrinsic worth of a bottle, and we also know that the price varies with the situation (the supermarket versus a high-end restaurant, for example).

Ariely wasn't testing his students' knowledge of wine. He was testing the power of anchoring. Leading the experiment was Drazen Prelec, a professor of MIT's Sloan School of Management. Prelec talked to his class about two bottles of wine. One was a 1998 Jaboulet Côtes du Rhône Parallèle 45. 'For those of you who don't know much about wines, this bottle received 86 points from *Wine Spectator*. It had the flavour of red berry, mocha and black chocolate; it's a medium-bodied, medium-intensity, nicely balanced red and it makes for delightful drinking.'

The second bottle was a Jaboulet Hermitage La Chappelle, 1996, with a 92-point rating from *Wine Advocate*. Students were asked to perform the following tasks: 1) Write the last two digits of their social security number on the top of a form. 2) For each bottle, write those last two digits next to the bottle as a dollar amount. So if the last two digits of a student's social security number were, for example, 23, the student would write $23 beside the bottle. 3) Indicate with a yes or no whether they would pay the dollar amount for the bottle. 4) Write down the maximum they were prepared to bid for each of the bottles, with the winner having to stump up the cash for his or her prize.

Ariely's results were remarkable. The students were heavily influenced by their social security numbers which served as anchors, even though they had no connection with the value of a bottle of wine. In Ariely's experiment, the students with the highest social security numbers (80 to 99) bid highest while those with the lowest numbers (01 to 20) bid lowest. For the 1998 Côtes du Rhône, low social security number students bid an average of $8.64 while high social security number students bid an average of $27.91. For the 1996 Hermitage, the low group average was $11.73 while the high group average was $37.55. Across a range of six products including wines, a book, a keyboard and a box of chocolates, students with social security numbers ending in 80 to 99 placed bids that were 216 to 346 per cent higher than those with social security numbers ending in 01 to 20.

We are easily swayed by anchoring. Ariely describes a second experiment where he pays volunteers to listen to a really annoying sound for thirty seconds.[7] One group is paid 10 cents to submit to the experience. Another is paid 90 cents. The experiment was designed to test whether the anchor mattered and Ariely chose 'listening to an annoying sound' because there is no market in annoying sounds. Nobody knows how much they 'should' be paid for this experience. They were then asked how much they would have to be paid to listen to the sound again. The 10-cent group were prepared to listen to the sound for a payment of, on average, 33 cents, while those in the second group demanded 73 cents for the same experience. The initial price expectation set by the experimenters altered the participant's perception of value.

The importance of setting the initial price is why a pay-what-you-want strategy is not the same as a strategy that harnesses the Curve. Value is created by context and varies from person to person. A pay-what-you-want strategy leaves a potential purchaser with a limited context within which to determine the value of a product.

In October 2007, Radiohead released an album, *In Rainbows*, that had an innovative pricing model. Anyone could download the album for free but they were invited to pay as much or as little as they liked for it. During the first year, *In Rainbows* sold 3 million copies, compared with 900,000 for their 2001 album, *Amnesiac*, and 990,000 for 2003's *Hail to the Thief*. Of those 3 million copies, 1.75 million were traditional, physical CDs. Another 100,000 came from a premium boxed set priced at £40 ($60). The rest was made up from the paid-for digital downloads, priced at anything from a penny upwards.[8]

ComScore estimated that 62 per cent of online customers downloaded the album for free while the remaining 38 per cent paid an average of $6, leading to a blended average of $2.26.[9] Radiohead disputed the figures but declined to provide their own more accurate ones, although they did say that 'in terms of digital income, we've made more money out of this record than out of all the other Radiohead albums put together, forever – in terms of anything on the Net'.[10] (This is partly because EMI did not pay the band for digital sales for some of their earlier albums because the contracts were written before the emergence of digital opportunities.) If you think these figures are on the low side, I would agree with you. Pay-what-you-want suffers from a lack of anchoring. It suffers from a lack of context, social proof and a mechanism to enable customers to understand where value lies.

A stronger example of a pay-what-you-want strategy is the Humble Bundle, a games site that allows customers not only to pay what they want, but to allocate their payment between the developer, charity and the Humble Bundle platform itself. The Humble Bundle uses a number of strategies to give customers a context for their spending and an anchor for premium value. In May 2013, the Humble Bundle was running a bundle of games from developer Double Fine. A user could enter any amount and get three games. If they paid 'more than the average', they would also get another title, *Brutal Legend*. This is a clever strategy which tends to move the average up over time. If they paid $35 or more, they could be part of Double Fine's new project, fully funded on Kickstarter and now in development. If they paid $70 or more, they would get a T-shirt exclusive to the Bundle campaign.

The Humble Bundle website displays a lot of data. It shows the average amount spent and the amount paid by the most generous customers. With thirteen days left to go, the Double Fine Humble Bundle had raised over half a million dollars.[11] Nearly 70,000 customers had spent an average of $7.89. The highest spend was $2,048. The second was $1,337.* The Humble Bundle has showcased what its audience is doing and created value for itself, its developer partners and its customers through a smart use of context.

Penn and Teller showed us how easily our taste and value expectations can be set by the marketing of a product and the environment in

---

* If you know why someone contributed that exact amount, gain one geek point.

which we consume it. Ariely has proven that we can be misled by any arbitrary number when thinking about price. The Humble Bundle shows that social context matters.

Our final example again returns to wine. This time, though, the topic is not the wine that we drink, it's the wine glasses that we drink from.

Riedel is a company that manufactures high-quality glassware. Its founder, Johann Christoph Riedel, was born in the Bohemian town of Neuschloß in the modern-day Czech Republic in 1673. After 250 years of trading, and eleven generations, the business is still family owned and run. Claus Riedel, the ninth generation of Riedels to control the business, died in 2004, but not before revolutionizing the way the company presented its products. According to the company, 'Claus Riedel was the first in history to recognize the effect of shapes on the perception of alcoholic beverages.' Claus concluded that the shape of the glass mattered. He didn't just mean the difference between red, white and sparkling wines. He meant every single grape.

Daniel Zwerdling of *Gourmet* magazine attended a Riedel-funded wine tasting in 2004. This is how he reported a Riedel expert describing how Riedel glasses work.[12]

> Before we take a sip, she instructs us to study the diagram in the centre of our tasting mats. It's labelled 'Taste Zones of the Tongue'. This 'tongue map', as she calls it, depicts the tongue as a kind of triangle that's divided into striped or dotted zones, like survey plots. There's the pointy tip, where the map says you taste sweet; the long, narrow sides, where you taste salt; the wider inner strips, where you taste acid; and, finally, the broad band along the back, where you taste bitter.
>
> The Riedel Company says it painstakingly designs the glasses to deliver the wine to a precise target on your own tongue's map every time you take a sip. As a result, Riedel insists, the wine will hit the exact taste buds that bring out the best flavour notes.

Riedel now sells expensive wine glasses tailored for individual grapes. A tasting set of four glasses ('contains one of each of the Vinum Bordeaux, Montrachet, Burgundy and Sauvignon Blanc glass') for $118. Two Cabernet Sauvignon/Merlot glasses for $59. A single Burgundy Grand Cru glass for $125.

The sales blurb for this expensive glass makes extravagant claims. Take the Burgundy Grand Cru:

> This glass was described by *Decanter* magazine as 'The finest Burgundy glass of all time, suitable for both young and old Burgundies.' Its shape, developed in 1958, represented a quantum leap in terms of wine glass design, and has earned it a place in the permanent display of the New York Museum of Modern Art. This 'beautiful monster' of a glass can take apart a lesser wine, mercilessly showing up its weaknesses. But a great wine – a top-class Burgundy, Barolo or Barbaresco – will be revealed in all its glory. The large bowl allows the bouquet to develop to the full, while the slightly flared top lip maximizes the fruit flavours by directing a precise flow onto the front palate. Certain wines and grape varieties require this type of controlled delivery. By ensuring that the fruit is highlighted while using the marked acidity of the wine to keep the flavours in balance, this is a glass that produces a superbly three-dimensional 'taste picture'.[13]

There is a problem, though. When people are walked through the 'Riedel' experience by Riedel staff, or by the present charismatic chief executive Georg Riedel, they report a heightened sense of quality. They believe that the wine is better quality and more enjoyable to drink.

Unfortunately, in the laboratory, without the benefit of a sales patter and heightened expectations, scientists can't find evidence that the shape of a glass makes any difference to your experience of wine. In one famous experiment researcher Frédéric Brochet of the University of Bordeaux demonstrated that wine experts can't even tell the difference between red wine and white wine. Brochet presented the experts with two glasses of wine. One contained a white wine. The other contained the same white wine dyed red with food colouring. Not one of the fifty-seven experts he asked was able to identify the wine as white.[14]

In a subsequent experiment, Brochet took an ordinary bottle of Bordeaux and decanted it into two bottles. One had fancy labelling and looked expensive. The other looked like an ordinary vin du table. Forty of the experts gave a positive opinion about the 'expensive' wine.

Only twelve were positive about the 'cheap' bottle, despite there being no difference between the wines except their presentation.

In a carefully controlled experiment, it turns out that Riedel glasses don't make wine taste any different, just as it turned out that experts struggled to identify a dyed white wine. It also doesn't matter.

We don't drink wine in carefully controlled conditions. We don't experience wine just by taste or colour or smell. We do it by look and the feel of the glass and in the context of our surroundings. We do it with our own expectations and with the expectations of those around us. The scientists who are trying to prove that when you strip out the extraneous elements there is no difference are missing the point. We never experience wine without all the extraneous elements. They are part of the experience and they contribute to our enjoyment. If we enjoy our wine more from a $125 glass, does it matter if on a scientific, taste-alone basis we are being fooled?

Zwerdling asked Frédéric Brochet whether his research showed that most of us can't tell good wine from bad.

> No, no, no, I'm not saying that. I'm saying that expectations have an enormous impact. People can, in fact, tell the difference between wines. But their expectations – based on the label, or whether you tell them it's expensive, or good, or based on what kind of wine you tell them it is, the colour – all these factors can be much more powerful in determining how you taste a wine than the actual physical qualities of the wine itself.

As Zwerdling puts it:

> Look, Brochet says, he's never studied wine glasses himself, so he can't prove what he's about to say. But the research that he and others have done on the science of expectation convinces him that they've found the key: Riedel and other high-end glasses can make wine taste better. Because they're pretty. Because they're delicate. Because they're expensive. Because you expect them to make the wine taste better.

Perhaps Mark Twain put it best. After his hero Tom Sawyer persuaded his friends to pay him to let them whitewash a fence for him by convincing them how much fun he was having doing it himself,

Twain said, 'Tom had discovered a great law of human action, namely, that in order to make a man covet a thing, it is only necessary to make that thing difficult to attain.'

Bigpoint's *DarkOrbit* is a browser-based space opera. By browser-based, I mean that you can play the game just by typing www. darkorbit.com into your web browser and hey, presto, you are in the game. No disc. No big download. Just straight into the game.

Bigpoint was founded in 2002 by Heiko Hubertz with an initial focus on sports games. In 2006, the company launched *DarkOrbit*, a free-to-play game where users fly, shoot and explore an extensive, detailed online galaxy. Over 80 million accounts have been registered for the game, and it is one of the most successful games in Bigpoint's arsenal.

Some of the most popular items in *DarkOrbit* are drones. Drones support your spaceship in battle, and come in various strengths ranging from the weak First Drone to the mighty Tenth Drone. Getting the Tenth Drone takes real commitment. Players have to work their way up from the First Drone to the Second Drone to the Third and so on, amassing the resources they need to get their level up as well as finding the necessary blueprints by scouring the galaxy. In 2011, Bigpoint decided to make it possible for players to buy the Tenth Drone for just four days.

Some players would already have the Ninth Drone, and would pay to upgrade it instantly to the Tenth. Some players would have no drones at all. If they wanted to go from zero to the Tenth Drone in one transaction, they would be able to do so for a limited time. The price was high: €1,000 ($1,400). During those four days, Bigpoint sold 2,000 Tenth Drones. That's not to say that they made €2 million. Some players were already part way through the upgrade path and 'topped up' their drone. But some players did spend the full €1,000 on a virtual good.[15]

For players deeply immersed in the world of *DarkOrbit*, these transactions made sense. They made sense because of the advantage they gave players, because of the emotional commitment those players had made to the game and because of the status it gave to players who owned a high-level drone. That status cannot exist in isolation. It needs to be part of a social context to have emotional resonance for the player. To understand that, we need to understand why free players are so important to a game like *DarkOrbit*. Free players are not a weakness of the free-to-play model: they are its greatest strength. It's time to embrace the freeloader.

7
FREELOADERS

In the dying days of the dotcom boom in 2001, I bought a sailing boat and spent four months sailing around the Mediterranean with my then girlfriend, now wife. As I was preparing for my trip, I travelled to Captain O. M. Watts, a yacht chandlery just off London's Piccadilly on Dover Street. It was a marvellous shop, full of ropes and fenders, oilskins and sextants, with an amazing blend of the highly practical and the beautiful but useless. In the back was a room full of Admiralty charts, covering the UK and much of the Mediterranean. With 2,500 nautical miles to sail, I had to buy a lot of charts.

While I was exploring the shop, working out which items I actually needed rather than just wanted, I noticed another guy wandering around it. He was short and balding with a pronounced beer belly that hung low over his blue jeans. His T-shirt was black, not very clean and could not have been designed better to emphasize, rather than hide, his gut. He carried a small bottle that was once used for Evian water, but now had a black-brown sludge in the bottom. Every so often, the man would remove the lid from the bottle, shift the quid in his mouth and spit a wad of tobacco juice into the bottle.

If it had been my shop, I would have kicked the man out. The shop owners didn't, and I ended up standing behind him in the queue. He took out a black American Express card and spent, if memory serves, in the region of £20,000 ($31,000).

You never can tell who your best customers are going to be.

I give masterclasses on how to make money from free-to-play games to companies who are making the transition from a traditional fixed-price model. In the model that most people are familiar with, customers pay upfront for a product. In the case of games, that used to mean paying $60 for a console game or perhaps $5 for a game on early generations of mobile phones. Now the iPhone and Android charts are filled with games that players can download for free and where fewer than 10 per cent of customers typically pay anything at all. Many traditional game makers view the 90 per cent of customers who never pay money directly as evil freeloaders, only a slight step above being evil pirates. This is a big mistake.

The first business model that most people propose when asked how they might make money from the 90 per cent of users who never pay is through advertising. That can come in the form of display advertising, the pop-ups and banners that we are familiar with, or in the form of lead generation, where a game maker gets paid if we follow an advert from their app to sign up for another game, join a gym or watch a sponsored video.

Advertising is a well-understood business, although it requires a different set of skills from those required to build an audience through the creation of high-quality content. The premise of the advertising business is simple. It is a cross-subsidy. Instead of us, the consumers, paying for something, we get it for free or at a discounted rate. To take the example of free-to-air television, the television broadcasters commission and transmit programmes to draw in audiences. Advertisers who want to sell products to those audiences pay the broadcaster to air their advertisements. We get television for free and we pay with our attention. The broadcasters earn our attention with programmes and pay for it by charging advertisers. The advertisers subsidize our free enjoyment. The same model is in place throughout the media, at events, as part of the revenues of many retail stores and elsewhere.

Advertising and lead generation have one very important limitation in a connected, online world. Advertising is a volume game. To make money in advertising you need large numbers of users and to be able to show them a reasonable number of ads. There is a perpetual trade-off between keeping the rates you can charge for your ads high by maintaining a focused, targeted audience versus increasing revenue by increasing the number of users or the amount of ads that you show. Advertising revenues inhabit the world of Mediocristan.

Advertising revenue models are best suited to businesses which have massive scale and preferably some form of distribution monopoly, like television broadcasters.* In an open market like the web or mobile apps, competitive pressures have a habit of driving advertising rates downwards. In many cases, it may be better to consider another value of freeloaders: as potential converts.

Getting real people to pay for a product is a great way of building a business or funding the creation of your art. It can be hard to tell whether a freeloader is going to be a freeloader for ever or, like our sailing friend, is going to convert into one of your best customers. Research from Chinese games firm Papaya suggest that customers who go on to be the biggest spenders – those who spend $100 or more per month – don't start spending until they have played the game at least eight times.[1] In a world where you are trying to build a relationship with your customers and let them spend varying amounts of money, it makes little sense to kick them out unless financial pressures make it essential that you do so.

The concept behind the Curve varies from the freemium model. In most freemium businesses, the product or service is offered free but users are charged for advanced features or functionality. Venture capitalist Fred Wilson, an investor in businesses such as Twitter, Tumblr, Zynga, Etsy, Meetup and Foursquare, describes the model as 'Give your service away for free, possibly ad supported but maybe not, acquire a lot of customers very efficiently through word of mouth, referral networks, organic search marketing, etc., then offer premium priced value added services or an enhanced version of your service to your customer base.'[2] The freemium business model has come under fire for creating a huge audience of freeloaders that cannot be sustained by the small proportion of users who do pay. Initial proponents of freemium such as software-as-a-service providers Basecamp and Huddle have moved away from a free offering either by eliminating it entirely or by switching to only targeting large corporations. With conversion rates of only a few per cent for most freemium businesses and often a real cost for supporting the freeloaders, the model didn't work for many businesses that tried it.

---

* Television broadcasting is actually an oligopoly, meaning control by the few.

It didn't work not because too many people paid no money but because the biggest fans couldn't spend enough money. They could spend only a fixed amount. Freemium became a volume game where companies had only two variables: the number of users of the service and the number who paid. In technical terms, freemium is often implemented as a business model that focuses more on audience size and conversion rate than it does on ARPU (average revenue per user). In a world of the Curve, allowing your biggest fans to spend lots of money is key. In freemium, the revenue you could make from your biggest users is often capped. Subscription businesses face a similar challenge. A fixed subscription caps the amount that your biggest fans are able to pay, forcing you to focus purely on acquiring new subscribers rather than servicing your existing customers so well that they want to spend more money with you.

The Curve adds a third element: variable pricing. It focuses not just on getting lots of users (which is difficult and expensive) and improving your conversion rate (which is hard) but on adding layers of value that allow users to spend ten times, a hundred times or even a thousand times the average. It is about allowing your business or art to thrive in Extremistan, not Mediocristan. It doesn't require a large volume of users to enable your business to make a profit, although a large volume can equal massive success. Just ask Supercell, maker of *Clash of Clans* and *Hay Day*. It doesn't require the very different skills of making great products or services on the one hand and talking to advertisers on the other, so a strategy that excludes advertising allows you to focus your efforts on satisfying your customers and fans. Instead of the only way to increase your revenues being to increase volume, you can expand either by growing volume, or by raising price, or both.

Tumblr, the microblogging site that allows its users to share photos, short comments and videos, is one of the top ten most visited sites in the US, according to audience measurement company Quantcast. In November 2012, it had 170 million unique users, who viewed 18 billion pages. Yet according to *Forbes*, the company made only $13 million revenue in 2012.[3]

In stark contrast stands Venan Entertainment, a developer of mobile games based in Cromwell, Connecticut. In 2011 the company released

Book of Heroes, a free role-playing game on iOS and Android mobile devices. The company doesn't have a huge audience for the game, getting about 100,000 unique players per month, and perhaps 25,000 unique players per day.* The company is on track to make $3 million in 2013.

Venan, with fewer than 200,000 unique users playing *Book of Heroes*, is making around a quarter of the revenues that Tumblr made in 2012. That's an audience of just 0.1 per cent of Tumblr's making 25 per cent of the revenue, through application of the Curve.

Freeloaders are not just sources of revenue. They are also one of the most potent sources of marketing. Marketers have long regarded word-of-mouth recommendation as the most powerful form of promotion, and one of the hardest to achieve. With the advent of social networks, sharing what you enjoy has become even easier.

The viral sensations of 'Gangnam Style' and the Harlem Shake happened at unprecedented speed due to the ease of sharing across the globe. Freeloaders are critically important in places like the App Store, where by downloading, using or spending in an app, users can contribute to its chart ranking. To be in the charts you either need to spend lots of money on customer acquisition, or you need your existing customers to love your game so much that they each persuade several of their friends to check it out. In reality you probably need elements of both. We have seen how Electronic Arts and others gamed the App Store so that their products appeared at the top of the charts on Christmas Day when consumers were opening their new iDevices. We also saw how the price war between Sony and Amazon over ebooks in the UK affected the charts when many ebooks were available for a very low price. I picked up a copy of *1,227 QI Facts To Blow Your Socks Off* for 20p for my Kindle in February 2013, a discount of 98 per cent from the publisher's recommended retail price. It was at number 4 in the paid Kindle store, behind *Life of Pi* by Yann Martel, *The Hundred-Year-Old Man Who Climbed Out of the Window and Disappeared* by Jonas Jonasson and *Safe House* by Chris Ewan, all of which were also available for 20p.

---

* Known respectively as MAUs and DAUs, or monthly/daily active users. The internet loves its TLAs.

The marketing value of users is enormous. We have already seen that in this world of social media, the big are getting bigger and the niche is getting more viable. Free users acting as viral marketing are vital to both elements.

There are some things in life that are unmissable. On TV, the Olympics, Queen Elizabeth II's Diamond Jubilee and the finales of certain shows have already been mentioned in Chapter 4. In 2012, every woman in my social sphere had to have read *Fifty Shades of Grey*. In my world of technology-savvy game players it was hard to fit in if you hadn't seen 'Gangnam Style' on YouTube, played *The Walking Dead* on your iPad or experienced *Angry Birds Star Wars*.

This is nothing new. Throughout the twentieth century we've had shared cultural experiences. The difference is that even in this era of time-shifting and streaming, of personalization and niche content, there are some experiences which we all want to talk about, to share, and to experience either in person or via social media. The big experiences benefit from being talked about. A lot.

So do the small ones. Word of mouth enables niche products to thrive. But word-of-mouth recommendation can be at its most powerful when acting on that recommendation is made as frictionless as possible. Technology is making it ever easier to go from a recommendation to a download or purchase. I can click on a friend's recommendation on a social site and go straight to a purchase page. The friction is reduced even more if the price of the product is free.

It turns out that 'free' is a very different psychological price point to 'cheap'. Psychologist Dan Ariely demonstrated this irrational behaviour that relates to free products in a famous experiment using Hershey's Kisses chocolates.[4] Ariely set up a table at a large public building. He offered two kinds of chocolates: high-quality Lindt truffles and ordinary Hershey's Kisses. A large sign above the table read, 'One chocolate per customer'. Customers could only see the chocolates and their prices once they stepped close to the table.

Lindt chocolates are high-quality Swiss chocolates that Ariely describes as 'particularly prized, exquisitely creamy and just about irresistible'. They cost Ariel about 30 cents each when he bought them in bulk. Hershey's Kisses are less special: the company makes 80 million of them every single day. Ariely started the experiment by setting the price of Lindt chocolates at 15 cents and Hershey's Kisses at 1 cent. 'We were not surprised to find that our customers acted with a great deal of rationality: they compared the price and quality of the Kiss with the price and quality of the Lindt truffle, and then they made their choice. About 73 per cent of them chose the truffle and 27 per cent chose a Kiss.'

The purpose of the experiment was to see what impact free had on people's rationality, so Ariely then lowered the price of both chocolates by 1 cent. The Lindt was priced at 14 cents while the Kiss was now free. 'What a big difference FREE! made. The humble Hershey's Kiss became a big favourite. Some sixty-nine per cent of our customers (up from 27 per cent before) chose the FREE! Kiss, giving up the opportunity to get the Lindt truffle for a very good price. Meanwhile, the Lindt truffle took a tumble; customers choosing it decreased from 73 to 31 per cent.'

Ariely repeated the experiment in different circumstances and with different conditions. His conclusion is that free is a very powerful motivational price. It gives us an emotional charge that increases the perceived value of what we are getting. More than that, we will often take the free option because it is perceived as being lower risk, as eliminating the possibility of loss. We often ignore the externalities (such as the time taken to download an app, or the limited amount of storage space we have on our iOS devices) because the lure of free is so powerful. Most importantly, Ariely shows that the difference between an app that is free and an app costing 99 cents is much bigger than the difference between $0.99 and $1.99. Even though a dollar is a tiny amount to pay for a game, an amount that most of us wouldn't flinch from spending on a cup of coffee with barely a thought, it is vastly, unimaginably, infinitely more expensive than free. (Expensive is very important too. That is covered in Chapter 9.)

David Barnard has first-hand experience of this. Barnard is an independent designer of productivity apps that he publishes on the App Store. His business, App Cubby, makes an app for keeping track of your car's fuel consumption and another, Launch Center Pro, which makes it easy not just to launch apps but to launch actions within those apps, such as 'Call Home' or 'Search Yelp for nearby coffee shops' from a single shortcut.

On 31 May 2012, Barnard released Timer, a simple-to-use app that improves on the built-in features of the iPhone. He priced it at 99 cents. Over the next three months, he saw nearly 9,000 downloads and $6,000 in revenue, but by August, downloads had slowed to a crawl. Barnard's development philosophy is that 'the future of sustainable app development is to give away as much value as possible and empower those who receive more value to pay more for it'.[5] So he decided to allow people to have the functionality of Timer for free, but to let people spend more on it if they want to with in-app purchases (IAPs). The IAPs were simply different themes: aesthetic choices which allowed people to customize how the app looked and the sounds it played when the timer was up. They started at 99 cents. The most expensive IAP was the Ultimate bundle, $9.99 for all the themes and sounds both in existence now and that App Cubby might release in the future. None of the IAPs were necessary to use the app.

On the first day that Timer went free, downloads jumped from just twelve copies to 25,000. The app has now been downloaded over 200,000 times, more than twenty times its installed base when it was paid. It has made $8,000 as a free app. More than half of the revenue came from the 672 people who decided to upgrade for the full Ultimate Bundle, choosing to pay $10 for an aesthetic upgrade to an app where the core functionality is available for free.

These results happened despite some challenges. The original paid app was featured by Apple. The free version wasn't. Barnard says he made a tactical error with the free launch too. He turned the product free without having the in-app purchases in place. He got a spike in downloads but there was nothing for them to buy for a long time. Despite these errors, by going free and letting those freeloaders who wished to spend money do so, he has an audience twenty times bigger than he had before, and a third more revenue. Barnard is a believer in the power of free.

The Curve is not dependent on having a free offering. The heart of the Curve is allowing customers to spend lots of money if they wish to. It doesn't require a starting point of zero, although that may increase your audience size. Many games companies are experimenting with a paymium business model where customers pay up front to buy the game and are then able to spend more on in-app purchases if they wish. It is not without risk – customers are more forgiving of something they got for free asking for money than something they have paid for upfront – but it does shield a traditional business against making the painful decision to offer its core product for free.

The Curve is a defence against piracy, where many customers can get your products for free. Piracy is not the real long-term threat. That comes when competition from new upstarts or brave incumbents pushes the price of anything that can be shared digitally to zero because the new player has figured out how to let the high spenders subsidize the freeloaders. Smart businesses and artists will start experimenting with ways to enable their biggest fans and best customers to spend lots of money on things they truly value now, before it becomes the only way to survive. They will make their mistakes when they have alternatives, and can survive some of the experiments failing. They will prepare for the moment when it is no longer possible to put a pay barrier between their end users and their product, service or art.

Then they will pick their moment. Different industries are at different stages of development. Games has already made the transition to free voluntarily. Music has done so involuntarily. Movies are still at a premium price point, both in theatres (sustainably) and on DVD (less so). I expect Penguin to charge for the ebook version of *The Curve* because it is not yet essential that all ebooks be free, although I think that day will come. If customers are still prepared to pay, it may be worth letting them do so, until you figure out how to make more money by allowing them to get the product for free and paying you more money further along the Curve.

Free is a powerful tool for getting users to your product, service or art. It is not that users aren't prepared to spend money on apps or music or online services. It is that their fear of loss is strong and when companies find a way to let them experience an app or music or a service for free, that fear is eliminated or reduced. That means more users in the ecosystems to be advertised to, to tell their friends or to move along the Curve to become high-spending customers.

They also provide the context within which users spend. The final reason why freeloaders are so important is because they act as gawkers. Gawkers are so critical to understanding the Curve that they have a chapter all to themselves.

8
GAWKERS

The male bowerbird is a peculiar creature.

Bowerbirds are medium to large passerines, a type of bird that is about the size of a Eurasian blackbird or perhaps a small crow. Their most significant distinguishing feature, at least as far as evolutionary biologists are concerned, is their habit of constructing a large 'bower' as part of the courtship ritual. For example, the male satin bowerbird, native to eastern Australia, builds a structure of sticks and twigs which he decorates with objects that he has collected, many of which are blue, yellow or shiny. Life became a lot easier for bowerbirds when the plastics industry began to manufacture blue clothes pegs and disposable pens with blue caps.

Female bowerbirds visit the bowers to inspect their quality. They will return to some of them to see the male's dancing display as well. Eventually, females will pick a mate, usually just one. That is the end of the male's involvement in the process of creating the next generation, so biologists have had to come up with an explanation for why male bowerbirds expend so much energy in building a bower that has no practical purpose – it doesn't protect from the elements, it doesn't protect from predators, it's not even a nest, the female has to build that on her own – and why the females use the quality of the bower, and the attendant dancing courtship ritual, to determine which suitor wins.

In 1975 biologist Amotz Zahavi put forward a theory to explain the profligacy of the male bowerbirds' behaviour. Zahavi proposed that certain traits that biologists struggled to understand – the bowers of the bowerbird, the tail feathers of a peacock – could be best explained by considering them as 'handicaps', signalling the ability to squander a resource simply by actually squandering it. In essence, the bowerbird is saying, 'Look at this lovely structure I have built. Look at the effort I have spent in building it. Look at the energy I have squandered flying across the land seeking out shiny pebbles and blue plastic gewgaws. I must have oodles and oodles of surplus energy to be able to feed myself and protect myself from predators while also doing this totally pointless thing. Wouldn't you love my genes to be passed on to your chicks, rather than the genes of my pathetic rival in the next bower who has only five sticks and a clothes peg to his name?'

Zahavi's handicap principle was initially controversial, although it has been influential in changing mainstream biological thinking. Geoffrey Miller, an evolutionary psychologist, has developed the idea of the handicap principle to how they affect sexual selection amongst humans. At the more positive end of this interpretation, Miller sees the human mind as having developed, for reasons more than simply for survival, a step beyond the simplistic understanding of Darwin's selection theories. He argues that those elements of the human mind that seem unhelpful for escaping predators and finding food – art, literature, altruism, creativity and so on – can be best understood as being about *sexual selection*. The human mind has evolved as a tool for aiding mate-choice by advertising intelligence, creativity or a number of other desirable characteristics.

The best of our species – our capacity for art, for charity, for love and for altruism – are sexual selection displays, used to display both the capacity of our brains and as fitness indicators using Zahavi's handicap principle. Anthropologists have identified other potential explanations for why humans are compelled to display their consumption or adopt certain behaviours, ranging from sexual selection to creating mutual obligations, cementing the alliance between groups or demonstrating status through waste. Miller sees conspicuous consumption as humans spending to prove that we have surplus energy to squander. The more we squander, the more energy we must have had in the first place, making us more attractive as potential mates. Marketing departments have leaped on this fundamental of human nature – that we need to use signals to evaluate the quality of potential mates – to convince us that the best way to display our sexual attractiveness is through the consumption choices that we make.

Miller's work builds on the work of Thorstein Veblen, a Norwegian-American economist who was one of the first to investigate the theory of conspicuous consumption in his 1899 work *The Theory of the Leisure Class*. Veblen gave his name to Veblen goods, a group of commodities for which people's preference for buying them increases as their price increases (because a higher price suggests a greater status) instead of decreasing as the economic law of demand would suggest. Common examples of Veblen goods are luxury wines and spirits, high-end cars, designer clothes and jewellery.

The Gawkers for whom this chapter is named are important players in a conspicuous consumption display. The purpose of conspicuous consumption, or indeed any sexual selection display, is to distinguish between individuals. Those choosing need to have something to see, while those displaying need to have an audience to which to display. In the context of the Curve, sexual selection theory suggests that many of the behaviours attributed to evolution by sexual selection involve a social context. An audience. Gawkers.

Robert Cialdini is one of my two favourite writers on how we perceive price and value. (The other is Dan Ariely.) Cialdini is a professor of both marketing and psychology at Arizona State University. His book *Influence: The Psychology of Persuasion* is a masterpiece that will help you understand how and why you buy things, and how to sell them.

Cialdini opens his book with an anecdote of the experience of a friend who ran a Native American jewellery store in Arizona. She had a collection of good-quality turquoise pieces that she just could not sell. It was not a problem of footfall: it was peak tourist season and the shop was full of customers, but the turquoise jewellery stubbornly stayed on the shelves. She moved them to a more prominent location. No luck. She told her staff to recommend them. Nothing.

Finally, as she went out of town on a buying trip, she left a note for her head saleswoman. 'Everything in this display case, price × ½', with the intention of clearing the stock, even if it meant she took a loss.

When she returned, she was pleased that all the stock was gone. She was even more pleased to discover that the saleswoman had misread the note. Instead of selling the turquoise pieces at half the usual price, she had priced them at double the usual price.

Cialdini explains it like this. We all use shortcuts in our lives. Mother turkeys will nurture anything that makes the *cheep, cheep* of a baby turkey, even if the thing going *cheep, cheep* is a stuffed polecat with a tape recorder playing the sounds of a chick where its intestines used to be. Male robins will let a perfect stuffed replica of a robin with no red breast feathers stay unmolested in its territory while it will vigorously attack nothing more than a clump of red-breast feathers placed there. These behaviours are called fixed-action patterns, and tend to be repeated in the same way every time when activated by a trigger-feature, something like the cheep of a turkey chick or the red breast feathers of a male robin.

In the case of the turquoise-buying tourists, the fixed-action pattern was a way of thinking, a cognitive shortcut that equated 'expensive' with 'good'. Most of the time, it is a good guide. On this occasion, the turquoise jewellery in Cialdini's friend's store seemed to be more valuable and more desirable when the only thing that changed about it was the price. It turns out that Native American jewellery is a Veblen good.

Cialdini goes on to comment that although the tourists made a wrong decision on this occasion, due to the pricing mistake made by the salesperson, they are probably, on balance, better off following the shortcut 'expensive = good' than not. Since the alternative is to become an expert valuer of everything that we might want to buy, from jewellery to wine to cheese to clothes, it makes rational sense to use the shortcut to avoid that effort, even if on occasion it fails us.

We've seen that conspicuous consumption may be a way of signalling surplus energy, something that is likely to be attractive to a mate (of either sex). Conspicuous consumption doesn't have to be confined to ostentatious displays of wealth, though. After all, the purpose of the consumption is to show that we have surplus energy, that we are able to feed, clothe, house and protect ourselves from predators while still splashing cash on Cristal champagne or Dolce & Gabbana clothes. Miller argues that marketers 'still believe that premium products are bought to display wealth, status, and taste, and they miss the deeper mental traits that people are actually wired to display – traits such as kindness, intelligence, and creativity'.[1]

There are many ways to signal a surplus of energy. People with three degrees are demonstrating that they can afford to spend their time in full- or part-time education while still feeding, clothing and housing themselves. My deep knowledge of the extended Star Wars universe or PC games of the 1990s is highly unlikely to have increased my sexual attractiveness, except through the handicap principle. People pursuing the 100 Thing Challenge, trying to live their lives with fewer than one hundred possessions, are demonstrating that they don't need the accoutrements that many of us take for granted in our lives.[2] For different people, they may harness the handicap principle through their charity work, through acquiring esoteric knowledge of fine wines, of football, of cooking, through an individual dress sense, through making their own jewellery. You can argue that almost everything we do can be traced back to the display of consumption in different forms.

That is not to say that all of these displays are purely self-interested, or designed solely to win a mate. They have become part of the fabric of our society. They are how we construct our identity and sense of self. They are part of how we create friendship groups and become part of a community. It is not necessary to believe that everything we do is done because others are watching; thousands of years of social evolution mean that these behaviours have become part of what it means to be human.

The handicap principle, signalling of social status, the desire for conspicuous consumption; these are all ways of thinking about our behaviours from an evolutionary biological point of view. It is also worth thinking about how these translate into everyday behaviours, and the language we use to describe them.

Much of what we do, consciously or unconsciously, is self-expression. We craft our own identities through the clothes we wear, the friends we choose, the objects we covet, the music we listen to, the books we read, the knowledge we seek out and the events we attend. We display that identity, consciously or unconsciously, as part of our daily lives.

My house is full of books. About a quarter of the wall space of my living room consists of floor-to-ceiling white-painted shelves filled end to end with them. About half of my living room collection is history. Braudel's *The Mediterranean* jostles against Andrew Lambert's *Admirals* and Ian Kershaw's masterful biography of Hitler. The other half is business books – Taleb's *Black Swan*, Chris Anderson's *Free*, Seth Godin's *Tribes*, Nicholas Carr's *The Shallows*, William Goldman's *Adventures in the Screen Trade*. These are the books I want people to know that I read when they first visit my house.

Upstairs, I keep my geekier books – Star Wars, Car Wars, the complete sets of the Sharpe novels by Bernard Cornwell and the Aubrey–Maturin books by Patrick O'Brian. Only people to whom I'm happy to reveal my inner geek get to see them. Increasingly, I find that when I buy genre fiction, crime, airport thrillers, and so on, I do so on my Kindle first, particularly if I am not sure whether I like the author enough yet to make them part of my displayed identity.

For me, what I read and, more importantly, what I choose to display that I read, are an important part of my self-identity. I am sure you will have noticed that the preceding two paragraphs are a conspicuous display of the breadth of my knowledge and erudition (and geekiness). It's about telling other people who I am.

Jonah Peretti, the founder of BuzzFeed, suggests that conspicuous displays are not limited to possessions. Many people pause to think before they share an article or a video on an online site. They pause to ponder what the fact of sharing says about them. 'Social sharing is about your identity. You want to say, "Look, I'm smart, or charitable, or funny."'[3]

Self-expression. Status. Identity. Friendship. Relationships. Mate selection. These elements are all intimately linked. They are also key to understanding how the Curve works in an online world. Before we can get there, though, we need to think about how the world has changed such that value is no longer only contained in the place that some people misleadingly call the real world.

'To understand why Zynga Inc. is among the tech industry's hottest companies, consider how it gets people to buy things that don't exist,' wrote Nick Wingfield of the *Wall Street Journal* in September 2011.[4]

'Marketing Fanciful Items in the Lands of Make Believe' was the headline above an article on virtual goods in *The New York Times* by Elisabeth Olsen in September 2010.[5] In 2009, Claire Cain Miller and Brad Stone wrote in *The New York Times*, 'Silicon Valley may have discovered the perfect business: charging real money for products that do not exist.'[6] It's like newspapers think that what readers value is the dead tree, not the words, thoughts, ideas and intellectual property that the dead tree pages contain . . .

The emergence of virtual goods as viable business models in the games industry took many traditional media commentators by surprise. They could understand a $50-billion global business for long-form games purchased on shiny gold DVDs and played on dedicated console hardware or high-end PCs. They could even understand when that same long-form experience was distributed via a fibre-optic cable to someone's home, using a service such as Steam or Xbox Live, rather than on a disc. What they found hard to understand was the consumers who would play a game entirely for free yet choose to spend $10 on a virtual farmhouse in Zynga's seminal title, *Farmville*.

Farmville was one of Zynga's early big successes.* Released in 2009, it allowed players to manage a virtual farm. They could plant crops, collect wool from virtual sheep and lay out fields, fences, orchards and duck ponds. The game was on Facebook and, importantly, it was free. Anyone could click on a link or a story in a friend's newsfeed and be taken straight into the game. At one point, Farmville was the most popular game on Facebook, with 60 million people playing it every month.[7]

Sixty million people. Other than massive sporting events like the Olympics or the Super Bowl, there isn't a great deal that can claim the attention of 60 million people. Of course, *Farmville* was free. It was monetized by selling virtual goods, items that didn't exist in the physical world but which enhanced the game. I bought a virtual farmhouse because my farm looked strangely empty without a focal point, and I was happy to spend $10 making my farm look better. Many critics scoffed at the foolishness of spending money on something that didn't

---

* Zynga's early lead in this market has disappeared as they failed to adapt to changing consumer preferences, but the business model is thriving elsewhere.

exist. Those critics seemed to believe that only the physical can have a value.

Is the value in a book the collection of dead trees, or is it in the ideas, thoughts and concepts contained therein? Is the value of a CD in the disc of shiny plastic or in the ability of the music it holds to absorb, entertain, or transport us? Is a DVD really a physical artefact, not merely a delivery device that contains the true value: the television series, the movie, the game software?

We have spent nearly 500 years understanding that books have value without realizing that they have two different elements of value. Books are an access device. Books are the content contained within that access device. For 490 of those years, this fine distinction has only been of interest to philosophers. That is suddenly no longer the case. The access device is becoming of less value to many consumers. The emergence of the ebook has shown a different, cheaper, more flexible way of getting access to the other valuable piece, the content. Similarly, the MP3 and other digital music formats have separated the CD into 'access device' and 'the music the device contained'. There remains enormous value in the content of a book, an album, a movie, while the value of the physical media that contains it is collapsing as new, better, cheaper ways of accessing content emerge.

There is, of course, a third value of the physical object: that of status symbol.* Based on the handicap principle or Veblen's ideas of conspicuous consumption, the book, the CD or vinyl LP and the DVD boxed set will continue to have value as means of self-expression and displaying status, knowledge or culture. This is part of the reason sales of vinyl LPs have been growing for the last five years, rising by 15 per cent in 2012 even as album sales fell by 11.2 per cent overall.[8]

Virtual goods such as my *Farmville* farmhouse have begun to fulfil the same roles that physical goods and experiences fulfil for many people. It's not about transience: no one argues that paying for an expensive gig or a safari holiday or a celebratory meal at a Michelin-starred

---

* There is a fourth value too: some people talk about the joy of turning the crisp pages of a hardback or owning the glistening vinyl of an album. I tend to believe that this is part of status, but accept that for some people, the fetishization of the physical is important in its own right.

restaurant is paying for something that doesn't exist, although it very quickly only exists in your memory. As we move towards an existence that intertwines the physical and the virtual, so our sense of what we value adapts to both realms.

Although that process of adaptation started many years ago, one development above any other allowed virtual goods to make the leap into the mainstream: social networking. It did that by transforming the nature of our friendships. On 14 September 2012, Facebook reached its billionth active user. A billion people, one-seventh of the global population, logged into Facebook in the thirty days before that date. That is a staggering statistic, but it is also one that has already transformed how we view friendships and, importantly for the Curve, virtual items.

Facebook has over 140 billion friend connections, implying that the average user has 140 friends.[9] These friendships are not the same as physical-world friendships. Facebook has not replaced the need or desire for humans to come together in physical proximity, to share a drink or food or an atmosphere in a combined experience. What it has done is taught us that we can build, maintain or strengthen human relationships in purely virtual environments. If relationships can work virtually, then many of the behavioural traits we display in the physical world are likely to migrate to the virtual world too, including displays that enhance our status or provide signals for sexual selection. In other words, if we buy physical goods or invest time, money and effort in acquiring or displaying specific knowledge or expertise to physical people in physical space, when we move those relationships into the online sphere, it makes sense for us to desire to buy goods or to display our knowledge, expertise, status and wealth in an online environment too.

Facebook took a billion users into a virtual space that was filled with human relationships. Along the way, it transformed our understanding of the distinction between the physical and the virtual, reducing its importance for many of us. That is not to say that there is no distinction. In fact, the physical is likely to have *more* value in the future, as it becomes more scarce and more important as a signal of our self-identity. It is to say that the migration of human relationships into an online space has made it possible for us to also see the value in spending money on things which exist only in that online space if they also, in some form, influence those human relationships.

Let me put it another way. A decade ago or more, my wife explained to me the significance of flowers, or indeed any similar small, non-event-specific gift. 'It's not about the flowers themselves, although they are lovely. It is about showing that you thought about me when I wasn't there, that you bothered to spend the time, effort and money on me, that you wanted to express that you were thinking about me.' The flowers are important, the gesture more so. (Virtual goods carry much of the same symbolism that my wife ascribed to flowers, or they can do in the right circumstances.)

I had a client who was designing a medieval virtual world in which users could buy virtual items to customize their avatar. Customers would be able to browse an online shop for greaves and breastplates, helmets and vambraces, new designs for their heraldic shields and pets to lie at their feet. I looked at the design and noted that there was no intention to allow users to look at each other's avatars. The company thought that people would choose to customize their avatar just because they could, not because they were aware that other people were looking.

'Let me ask you this,' I said. 'When you are at home, on your own, with no one looking, do you dress up in your finest clothes, or do you slob out in tracksuit trousers and an old T-shirt?'

Most of us don't take much care of our appearance when we know that no one is looking. The same is true in an online environment. Zynga faced the same problem with *Farmville*. Despite the intensity of their notifications to users, which reached sufficiently spam-like levels that Facebook moved to shut down the viral channels that Zynga was using, users were not visiting each other's farms. Zynga responded by adding a small, seemingly pointless minigame. While I was harvesting crops one day, a pop-up box appeared on the screen. 'There are crows eating the crops of your friend, Leonie. Will you scare them away?' I clicked yes (who wouldn't want to help a friend in need?) and the image of my farm on my screen was replaced by the image of Leonie's farm. Overlaid on top I saw a new pop-up screen congratulating me on scaring away the birds and granting me some virtual currency for my trouble.

Because it is my profession, I spent some time looking at the screen, thinking about what Zynga was trying to achieve with this process. It can't have been to add challenge or a meaningful new layer of game-play to the game. All I did was click on the button and turn up at Leonie's farm and the birds were scared. It was a very passive experience. While I was thinking, I noticed that Leonie had a bigger farmhouse than I did. She had a duck pond. I scrolled around the map and looked at how she had arranged her fields. I admired her orchard.

Which was when it struck me. Zynga was strengthening my aware-ness that *Farmville* was a social game, with all the social consequences that entailed. Leonie was displaying her prowess as a *Farmville* player, her aesthetic choices, her personal style. I was looking at it, and I now knew that other people, going through the same process, would end up looking at my farm. I immediately clicked back to my farm and started improving it. When I know people are looking, I don't wear tracksuit trousers and an old grubby T-shirt.

That is not to say that virtual goods only have value if other people are looking at them, in the same way that, in the physical world, we don't only get satisfaction or validation from the way other people view our possessions or achievements. I use the example of people visiting each other's farms to see their virtual possessions and achieve-ments as an illustration of how our awareness of the social nature of online experiences has led to us having an understanding that the vir-tual has value. Once this idea has taken root, it is possible to buy virtual goods for personal satisfaction or self-expression, not simply for display. It is harder to market them without the idea that other people will see them, but not impossible.

Sociologist Nathan Jurgenson has a name for the artificial distinc-tion between our physical self and our online self. He calls it *digital dualism*.[10] To a digital dualist, the physical world is 'real' and the digital world is 'virtual'. Like Neo in *The Matrix*, we can either exist in a real physical world (Zion), or an idealized, fictional virtual world (the Matrix) but not both at the same time. This reductionist view believes that social media lead people to trade the rich, physical and real nature of face-to-face contact for the digital, virtual and trivial nature of Facebook. It is prevalent in books such as Nicholas Carr's *The Shallows*, Evgeny Morozov's *The Net Delusion* and Andrew

Keen's *The Cult of the Amateur*. Jurgenson also believes that the arguments are flawed owing to a systematic bias to see the digital and the physical as separate; 'a zero-sum trade-off where time and energy spent on one subtracts from the other'. As Jurgenson says, this is a fallacy.

On a personal level, my three closest friends live far away from my home in London. One is in Washington, DC, one in Oman in the Middle East and the third in a tiny village north of Belfast. I communicate with them regularly via digital channels like Facebook, Twitter, Skype and email when in a bygone era I would have communicated by letter. The two or three occasions a year when I meet up with them are significantly enhanced by the regular communications we have had electronically. At the other end of the spectrum, I work from home and my equivalent of the water-cooler is Twitter. There are people whose names I do not know but whose Twitter handles I recognize instantly. These people are becoming friends, but I'm not ready to count them as *real* friends until I have met them for a drink or a coffee. Twitter is a starting point or a continuation of a relationship in the physical world, but the two are inextricably intertwined.

The dangers of digital dualism are manifold. Writers and commentators who persist in this artificial distinction perpetuate the idea that change is bad. They imply that the physical is intrinsically better than the digital, when it would be more accurate to say that certain experiences may be more or less enjoyable, informative, educational or enlightening in the physical world, the digital world or the crossover between both. They ignore the day-to-day reality that an increasing proportion of the population (remember those billion Facebook users) exist comfortably in both worlds regularly. They refuse to acknowledge that humans adapt their behaviour to changing technologies with amazing rapidity, or they acknowledge it and find it disappointing because it doesn't fit with an idealized perception of how the world ought to be.

From a business perspective, it is also dangerous. The first manifestations of a digital strategy involved taking the existing physical product and converting it into a digital format. (Actually, you could argue that the first version was mail order delivery, and that Amazon is not a truly digital business. You would be right, in that Amazon's delivery business is still resolutely physical for the majority of the items it sells. However, the Amazon *catalogue* is digital, which is what enables the site to have such an enormous range.) The thinking in this form of 'going digital' is that consumers have already understood the value of the product, because it existed in a physical form. The business people who designed products, sold products and marketed products could understand this product offering, because they were essentially saying, 'We have taken this physical artefact – a compact disc containing *No Angel* by Dido, a box containing every episode of *The Simpsons* on DVD, a black plastic case containing a shiny disc that holds *Finding Nemo* – and made it into a digital artefact *without changing its fundamental essence in any way.*' This perception saw the physical and the digital as two separate realities, with the ability to convert between them.

The new business opportunities eschew this digital dualism. Jurgenson calls the opposite of digital dualism 'augmented reality', a phrase that I hate. I hate it because it has been a buzzword of games for nearly a decade, as companies tried to convince us that we want games played in the real world, virtual reality goggles, a holographic projection of digital information onto our perception of the real world and a dozen other dead-end technologies. I think it is a tainted term. I prefer digital holism, the idea that the two realities of the physical and the digital, while not being the same, cannot be understood without reference to the other.[11]

Digital holism is why consumers will buy ebook readers and download cheap or free books and then go out and buy that same book in hardback. It connects our understanding of friendships in the real world with our preparedness to help out people we only know virtually in an online game. It is the marketing journey that businesses need to take customers on as they move from slightly interested visitor to a website to a fully engaged, deeply committed superfan spending tens, hundreds or thousands of dollars on items that exist in the physical reality, the digital reality or both.

In 2007 Ian Livingstone, author of the *Fighting Fantasy* game books and life president of video game maker Eidos, visited South Korea. On his return, he started talking about a new business model that had become amazingly successful there. The prime example was *Kart-Rider*, a game so popular that within the first year 12 million Koreans, one quarter of the population, had played it.[12] The game involved racing cartoon-like virtual cars around a virtual racetrack against other, real players. The game was free to play, but in the run-up to Christmas 2007, the company behind *KartRider*, Nexon, decided to allow its users to buy Santa hats to wear while racing. They put them on sale for $1 and, according to Livingstone, they had sold a million hats within a week.

Game developers in the Western world were amazed. A Santa hat probably cost an afternoon of an artist's time to make, if that. Yet here it was generating $1 million in a week. It looked like a licence to print money. The developers were missing one very important fact: the players were not paying for the game at all. They were not paying for the expensive game engine that managed the steering, collision detection, animation and graphics that formed their entertainment experience. They were not paying for the design of the tracks. They were not paying for the work that went into balancing the performance of the different cars, the artwork of the characters, the points system or anything else. They were not paying for content. They were only paying for hats.

The precursor to *KartRider* was *Quiz Quiz* (now *Q-play*). Nexon didn't plan on a virtual goods business model. In 2001, when the trial period of free membership ended and they announced they would shortly start charging fees, membership plummeted by 90 per cent. Nexon made membership free again and experimented with creating wigs, hats and shirts to decorate the avatars representing players in the quiz. The cosmetic items soon generated over $150,000 per month.[13]

In this world of digital distribution, where it can be trivially cheap to distribute content and where Bertrand competition dictates that prices will tend to move to the marginal cost of distribution, content will tend to be free. Instead, consumers will pay for things that they value, like self-expression, identity, status, expressions of friendship, and so on.

If you think that spending $1 on a Santa hat is foolish, consider this: do you spend more than $1 every year on holiday celebrations or decorations. If you say no, you are either a curmudgeon, a liar or a hermit. I think that spending $1 on a Santa hat as part of a social celebration in a place (albeit a virtual place) where I am surrounded by my friends seems cheap, and a darn site cheaper and better for the environment than buying a pair of novelty reindeer antlers for the office Christmas party.

The first person who bought a Santa hat in *KartRider* might have thought, *Look at me, I'm the first person to have a Santa hat. Aren't I cool?* The next buyers might have wanted to be early trend setters. Then players will have started to think, *Everyone else has a Santa hat, I'd better buy one.* The Santa hat satisfies different urges: the desire to celebrate, to be first, to stand out, to fit in, to share an experience with friends and acquaintances and to have fun. Not bad for only $1.

We've established that people spend money on virtual goods for many of the same reasons that they buy goods in the real world. We've established that companies need freeloaders to provide the context within which people will choose to spend money. We've also established that in a competitive environment, the economic rule of Bertrand competition tends to push the price of goods to their marginal cost which, in the case of digital assets, can be as close to zero as makes no odds. We also know that when your product goes free, you no longer get a fee from all of your customers. Many of them will never spend any money with you at all. If only 10 per cent of your customers are going to pay you, when previously 100 per cent of them paid you, how are you going to be able to afford to pay for the creation of new content or products?

To answer that question, we need to meet another type of customer. Enter the superfan.

9
SUPERFANS

Phish are a peculiar band. Their music is hard to define. They are a band that many fans think are best experienced live rather than via a recording. They have played together for so long, improvising, experimenting and performing, that no two gigs are alike. They've been going for thirty years yet only one of their albums has been in the top ten Billboard rankings. They've released over 800 songs and none of them have been radio hits. They have only made one music video in all that time.[1]

Yet, between 2008 and 2012, Phish made over $120 million from touring. In 2012 they grossed $28.1 million, more than Radiohead, Metallica or a resurgent Neil Diamond.[2] Because Phish gigs are so heavily improvised, fans fear missing out by not attending. The fans who do go trade recordings of the live concerts with each other, a practice which the band encourages. John Ellis first saw them play in Toronto in 2002, since when he has been to more than fifty gigs.* I asked Ellis how much money he had spent on Phish.

'At least $1,000 on the gigs. More when you add petrol and motels and food. Hundreds on CDs. Then T-shirts, books and so on. Perhaps $2,000.'

Ellis is one of Phish's superfans.

*

* 'John Ellis' is a pseudonym. Ellis was happy to admit to his American and Canadian friends how much he has spent, but now he has emigrated to England and is embarrassed to admit it to his British friends who don't 'get' Phish.

Sharna Jackson is a thirty-year-old mother of one. By day she is employed at the Tate Gallery, trying to interest children in the art and artists housed in her workplace. By night she explores a gothic fantasy of Victorian London in an online game called *Echo Bazaar*.[3]

The brainchild of Alexis Kennedy, chief narrative officer of Failbetter Games, *Echo Bazaar* is part familiar, part intoxicatingly different. Described as 'a free browser game that only takes a few minutes a day to play', *Echo Bazaar* introduces players to a world of peasoupers and squidmen, detectives and nightmares through a series of short, interactive vignettes.

Jackson has spent over £250 ($400) on *Echo Bazaar*. 'I love the game. I love the content and I love how the writers have evoked such an intriguing world. *Echo Bazaar* is brilliant because it is free. You can play it even if you have no money. You get a limited number of actions every day for free, and when I first played, I blew through all of my actions really fast. I spent money so I could get more access to content. I'm still spending.'

Whether she's at work or at home, Jackson always has a browser window open, so she can see how many actions she has available to her. Her office computer is littered with giant Post-it notes showing her progress towards different goals. She is a superfan of *Echo Bazaar*.

We have met superfans throughout this book and will meet more. The players of *Clash of Clans* who spend thousands of dollars on the game. The supporters of Victoria Vox who paid $1,500 to hear her play a gig in their home. The people who pay $275 to attend a baking course in Vermont or £4,000 ($6,000) for a four-day residential cookery masterclass with Michelin-starred chef Raymond Blanc at Le Manoir aux Quatre Saisons.

Kevin Kelly was one of the first proponents of the idea of relationships with true fans, rather than with the mass market, as being the future route through which independent content creators would be able to fund their existence. Kelly, the founding executive editor of *Wired*, set out his views on how artists would be able to survive in an online world in a 2008 blog post entitled '1,000 True Fans'.[4] Given that the long tail has increased both competition and downward pressure on prices, Kelly asks the question: 'Other than aim for a blockbuster hit, what can an artist do to escape the long tail?'

Kelly answers his own question by talking about what he terms 'True Fans':

> A creator, such as an artist, musician, photographer, craftsperson, performer, animator, designer, videomaker, or author – in other words, anyone producing works of art – needs to acquire only 1,000 True Fans to make a living.
>
> A True Fan is defined as someone who will purchase anything and everything you produce. They will drive 200 miles to see you sing. They will buy the super deluxe re-issued hi-res box set of your stuff even though they have the low-res version. They have a Google Alert set for your name. They bookmark the eBay page where your out-of-print editions show up. They come to your openings. They have you sign their copies. They buy the t-shirt, and the mug, and the hat. They can't wait till you issue your next work. They are true fans.

Kelly's blog post is, inevitably, short and simplistic. He has been criticized for not understanding the true costs of making content. His contention that $100,000 is enough for a creator to live on has been criticized for ignoring the reality that many creative endeavours combine multiple talented people (even though his blog post says that if you have more than one creator, then you need to multiply the number of True Fans you need by the number of creators involved). Yet his idea – that the future of creative endeavour is more about making a connection with a limited number of committed fans, rather than relying on getting a lucky break – is more true than ever before.

The concept of the True Fan has evolved since Kelly's original post. The technology has evolved too. The web has made it cheaper than ever before to connect with fans while production costs continue to fall. Yet the key transition is less about technology and more about how artists have chosen to build their audiences and sell to their fans. As we've already seen, it has become incredibly cheap to distribute content to fans. The iPhone, the web, the Kindle, the music streaming service and many other technologies have made it ever cheaper to reach a wide audience. (It has also made it much harder for an individual piece of new content to be found.) It is now also easier than ever to find fans who love what you do and who are willing to pay lots of money for things that they value. My primary criticism of Kelly's thesis is that he was not thinking big enough when judging how much a fan would pay for products. His fans are not superfans. True Fans might spend an average of $100 a year, in Kelly's theoretical example, but we know that averages are misleading. Businesses and creatives who struggle to embrace Kelly's ideals are fixated in old-world thinking where an average is the price that most people paid. The web has freed us from the tyranny of the physical by allowing us to experiment with much more variable forms of funding. The truth is that the amount people want to spend is variable. Very, very variable.

Ian and David Marsh are twin brothers from San Diego. Their company, NimbleBit, makes games for mobile platforms, particularly the iPhone. Ian is the main programmer while David is the artist. 'It really worked out well that one of us got the right brain and one of us got the left brain,' says Ian.[5]

Initially, they charged up front for games like *Scoops*, a simple arcade game where players tried to build the tallest dessert they could by tilting their phones to catch falling scoops of ice cream. The game sold well, but NimbleBit decided to experiment with a different price point. They dropped the price to free, and made it possible for players to spend money to change the artwork in the background. Themes include monsters, cupcakes, burgers and hats, each of which could be unlocked for 99 cents. The game ended up making around the same amount of revenue as before but with a much larger player base.[6] The Marsh brothers decided that if they had the choice between a game that was profitable with a small user base or a game that was profitable with a large user base, they would rather go free and have more players. In September 2010, NimbleBit announced that all their games in the future would be free.[7]

This decision was to stand them in very good stead when they launched a game that they had designed to be free from the ground up, *Pocket Frogs*. In *Pocket Frogs*, players collect, breed and sell cute little frogs, each of which have a different combination of colours and patterns. The game is free to download and can be played without ever spending a penny. Players can, however, choose to spend money on in-app purchases using Apple's in-game store. As Ian explains, 'All of the content in the game can be accessed whether you use the in-app purchase or not. Stamps can be earned in the game (or purchased), which instantly deliver frogs and other items you order in game or find in the pond. Potions can be earned in the game (or purchased), which instantly mature a frog.'

The game proved a very popular title. It launched in September 2010 and shot straight to number 3 in the Apple Top Free charts. By 4 January 2011, the game had been downloaded 4 million times and at its most popular 350,000 people played it every day.[8] *Pocket Frogs* remained in the top hundred grossing games on the App Store for a year. (If that doesn't sound impressive, remember that when *Pocket Frogs* was released, there were 46,466 games available in the App Store. By the end of 2012, that number had grown to 128,125.)[9] NimbleBit had a hit on their hands.

What is even more impressive than the downloads was the revenue. NimbleBit is a private American company and doesn't release full financial data. The brothers have nevertheless been open with their data to help people understand the benefits of the free-to-play model. They provided a breakdown of the split of the revenue from their different in-app purchases. Remember that apart from a limited amount of advertising, this is the only revenue that NimbleBit was making from *Pocket Frogs*, a game they were giving away for free to millions of users.

To make it easier for consumers to make a choice of how much IAP they wanted to buy, *Pocket Frogs* had only three price points. For 99 cents, you could buy a pack of ten potions. For $4.99, you could buy a pack of 100 potions. For $29.99, you would get 1,000 potions. (The same pricing applied to buying the stamps that accelerate the speed at which products bought from the virtual store were delivered. A virtual DHL, if you will.)

People spending $29.99 on an iPhone app? Really? Yes, really. Fifty per cent of purchases were of the 99-cent pack. The $4.99 pack accounted for 42 per cent. The expensive $29.99 pack represented only 8 per cent of transactions. It might seem as if 8 per cent was hardly worth the bother, until you look at the breakdown by revenue, rather than by volume, shown in Figure 2.

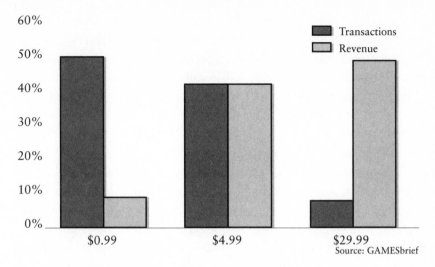

Figure 2: NimbleBit's *Pocket Frogs* revenue breakdown

As Figure 2 shows, the story is very different when the source of revenue is analysed. NimbleBit's 99-cent purchases accounted for just 9 per cent of its revenue from *Pocket Frogs*. The $4.99 pack stayed steady at 42 per cent, but the expensive package that attracted only 8 per cent of purchasers showed its true value: it made up 49 per cent of NimbleBit's revenue from the game.[10]

At the time NimbleBit launched *Pocket Frogs*, the general strategy with a free iOS app was to use it to drive sales of a premium version, the so-called Lite + Premium strategy. The Lite game would offer stripped-down elements of the full game, or be heavily filled with ads. The Premium offering would be more full featured, but given downwards pressure on the amount that consumers were prepared to pay for apps, was typically priced at 99 cents. If NimbleBit had followed the traditional strategy, they would have left 91 per cent of the revenue that they made from *Pocket Frogs* on the table.

If a superfan of *Pocket Frogs* spends $29.99 (and many spend much, much more), NimbleBit is making nearly half its revenue from the 8 per cent of its audience who are superfans, the audience who love what they do and even ask the developers to build more things for them to buy.

That 8 per cent is not 8 per cent of the audience. It is 8 per cent of the *paying* audience. *Pocket Frogs* is a free game. Only about 4 per cent of users convert to spending any money at all.[11] So half of Nimb-leBit's revenue comes from just 8 per cent of 4 per cent of their audience, or slightly over 0.3 per cent of the people who are playing their game. In the first week, half a million people downloaded that game, perhaps 20,000 of them spent money and half the income came from just 1,600 players. Which is not far off Kelly's 1,000 True Fans. I estimate that the game made at least $3 million in the first year, all through harnessing superfans.

You may think this was just a fluke, that NimbleBit got lucky with *Pocket Frogs*. If so, they got lucky again in July 2011, when they launched another freemium game, *Tiny Tower*, in which players strove to build a thriving tower for their little computer people, Bitizens, to live and work in. Again it was entirely free to play, with the ability to pay for virtual currency. Players spent in a similar pattern. The 99-cent package was the most popular transaction, making up 45 per cent of all purchases, but less than 11 per cent of revenue. That low price package made up nearly half the volume, but represented a small fraction of the total income.[12] The most expensive IAP, priced at $29.99, made up only 4 per cent of transactions but nearly a third of revenue.

Perhaps this outcome is unique to NimbleBit? Not a bit of it. We've already seen that, for Bigpoint, 80 per cent of their 2009 revenue came from just 23,000 players. Hundreds of players were prepared to spend up to €1,000 ($1,300) on a single virtual good, the Tenth Drone, in *DarkOrbit*. *Clash of Clans* has superfans who have spent over $5,000. I have clients where individual customers have spent over €10,000 on a single game.

Simon Read is the developer of *New Star Soccer*, a game that took the iPhone charts by storm in 2012. Read released the game as a free title in March 2012. In June it was the top-grossing game in the App Store. The game was sufficiently compelling that an unusually high number of customers converted to paying users, around 39 per cent. Read sells packs of in-game currency that players can use to acceler-ate their progress through the game. At one point, the total sales of the six cheapest in-app purchases, priced at between 69p and £5.99, had generated around $50,000 in revenue. The £9.99 package had generated over triple that amount, $160,000, around 15 per cent of

Read's total revenue, despite only being 1.7 per cent of the total purchases. At its peak, *New Star Soccer* was bringing in $7,000 per day.

Across the games world, the understanding that going digital enables you to offer your customers the ability to spend as much or as little as they want is not only good for customers, allowing them to choose the price points that they are comfortable with, it is good for game makers too. They are not replacing physical dollars with digital dimes. They are replacing physical dollars with nothing for some digital customers, digital dimes for others, digital dollars for yet others and digital tens or hundreds or thousands of dollars for customers who love what they do. They are making more money than they could have made in a pre-digital age, and we are seeing the pattern repeated again and again.

Critics of the free-to-play business model in games, looking at some of these very high spenders, leap to the conclusion that these purchases must be made by mistake. They claim they are made by children who do not know, or perhaps care, what they are doing, or by grown-ups who are manipulated by misleading messages in the game into buying something that they had no intention to buy.[13] There is no doubt that children can buy IAPs by mistake if their device is not set up correctly. The tabloid press loves to leap on a story like this, and there is still work to be done to ensure that people cannot buy virtual goods by mistake.*

Yet the criticism does not stack up. These games are seeing very high repeat usage. They are seeing the same users buying virtual currency and goods in their games over a long period of time, implying that players do understand what they are doing. As Torsten Reil, CEO of NaturalMotion, the publisher of hit iOS game *CSR Racing*, says, 'Free-to-play games are not about exploiting poor impulse control or being misleading, because then you get buyer's remorse. People with buyer's remorse won't pay again.'

---

* If you let your children use your Apple device to play games, make sure that they do not know your password and that the App Store is set to require a password every time a purchase is made. I would also like to see a 'child' mode, similar to an 'airplane' mode, which can be enabled very quickly so that if I hand my device to my kids, I can be absolutely confident that they can't spend any money on it.

The pattern of seeing substantial revenue from a limited number of players is not exclusive to the games industry. Trent Reznor made $750,000 in the first week of sales of *Ghosts I–IV* from the 2,500 people who bought the Ultra-Deluxe Edition. His total revenue that week was $1.6 million, meaning that the superfans represented 47 per cent of his revenue, but only a fraction of the number of people who bought the $75 Deluxe Edition, the $10 CD or the $5 digital download. Victoria Vox made over a third of her pre-order money from the five fans who wanted her to play in their house. App Cubby makes more money by giving its app away for free and allowing some users to spend ten times the average purchase price than it did when every customer had to pay.

In a world before it was possible for companies or creators to offer a wide range of price points to allow fans to spend as much or as little as they wish, they had to find a price that would work, on average, for the most number of people while still delivering a decent profit. They tried to squeeze prices down while maintaining their profit margins. They had to find the single price that would balance what the market would bear with the economies of scale they could achieve in production to deliver the highest profit. Now companies and creators are instead having to think about how they can allow users to experience what they have for free, while letting their biggest fans spend lots of money on things they value. Where is the best place to see this in action? In the world of crowdfunding.

10
THE POWER OF THE CROWD

Tim Schafer makes unpopular games.

At least, that was what he kept being told by the gatekeepers he needed to convince to be able to keep making the games that he loved. Luckily for the rest of us, Schafer is not someone who likes playing by the rules that others set. His big break into the industry came in 1989, when he was studying computer science at the University of Berkeley. He applied to Atari, then in its heyday of game-making cool. He was rejected. He applied to Hewlett-Packard. He was rejected. He built up a 'pile of rejection letters, most of them from jobs I didn't really want'.[1]

Then, on a bright summer day, he saw an advert in the campus career centre for an assistant designer/programmer at Lucasfilm's Games Division. Lucasfilm was the games arm of George Lucas's media empire and Schafer was a fan. The list of job requirements included, alongside the usual platitudes like 'excellent verbal and written communication skills' and 'work as a member of a team' an interest in computer games, a strong imagination and a great sense of humour. Schafer called right away and was put through to David Fox, who was handling the appointment. As Schafer tells it, 'I told him how much I wanted to work at Lucasfilm, not because of *Star Wars*, but because I loved *Ball Blaster*.

'"*Ball Blaster*, eh?" he said.

'"Yeah! I love *Ball Blaster*!" I said. It was true. I had broken a joystick playing that game on my Atari 800.

'"Well, the name of the game is *Ball Blazer*," Mr Fox said curtly. "It was only called *Ball Blaster* in the pirated version."'

Schafer figured that was the end of his hopes of working at Lucasfilm. Fox ended the call by suggesting that Schafer send in his résumé and a covering letter describing his ideal job. He did no such thing. Instead, he wrote and illustrated a two page 'semi-graphic adventure', printed it out on an Atari 800 dot-matrix printer and mailed it in.

```
Your quest for the ideal career begins, logically
enough, at the Ideal Career Center. Upon entering,
you see a helpful looking woman sitting behind the
desk. She smiles and says

'May I help you?'

>SAY YES I NEED A JOB

'Ah,' she replies, 'and where would you like to work,
Los Angeles, Silicon Valley or San Rafael?'

>SAY SAN RAFAEL

'Good choice,' she says. 'Here are some jobs you might
be interested in,' and gives you three brochures.

>EXAMINE BROCHURES

The titles of the three brochures are as follows:
'HAL Computers: We've got a number for you,' 'Yoyo-
dine Defense Technologies: Help us reach our destructive
potential,' and 'Lucasfilm, Ltd.: Games, Games,
Games!'

>OPEN LUCASFILM BROCHURE

The brochure says that Lucasfilm is looking for an
imaginative, good-humored team player who has excel-
lent communication skills, programming experience,
```

and loves games. Under that description, oddly enough, is a picture of you.

>SEND RESUME

You get the job. Congratulations! You start right away.

>GO TO WORK

You drive the short commute to the Lucasfilm building and find it full of friendly people who show you the way to your desk.

>EXAMINE DESK

Your desk has on it a powerful computer, a telephone, some personal nicknacks, and some work to do.

>EXAMINE WORK

It is challenging and personally fulfilling to perform.

>DO WORK

As you become personally fulfilled, your score reaches 100 and this quest comes to an end. The adventure, however, is just beginning and so are your days at Lucasfilm.

THE END

Schafer got the job, or rather the 'full-time temporary project position', on a salary of $27,000. Schafer's first big project, to which he was assigned as writer and programmer, was *The Secret of Monkey Island*, one of the best-loved adventure games of all time. The game was the brainchild of LucasArts designer Ron Gilbert but Schafer and fellow writer-programmer Dave Grossman wrote about two-thirds of the dialogue and had a strong influence on the game's comedy style.[2] Schafer went on to work on the sequel, *Monkey Island 2: LeChuck's Revenge*, and on other LucasArts titles *Day of the Tentacle*, *Full Throttle* and *Grim Fandango* before quitting to found his own business, Double Fine, where he created what some call his best game to date, *Psychonauts*, released in 2005.

During those fifteen years, the games industry changed dramatically. Expectations rose and budgets soared faster. When Schafer was playing games as a student, those games could be made cheaply by one person working for a year costing, according to Gilbert, 'thirty or forty thousand dollars'.[3] *The Secret of Monkey Island* had a budget of approximately $200,000 and, while sales figures are unclear, Schafer is on record as saying, 'In the early nineties, we were really excited if we sold 100,000 copies of a PC adventure game.'[4] *Full Throttle* took a year and a half to make and cost over a million dollars. *Psychonauts* took five years and, by early 2007, had sold half a million copies.

That's where the gatekeepers came in. Schafer cut his teeth on old-school computers, particularly the PC. But the mid-2000s were the era of the console. Shooters such as *Halo 3* or *Call of Duty 4: Modern Warfare* sold more than 3 million units in the US alone. Against that, a title that took three years to make and only sold half a million units globally was a tough sell. It looked as if the era of the types of adventure games that had made Ron Gilbert and Tim Schafer famous was over.

Schafer and Gilbert had been successful when the video games market was young and populated with people who would puzzle out solutions to challenges over time. They created a fan base who loved what they did because of the challenge, not despite it. They had even joined that pantheon of maybe a dozen game designers who are known to the gaming public by name. They had a fan base.

Schafer believed that the point-and-click adventure was not dead. Publishers didn't agree with him. 'If I were to go to a publisher right now and pitch an adventure game, they would laugh in my face,' he said.[5] The gatekeepers were doing their job of managing risk by making variants on the games that sold large volumes, mainly first-person shooters involving ever more realistic graphics of space marines or modern-day soldiers. But, as Schafer says, 'What if there are a lot of adventure game fans out there who want an adventure game? I wonder if there is some way I could talk to them directly. Cut out publishers altogether.' In February 2012 Schafer launched a Kickstarter campaign to create a new adventure game, a game for adventure game fans that would be funded by adventure game fans.

Kickstarter is the best known of the crowdfunding platforms that emerged in the early 2010s as a new way for creators to fund their works. Instead of relying on gatekeepers, a creator can turn directly to the fans. A Kickstarter page typically consists of a video describing the project, some text and a variety of 'pledge' tiers. Rewards for pledges range from getting a copy of the product up to exclusive tiers like having dinner with the creator or appearing in the work directly. The tiers are only limited by the imagination of the creator (and some practical considerations like cost and logistics). Importantly, these tiers do not give backers a financial stake in the success of the project. They are perhaps best thought of as pre-orders of projects that a backer would like to see come to fruition, and they come with the risk that the project, like any creative project, may fail.

Tim Schafer set out to raise $400,000 with his Kickstarter campaign, of which $300,000 would go towards the game and $100,000 would go towards the television crew who would film the process of making the game for a documentary programme. His tiers, like many Kickstarters, ranged from the cheap to the very expensive.

For $15, backers would get the finished game, exclusive early access to the beta test on Steam, and access to the video series and the private discussion forums. For $30, you could add an HD download of the documentary series and the soundtrack of the game. For $60, backers would get a PDF version of the *Double Fine Adventure* book 'filled with 100+ full colour pages of concept art, original photos, developer bios, excerpts from the game's script, deep dark secrets, and more!' For $100, backers would get the Special Edition box set. This contained the game disc and the DVD of the documentary, an exclusive T-shirt and poster and thanks in the game credits.

Schafer didn't stop at $100. For $250, Schafer offered 900 limited edition *Double Fine Adventure* posters signed by Schafer, Gilbert and the rest of the design team. For $500, you would get a physical copy of the *Double Fine Adventure* book signed by Schafer. For $1,000, you could be one of a hundred people to have a mini-portrait drawn of you in the style of the game. For $5,000, you could get one of ten original paintings of art used in the final game and for $10,000 you could get all of the previous reward tiers as well as lunch with Tim Schafer and Ron Gilbert and a tour of the Double Fine offices.

The *Double Fine Adventure* project was launched on 8 February 2012 with a target of $400,000. They achieved their target on the first day. A month later, the funding process came to an end on Kickstarter and *Double Fine Adventure* was declared funded having raised $3,336,371 from 87,142 backers.[6]

The mathematically minded amongst you will already have worked out that the average pledge level was about $40, which is roughly in line with the cost of a new PC game bought in a box from Amazon or on Steam.* If you've been paying attention to the Curve, though, you'll know that averages are often misleading, as indeed they are in this case.

Figure 3 shows the breakdown of the tiers, with the number of people who pledged against each tier.[7]

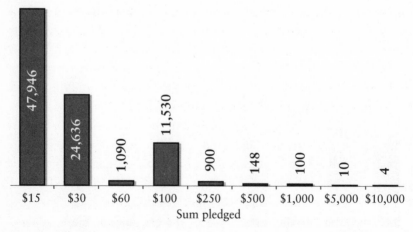

Figure 3: *Double Fine Adventure* funding chart: number of pledges per tier

* To be precise, $38.26.

Unsurprisingly, the vast majority of pledges were at the cheapest price point of $15. There was a spike at $100 because that tier was great value to serious fans, but even so, only about a quarter of the number of people who pledged at $15 pledged at $100. The remaining pledges at the high price tiers seem unimportant in this chart, particularly to anyone used to focusing on volume, not price, as the metric of success. That perception changes if we consider the amount of revenue generated by each tier, as Figure 4 shows.

When you look at the tiers this way, the picture changes radically. The vast majority of the backers – the 55 per cent who pledged $15 – represent just 22 per cent of the revenue. That small spike at $100 becomes the largest bucket of revenue and those higher tiers, with hardly any backers in them, are responsible for a significant proportion of the revenue.

We can take the analysis further. Backers pledging $1,000 or more represented 0.1 per cent of the backers but 6 per cent of the revenue. Backers pledging $250 or more represent 1.3 per cent of the backers but 15 per cent of the revenue. Backers pledging $100 or more represent 15 per cent of the backers and 52 per cent of the revenue.

One way to look at it is this: if Double Fine had gone down a traditional funding route, they would have sold their games for $15. Assuming everyone who pledged $15 or more would have bought the game, they would have made roughly $1.3 million, or just 40 per cent of

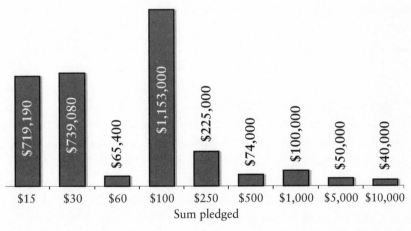

Figure 4: *Double Fine Adventure* funding chart: revenue generated per tier

the revenue that they made by having tiers that enable fans to spend lots of money on things they truly value. Instead, by unleashing the Curve and allowing fans to spend a variable amount, they were able to create one of the most successful crowdfunding campaigns of recent times.

Kickstarter describes itself as a 'funding platform for creative projects. These projects include everything from films, games, and music to art, design, and technology. Kickstarter is full of ambitious, innovative, and imaginative projects that are brought to life through the direct support of others.' Since its launch on 28 April 2009, over $450 million has been pledged by 3 million people funding more than 35,000 creative projects.

To many, Kickstarter is seen as an alternative to publishers with their gatekeepers, risk management and difficulty in taking innovative leaps. Yet its real, unnoticed success is that it has allowed creators to let their biggest fans spend variable amounts of money on things that they truly value. For *Double Fine Adventure*, we saw that backers who pledged over $100 were 15 per cent of the pledgers but more than half the revenue. We see this sort of distribution again and again.

It's hard to talk about new business models and the internet without talking about Amanda Palmer. Palmer started her career as a street performer in Cambridge, Massachusetts, was one half of the band the Dresden Dolls and released albums with Roadrunner Records, a label she was eventually to split from in acrimonious circumstances. In April 2012 Palmer launched a Kickstarter campaign to raise funds for her next album, which was to become *Theatre Is Evil*. She offered a range of pledge tiers from $1 all the way up to $10,000. For $1, fans would get a digital download of the album. For $5, the download and a lot of extra material: 'the lyrics, band photos, handwritten stuff, extra artwork, drafts, anecdotes, and of course . . . naked pictures. We love naked.' At $50, a limited vinyl edition 'on two 180 gram black records in a gatefold package. Includes a set of heavy-stock inserts with artwork, lyrics, and photographs.' It would cost $300 to attend one of the launch parties in Berlin, London, New York, San Francisco, Los Angeles and Boston and $500 for Palmer to be sent a black and white photo of anything and 'I'll re-render it via the magic of sharpie on hardboard & mail it to you with heaps of love. I'm a pretty good artist when I try.' For $1,000, fans would get the complete package: a turntable painted by Palmer, the album on CD and vinyl, the collection of 7″ singles and the signed copy of the artbook.

For the serious fans, or those who could gather a bunch of friends to join in, $5,000 bought a house party at which Amanda Palmer would play a gig. And for $10,000: an art-sitting and meal with Palmer, when a fan could spend an afternoon or evening with their idol. 'We'll get together in a space that makes sense & I'll draw you from life, naked or clothed.'

There were other tiers. Some tiers sold out, some didn't. Palmer became the first musician to raise over $1 million from pledges on Kickstarter: $1,192,793 from 24,883 backers. Her average pledge was $47.93, significantly higher than Tim Schafer achieved for *Double Fine Adventure*, and much more than a music fan would expect to pay for an album.

Again, the secret was in the upper end of the tiers. Palmer generated nearly half her income (48 per cent) from the 3.8 per cent of backers who pledged $250 or more. Two-thirds (66 per cent) came from backers pledging $125 or more. That means that those backers who were prepared to spend on the signed art book and a copy of the album, or on higher tiers, represented just over a tenth of the total audience (10.3 per cent) but provided the majority of Palmer's income. The thirty-four backers who paid for Palmer to come to their house for a party, paying at least $5,000 a pop, were just 0.15 per cent of the audience but represented 15 per cent of the income.

Across successful crowdfunding projects, we see a recurring pattern: around half the revenue comes from around a fifth of the audience. We've seen it for David Braben's remake of *Elite*, the 1980s video game that made him famous (to Europeans – particularly Britons – of a certain age, at least). We saw it with Charles Cecil's sequel to his *Broken Sword* games. Indiegogo, another crowdfunding site, says that the $100 reward tier makes more money for artists using its platform than any other tier and makes up nearly 30 per cent of total funds raised. Rewards (Indiegogo calls them perks) priced at $50, $100, $500 and $1,000 make, combined, 70 per cent of the total income of campaigns on the site. Rewards priced at $500 and $1,000 generate more than 25 per cent of income.[8]

Crowdfunding is important for understanding the future of publishing. Not because it will replace publishers, although it might, but because it shows how when you have a one-to-one relationship with your fans, unmediated by retailers and trade buyers and a sales force and so on, you can experiment with offering a range of products at a range of different prices that have different levels of emotional resonance with your fans. Kickstarter is simply showing us, in a very public, visible way, how variable the demand curve really is. It is new not because it democratizes fundraising, although it does do that too, but because it uses the power of the web to enable creators to let their biggest fans spend lots of money on things they truly value.

For some people, that is spending $10,000 to be painted in the nude by a musical heroine. Each to their own. Which is the very beauty at the heart of Kickstarter.

A common criticism of Kickstarter and similar crowdfunding initiatives is that many of the most visible successful campaigns are undertaken by companies or individuals who were previously encouraged, nurtured and enabled by the traditional media structures. Tim Schafer had games published by LucasArts, Majesco and Electronic Arts, all traditional video game publishers. Amanda Palmer was signed to Roadrunner Records, a label that was partially acquired by Warner Music Group in 2007.[9] Trent Reznor was signed to TVT Records and then to Interscope, a subsidiary of Universal Music. 'Of course these people can make crowdfunding work,' cry the critics. 'They are simply taking advantage of the publicity and early career enhancing activity that a publisher can offer and then milking it for all they're worth, while the original publisher – who invested to create them – gets nothing.'

Yes and no. The big successes on crowdfunding sites are not all well-known creators going solo. Stuart Ashen is a comedian from Norwich in the east of England. In 2006, Ashen started a YouTube channel in which he showcased terrible electronic devices. In the last seven years he has made 240 videos which have been watched a total of 64 million times. Ashens, as he is known on YouTube, has 280,000 subscribers to his channel.

In 2013, Ashen decided he wanted to make a feature film.

Commercially, his YouTube channel is part of Channelflip, a multi-channel network that helps creators make money on YouTube, largely through advertising sales. Channelflip is part of Shine, the television production arm of News Corporation founded by Rupert Murdoch's daughter Elisabeth and creator of shows such as *Masterchef*, *Merlin* and *The Biggest Loser*. Channelflip agreed to fund two-thirds of the production budget of Ashen's movie. To fund the rest, Ashen turned to his fans.

Ashen used Indiegogo to ask for $50,000 to round out the production budget.[10] (A crowdfunding campaign is also a useful test of market demand.) Rewards ranged from $10 for a thank you and $25 for a copy of the DVD of the movie up to $7,500 to have the unique chance – there was only one available – to appear as a cameo in the film. In thirty days, the project raised $73,690, nearly 50 per cent more than Ashen was seeking. Justin Gayner, creative director of Channelflip, told me:

> We decided to test the crowdfunding waters with Stuart Ashen because we thought it would be one of the hardest ideas to get funded this way. You almost never see Stuart in his videos. You just see his hands, reviewing the tatty tech devices on a distressed brown sofa. We weren't testing crowdfunding with a celebrity face like Alex Day or Carrie Fletcher. The question was whether a pair of hands and a funny voice-over had enough of a connection with fans to make them want to give us money. If we can make it work for this project, it's got a great chance of working for all of our other creators.

Well-known names can certainly find it easier to raise money. Fans pledged $5.7 million to make a *Veronica Mars* movie that Warner Bros refused to finance. Zach Braff, one of the stars of *Scrubs*, raised over $3.1 million to make *Wish I Was Here* with no studio interference. Many successfully crowdfunded film and game projects have established creators attached to them, because they bring an existing fan base and, in the eyes of the fans, reduce the risk that the project won't happen.

Amanda Hocking had never been promoted by the Establishment when she found self-publishing success at Amazon. Alex Day, the musician who reached number 4 in the UK charts without the support of a label, has never been promoted by the Establishment. Nor has Victoria Vox. Nor has the team behind *Chronicles of Syntax*, a UK-based production team making a TV-style thriller. Freddie Wong built a huge audience on YouTube and, in 2011, used Kickstarter to raise $275,000 to create a nine-episode web television series called *Video Game High School*.[11] In 2013, he turned to Kickstarter again to fund a second series, raising over $800,000.[12] Reaching an audience no longer needs the Establishment, as we've seen in previous chapters. Making money from your audience no longer needs the Establishment, either.

In fact, being an established artist does not guarantee crowdfunding success. On 28 January 2013, Björk launched a Kickstarter to raise £375,000 ($580,000) to port a successful iOS app called Biophilia to Android and Windows 8. The project was cancelled after ten days when the campaign had raised just £15,370 ($23,000).[13]

Biophilia was a hybrid app designed to help teach people, particularly kids, about music in an engaging way. Each song on the Biophilia album has its own interactive interpretation in the app and, for example, 'Thunderbolt' teaches how arpeggios work through manipulating lightning while 'Moon' uses the tidal pull to drive sequencers and 'Solstice' uses pendulums to explore counterpoint.

The campaign failed for many reasons. Fans were not being asked to be part of the journey of bringing a creative project into existence: Biophilia already existed and was released for iPhones eighteen months previously. Also, £375,000 is a lot to ask for a port of a mobile app and the estimate that it would take eight programmers five months seemed high to many observers. Many of Björk's fans, probably the richer ones, already had Biophilia for the iPhone and had little incentive other than altruism to contribute to the Kickstarter campaign.

The main reason, however, is that Björk doesn't seem to have cultivated a direct relationship with her fans. She may have over 400,000 followers on Twitter but her feed is a litany of announcements and statements that read like the output of a public relations intern. Her feed shows around sixty tweets in 2012, every one of which read as if someone else wrote it. She mentioned the Kickstarter campaign once while it was live. *Billboard* said, 'Most [of Björk's tweets] were one-way messages ("presale begins now", "pre-order a copy", etc.) that show a lack of conversation with fans. It's hard to imagine an artist forging a close relationship with her fans these days without being active on Twitter.' Björk proved the point. She may have had 2.6 million Likes on Facebook, but she does not have the connection with fans that encourages them to respond when she asks for help.

This is one important element of the Curve. You need to have the base to talk to. Having 2.6 million people press a Like button on Facebook is not what matters. What matters is how many of them love what you do enough to rally round and support you when you ask. When Tim Schafer asked, 87,000 people supported him; 25,000 helped Amanda Palmer. When Alex Day asked his 600,000 YouTube subscribers how many would be willing to help him get 'Forever Young' into the charts, about 2,500 people emailed him to say they would help.

An artist who treats fans as a replacement for the record label is not going to succeed. The Curve requires creators and businesses to build relationships with customers and let those who want to spend money do so. The Curve is the glue that connects the two: the link between the power of free to turbocharge your message across the web and the potential to enable your biggest fans to spend lots and lots of money with you.

The secret of the coming of the crowd is not that it replaces publishers but that anyone who creates anything no longer has to treat every customer equally, regardless of their desire. They can, cost-effectively, allow different people to spend very different amounts on very different things. There is one significant downside. Gatekeepers used to control access to the market, but they bundled that access with a bunch of other services: sales, marketing, community management, PR, finance and so on. If anyone can get to market now, those roles are still important and need to be fulfilled.

I am a self-published author. I have four books on the business of games available in hard copy and on Kindle, as well as a website with three to four original articles every week. It is too much for me to manage alongside writing, consulting and designing games. I have a team of five freelancers who support me – two writers, a web designer and a coder, together with a virtual PA. None of them works with me full time, but I have a team and I couldn't do what I do without them.

This is not true just for me. Amanda Palmer had a large team behind her successful Kickstarter campaign. Double Fine is a studio of sixty-five people. Alex Day doesn't have a team but finds himself often distracted by email rather than creating content or connecting with his fans. The revolution of the Curve is not that the role of publishing goes away, but that creators can now choose who gets to do it. It is a choice.

Choice is the biggest change that the emergence of crowdfunding, the ending of the tyranny of the digital and the demise of the gate-keeper has had on the market. Choice doesn't mean that businesses who are expert in bringing products, services or art to market no longer have a role. It just means that they no longer have monopoly control over distribution. Anyone who makes something now has an alternative to accepting whatever terms they are offered simply to see their creation available to consumers. The howls of protest from incumbents are not the howls of businesses fearing that they are obsolete: they are the howls of businesses realizing that the premiums they have been able to charge for scarce access to the market are erod-ing and they are going to have to change the way they do business.

We've seen how the web has enabled people who make things to connect with fans. We've seen how Kickstarter and other initiatives have exposed in detail how fans are prepared to spend wildly differing amounts of money on things they truly value, giving us an insight into how creators and businesses will need to think about what they create – and what their customers will demand – in the twenty-first century. We've focused on what for many of us are the industries which are likely to be disrupted by the internet: movies and books and games and music. What we haven't considered yet is how this will affect the industries that just aren't prepared for the threat of casual piracy. Where one of the biggest threats facing their financial future is that their biggest fans might choose to share what they do entirely for free not because they are mean but because they are excited. Because they want to share that excitement with their friends, and the friends of their friends.

That threat is coming to physical manufacture soon. Welcome to the world of 3D printing.

11
MAKE-IT-YOURSELF

What happens when anyone can manufacture anything they can see, whenever they like?

What happens if you can take a few snaps with the camera built into your phone, send it to some clever software that turns it into a 3D model, and produce it on the 3D printer sitting on the counter in your kitchen? There's a long way to go, but we are heading in that direction. If you make physical things for a living, and you want to avoid going the way of the music industry, now is the time to start thinking about how to deal with a world of digital manufacturing.

We have explored what has happened to the products that have already made the transition from physical atoms to digital bits. It becomes easy to share them. It becomes easier for fans to become pirates. As it becomes cheaper and easier to distribute books and games and music and films, so fans find it easier and more desirable to share them, or to find ways to own them without paying. It becomes possible for competitors to find new ways to give stuff away for free and to find different ways to pay for the production by building close relationships with fans. Businesses and creators who make physical items – widgets, jewellery, kitchen utensils, spare parts – have been spared the impact of digital and casual piracy.

But not for very much longer.

Chris Thorpe always wanted to be a boffin. 'When I was younger, I always really wanted to be a boffin. Maybe that's why I did a chemistry degree – the lab coat came with the course.'[1]

A boffin may be a peculiarly British expression. It's an egghead. A scientist of a particular breed. It's the phrase used by tabloid newspapers whenever they talk about science, as in the headline the *Sun* used to report on proof of the existence of the Higgs Boson: 'Boffins spot "God particle".'[2] Thorpe is hoping to be at the forefront of the new breed of boffin-entrepreneurs.

In November 2012 Thorpe travelled to the Bala Lake Railway in the mountains of North Wales. The railway is a charming narrow-gauge tourist railway laid on the trackbed of a former standard-gauge railway along the side of the lake. Thorpe was not just going to view the railway, though. He was going to see and record for posterity one of her famous engines, *Winifred*.

Winifred is a narrow-gauge steam engine built for the Penrhyn Slate Quarry in 1885. Her working life lasted eighty years, starting in the reign of Queen Victoria and ending in the reign of Queen Elizabeth, encompassing two world wars and countless technological changes. In 1965, the Penrhyn Quarry decided to sell its steam locomotives and three of them, including *Winifred*, were bought by Tony Hulman, an American businessman who ran the Indianapolis Motor Speedway. Hulman planned to make them part of a new museum he was building. The museum never happened and *Winifred* spent most of the next half-century sitting in dry storage in the shadow of the Indy 500 grandstands.

In 2012 she was returned, in almost the same condition she left, to Bala, home to four other similar quarry locomotives. Thorpe made a pilgrimage to see her. Not just to see her, but to record her in glorious 3D. He partnered with laser-scanning experts Digital Surveys who in the course of a single afternoon took fifteen detailed laser scans of *Winifred* and 1,000 high-resolution photographs. They took the data from the scans and images and, at a cost of just £4,500 ($7,000), converted it into a complex 3D model that could be used to reproduce *Winifred* at will. Which is just what Thorpe did. He placed an order with Sculpteo, a business that allows you to upload a model and have it printed by a 3D printer at their facilities just outside Paris. A week later he had a 1:25 scale model of *Winifred*, accurate to the bent brake handle and the dents in her dome.

The experiment with *Winifred* was part of the launch of Thorpe's business, the Flexiscale Company. Thorpe uses modern surveying methods on real-life objects, like the laser scans he took of *Winifred*, to make precise three-dimensional plans. Flexiscale then splits the plans up into kits that are simple but aim to be fun to assemble, detail and paint. The kits are produced on demand using 3D printing. The thing that is special about Flexiscale is that a customer can order the kit at any scale they want. Every kit is printed on demand, individually. The 3D model is accurate at a 1:1 scale, that is to say full size. The only limits to the size at which the items can be printed are the consumer's desire to pay and the physical capacity of the printer.*

On Flexiscale's website today, you can buy a Dinorwic Quarry Slate wagon, a simple vehicle once used to carry slate around Penrhyn Quarry. Flexiscale has three scales available: a 16mm model costing £34.50 ($55), a 9mm scale costing £22.50 and a 7mm scale costing £14.50. All printed on demand and all using the exact same underlying geometry stored as a digital file on Flexiscale's computers.

Thorpe estimates that the model-train market is worth £100 million annually in the UK alone. He hopes to disrupt the two major incumbents, Hornby and Bachmann, by harnessing a community of modellers and train fans to help him create, curate and manage a huge array of three-dimensional computer models that can be used to create replicas at any scale on demand. Thorpe is connecting two technological revolutions – the cheap cost of distributing digital files and the ability to produce cost-effective, physical items one-by-one using 3D printing technology – to change the way people think about making models.

As he does so, he will have to wrestle with the challenges that have faced the music industry for the past decade: if people love what Flexiscale does, they will want to share it. If the thing they want to share is digital, they can make and share a perfect replica, while still keeping the original for themselves. Casual piracy has just come to the manufacturing world.

Thingiverse is a website filled with 3D models. It currently boasts over 30,000 digital models that can be downloaded and manufactured

---

* There are few 3D printers in the world that could print out a full-size model of *Winifred*. Yet.

using laser cutters, CNC (computer numerical control) machines or 3D printers. It offers a holder to turn your iPhone into an electronic picture frame, a drain trap that can be scaled up and down to fit the size of your plughole and earrings in the shape of Captain America's shield. Many of the items can be adapted or customized to your exact specification.

Meanwhile, Defense Distributed, a Texas-based company run by twenty-five-year-old law student Cody Wilson, gained notoriety in 2013 when it announced that it had successfully fired the 'Liberator', a gun that had been created on a 3D printer. In the two days that the files were available on the web before the State Department asked Defense Distributed to take them down, they were downloaded more than 100,000 times.[3] With those files now spread around the web, it is only a matter of time before they resurface. While gun experts remain sceptical about the danger posed by the Liberator and warn of the risk that it might explode in the firer's hand, the control that governments have on access to firearms has just become a little bit weaker. To understand the importance of the Liberator files, it is helpful to understand how digital manufacturing works.

Digital manufacturing is a three-step process. First, you need a data file that contains the three-dimensional geometry of the object to be printed. Users can make these themselves in computer-aided design (CAD) software packages, they can scan the objects as Chris Thorpe did with *Winifred* or they can download existing files from the web. The data file is interpreted by software (step two), sent to the hardware (step three) and, hey presto, the object appears. It doesn't always appear fully formed: the Liberator handgun comes in fifteen pieces that have to be assembled after manufacture. The final piece, the firing pin, needs to be metal and is not currently printed, but a nail that can be purchased from any hardware store will do the job.

A 3D printer is not dissimilar, in principle at least, to the ordinary inkjet printer that sits on the desk in my office. There is a print-head that moves backwards and forwards, left and right, just like an inkjet. To create objects in three dimensions it needs an additional motor that moves up and down as well. On some printers, the bed on which the object being printed rests stays stationary while the print head moves around it. On others, the print head stays still and the object is moved.

The term 3D printer covers many different manufacturing techniques. Some 3D printers such as the Makerbot use a technique called fused deposition modelling (FDM), an additive process where plastic is melted and squeezed through a small heated nozzle. The plastic hardens to form layer on layer to build the model. More expensive machines use lasers either to harden liquid resin in a bath (stereolithography or SLA) or to harden layers of powdered metal, plastic or ceramic (selective laser sintering or SLS). Machines based on lasers can use a wider range of materials than the plastic-extruding ones and have a higher resolution, but are much more expensive. The Liberator handgun was printed on a second-hand Stratasys Dimension SST that cost $8,000 while a Makerbot 2 can be bought new for $2,199.

3D printers can work in a variety of plastics, in metals like stainless steel and silver, and in ceramic. The market is changing so rapidly that materials are improving in quality, decreasing in price or both at a fast pace. Anyone starting out in digital manufacturing in 2013 can expect rapid improvements in both quality and price, year by year.

Alice Taylor is chief executive of Makielab, a London-based company that aims to use 3D printing to take on the might of Hasbro and Mattel in the market for dolls.[4] Makielab allows users to design their own personal doll on a web page or tablet. They can change the shape of the doll's face, its nose, eyes and ears. They can choose different skin tones. They can personalize their online doll to make it completely unique in the entire world. Then, for just £70 ($105), they can get the unique, personalized, 10-inch poseable doll custom printed and posted to them.

'Moore's Law is at work here', says Taylor.* 'A commercial grade printer can cost anywhere between $50,000 and half a million dollars, but the quality is going up, prices are coming down and the results are amazing. Even in the first year of Makielab, we've seen the

---

* Moore's Law was proposed by Intel co-founder Gordon Moore, who noted in 1965 that the number of transistors on an integrated circuit doubled every two years, and predicted that it would continue to do so. It has continued to hold true for half a century, and in practice Moore's Law has tended to apply to other elements of computing capability such as memory capacity and bandwidth as well as processor speed. There are two alternative practical results for a product that follows Moore's Law: every two years, you'll get twice as much for your money as you did before, or every year the price of that processing power, storage or bandwidth will halve.

quality of the Makie dolls improve substantially as our printing partners have improved their processes.'

Makielab's vision is to have a virtual world or game where players can come in, design the virtual Makies, create new items for them, play or just hang out. That will be free, although there may well be charges for virtual items, the model that has worked so well for free-to-play games elsewhere. Some players will choose to make a physical Makie. Some of those will continue to spend money on physical items for their Makie: clothes, hats, accessories and so on. Makielab finds new customers through its website and tablet experiences (as well as through more traditional PR stunts like presenting personalized dolls to Prime Minister David Cameron and Prince Harry). Those customers who choose to spend will start by paying £70 for the basic doll. Superfans can buy multiple personalized dolls, and spend lots more money on accessories and accoutrements.

So Makielab is a Curve business. It grows its community through free digital content, and it allows those who love what it does to spend lots of money on things they value. Taylor and the team at Makielab are not fighting free or just targeting the expensive. They are embracing both ends of the Curve and everything between.

Taylor is under no illusions that this new world comes with challenges for intellectual property. 'I think that one of the biggest issues is going to be copyright and trademark. Anyone will be able to pick up anything, scan it into a computer and replicate it easily. What does that mean for the person who made the original? I believe the solution is to design for piracy: most often it's simply a service issue: pricing or access, for instance.'[5]

Taylor's comment is one that everyone who manufactures anything should take to heart. When every physical object can be reduced to a digital file, availability is no longer the only consideration for end users. If they want something they can visit Thingiverse, The Pirate Bay or BitTorrent to download a legal or illegal version of it. For many that is a terrifying vision of the future, where manufacturers have no place and every home is a factory. But while we are heading in that direction, this is not going to happen to manufacturing at the same pace that it happened to the record industry – if manufacturers start now, there is time to adapt to be successful in the digital age.

Let's start by considering what 3D printing and the associated digital manufacturing pipeline excels at, and where it is weak. If you want to produce lots of the same item very cheaply, traditional ways of manufacturing are still likely to be far superior to 3D printing. Injection moulding involves a heavy spend upfront to create the tooling for the mould, say $10,000. If you only produce one widget, you are paying $10,000 plus a few pence for the raw materials. If you making a hundred widgets, it's $100 each plus the raw materials. By the time you are making a million, the initial set-up costs are a trivial fraction of the per-unit price. Injection moulding means that the underlying cost of a product like a Barbie doll is less than a tenth of the retail price, with most of the value being captured by the retailer and Mattel, the owner of the brand.[6]

With 3D printing, creating a single widget would be much cheaper than with injection moulding. Let's say the first widget cost $20, compared with $10,000 plus a few pence in the injection moulding process above. The second widget costs $20. So does the third. So does the millionth. There are no economies of scale in this model. If you think of 3D printing as a direct replacement for traditional manufacturing methods, you would be right in thinking that it sucks.

The benefit of digital manufacturing is the new opportunities that it brings to do things differently. Digital manufacturing subverts the old order. It changes manufacturing in two fundamental ways: it changes the prototyping and creation of new products; and it changes what can be manufactured cost-efficiently.

In the days before digital manufacturing, it was hard to be an inventor. In his book, *Makers*, Chris Anderson tells the story of his maternal grandfather, Fred Hauser, a Swiss émigré with twenty-seven patents to his name. Only one of them ever saw the light of day as a product, an automatic sprinkler system licensed and manufactured by Moody and called the Rainmaster. Hauser patented his idea in 1943. It took seven years, lots of pitching and substantial legal fees before a product based on his patent reached customers.

Hauser was trapped by the tyranny of the physical. He had to negotiate with many potential manufacturing partners to find one who was prepared to turn his idea into a product. Each one had to do market research and feasibility studies to determine if there was a market for his product (although I'm sure some rejected it based on nothing more than gut instinct). Moody had to decide if the initial investment in the manufacturing capability for the Rainmaster was worth it. The success of Hauser's product was in the hands of the gatekeepers who controlled the means of production: the factory owners and manufacturers.

That is not true any more. If Hauser wanted to give his invention away for free, he could upload it to Thingiverse and those early adopters with access to a 3D printer could make a sprinkler system for their garden in the course of a weekend. If he wanted to commercialize it, he could print it himself on a 3D printer. He could sell it via his own website and start to build a community of gardeners to help him to adapt and improve his product to meet their needs. He could take the sprinkler system to garden shows and fêtes and sell his products one-by-one. He would get feedback from real users which would allow him to improve on his product with every iteration, and in the world of 3D printing, every single copy can be a new iteration. Some customers might want a small system for an urban patio, others an enormous set of sprinklers for a rural estate. They might pay a premium for Hauser to visit them to advise on the system and to install it. Hauser would have harnessed the Curve.

If that all sounds like a lot of work, that's because it is. Nothing about the Curve says that you can sit back and make money for doing nothing. The ending of the tyranny of the physical and the erosion of the role of the gatekeeper mean that more people will be able to test their ideas in the open market than ever before, although finding customers will still be hard. Many will fail. Others will create viable businesses that would not have been viable at the scale needed under the old manufacturing model. A few will create huge businesses which will compete directly with the industrial titans of the twentieth century. Inventors and creators will spend more time talking to their customers, the people who actually use their products, to iterate on, improve and refine their ideas. Digital manufacturing will enable products to get better faster.

The second change is that personalized manufacturing changes what is cheap and what is expensive. In the traditional manufacturing model, it is the fact that every single product is identical that makes it so cheap. If the objective is to reduce the price as much as possible, it is critical that you make as many of the same thing as possible. If that means that each customer has to have exactly the same product as everyone else, so be it. That's why Henry Ford is reputed to have said his customers could have their Model T any colour they wanted as long as it was black. It is the sacrifice consumers had to make to get a high-quality product at a very cheap price. These limitations are different for personalized manufacturing.

When you are manufacturing from a digital file to a 3D printer, you can make every single product unique. Gone is the need for expensive set-up fees and the requirement for scale (although the unfortunate corollary is that economies of scale have gone as well). If a computer is driving the manufacture of each single item, it can make each one different. The items can be complex too, because a computer can just as happily perform the calculations to print out a complex model of the Eiffel Tower as those for a simple cube. Inventors and creators will be able to make mistakes because they can fix the mistake before the next product rolls out of the 3D printer.

You get variety, complexity and flexibility at no extra cost. These properties are no longer scarce, and successful businesses will work out how to take advantage of this new abundance. On Thingiverse, there is a whole category of 'Customizable things'. You can get collar stiffeners that are monogrammed and personalized for you. You can make a pair of dice with customized text on each face. You can manufacture a hundred key fobs and make every one of them different.

This is a very different proposition to traditional manufacturing. If you want to make tens of thousands of the same item, traditional methods are likely to be more cost-efficient. But consumers are going to start seeking out the personalized more. As we move through the journey from commodities (is it available?) to goods (how much does it cost?) to services (is it high quality?) to experiences (how will it make me feel?), manufacturing is only just beginning to offer that personal, social, emotional bond that is where real value will be created in the twenty-first century.

If you type 'overdesigned lemon squeezer' into Google and hit the image search, it is likely that half of the images that you see will be of

159

the same product. A tall, spindly, bulbous blob on three slender legs, it looks like a three-legged arachnid or the tiny offspring of one of the invading Martians from *The War of the Worlds*. It is one of the most iconic pieces of kitchen equipment ever designed.

In 1989, Italian manufacturer Alessi asked Philippe Starck, the French designer, to come up with a new lemon squeezer. The result was the Juicy Salif described above, twelve inches of cast aluminium that was almost, but not entirely, unpractical. It's hard to use on a kitchen surface given its height. It takes up a lot of space. The grooves are hard to clean. It is quite pretty, though.[7]

The Alessi lemon squeezer costs £48 ($72) from the online website of British department store chain John Lewis. A digital model of this iconic design is already available on Thingiverse and it won't be long before I can print a bootleg copy, at any size I like, in resin, plastic or stainless steel. People who love Starck's work will want to tell their friends. To share it. Some of them will send digital files containing everything you need to know to make one of your own in your very own home. In a stroke, manufacturers have a new intellectual property risk to worry about. They don't have to worry about organized gangs of criminal counterfeiters creating knock-off assembly lines; they will have to worry about the piracy taking place in every house in every nation in the world.

They are not ready for that.

A Makerbot Replicator 2 is an amazing piece of kit. In December 2012 I went along to the Wired pop-up store on London's Regent Street to watch one in action. The head moved across and around, pumping out layer after layer of gloopy plastic, depositing and building the 3D shape of a Christmas angel, perfect for hanging on the Christmas tree. I brought one home with great delight, marvelling at how I had seen this thing manufactured before my eyes. I showed it to my wife.

'I'm not sure what you're excited about. It doesn't look as good as any of our other decorations. I wouldn't have paid 50p for that in a market.'*

---

* I didn't pay anything for it. My four-year-old son was watching the printing process with rapt attention and the Wired assistant was kind enough to give it to him.

She was right, of course. 3D printing is still in its infancy. The Makerbot Replicator 2 costs $2,199. It is aimed at 'prosumers', those early adopters for whom the fact that you can manufacture whatever you like is the heart of the product, not the quality of its finish. Alessi, which can afford the significant upfront cost of creating a production line optimized for churning out thousands of Juicy Salifs, has nothing to worry about. Yet.

Clay Christensen is the author of *The Innovator's Dilemma*, the classic work on how disruptive technologies are at first derided by incumbents before overtaking and ultimately destroying them. His book focuses on how many of the businesses that are destroyed fail not because they do anything wrong, but because they do everything right. They focus on quality. They deliver what their customers want and would pay for. They improve. Meanwhile, some scrappy little business has a product that costs a tenth of the price of that offered by the incumbent. It isn't as good. It lacks features, or quality, or something that the incumbent believes gives it a long-term sustainable advantage. Over time, the upstart competitor gets better. It keeps its prices low but it adds features. It improves that quality. It starts to be a viable alternative to early adopters, and then to the mainstream. It knows how to deliver an experience in a way that the incumbent can't match. One day, the incumbent wakes up and realizes that its competitor can make an equivalent product for a much lower price, and goes out of business.

That's where we are with 3D printing at the moment. To the management at Alessi, comparing their Starck-inspired kitchenware to a knock-off 3D-printed lemon squeezer, it might be hard to imagine the Makerbot as a real threat. The whole point of an Alessi lemon squeezer is that it exudes quality. Quality of design. Quality of raw materials. Quality of manufacture. A rip-off 3D print in striated plastic doesn't fit the bill.

Meanwhile Makerbots and other 3D printers will get better. Someone will take the 3D image of the Starck classic and improve it. Maybe they'll make its legs a bit shorter so you don't need to raise your shoulders or stand on a chair to squeeze a lemon. Maybe they'll experiment with different grooves that clean better in a dishwasher. Maybe someone will adapt one that will fold, or come to pieces for easy storage. I don't know what they will do.

Which is the heart of the threat to the traditional business. Most businesses that make physical products are used to being one of the few organizations with the time and resources to experiment with a product, to take the risk on a production run and to bring it to market. In the world of 3D printing, experimenting becomes incredibly cheap. Ordinary consumers become designers and manufacturers. All those tinkerers and makers in the general population get to tinker and experiment with new designs. Many, maybe most, of the alterations that are made will make the product worse. Some, a few, will improve it. Those improvements will spread through the web as people search for 'overdesigned lemon squeezer that works'. Alessi's lock on what gets made will be over.

In 2000, to celebrate the tenth birthday of the Juicy Salif, Alessi launched a limited edition. Ten thousand pieces were produced. Each was gold-plated. Each was individually numbered. You can currently buy one for $640.[8] It has no use as a lemon squeezer, because the citric acid in the lemon juice would discolour the gold. It is an expensive artefact, much like the Ultra-Deluxe Edition of *Ghosts I–IV* that Trent Reznor released to his biggest fans.

This, in fact, may be Alessi's salvation. Instead of being a volume player, trying to keep the price fixed while driving up revenues by selling more units, Alessi could go the other way. It could give away the designs for its products, which is not much of a concession, given that anyone with a hand-held scanner and the product in question will be able to produce a 3D geometry file in a matter of moments. It could still make the basic product for those who don't want the hassle of making it themselves. It could have a version available at $100, $1,000, $10,000, each tapping into some emotion of status, exclusivity, belonging, self-expression or whatever.

In short, Alessi will move away from the business of making things and move towards the business of making people feel. That is how to fight casual piracy in the internet age.

Bill Gates, the founder of Microsoft, says that we overestimate the short-term impact of technology but underestimate its impact in the long term. That is where we are with 3D printing. In my lifetime I expect that as many homes will have 3D printers as currently have

2D paper printers. The process will be slow. First, the early adopters will take their expensive playthings and use them as a hobbyist would, simply for the fun of doing. Next, local convenience stores will start having their own 3D printers so every town will have its own. Just as every town once had a shop that processed camera film, it will instead have a 3D printing shop, in many cases occupying the same premises. In the same way that most of us could, if we chose to, print out our holiday snaps on our own home printers yet often conclude it is easier to upload them to a website and collect the finished, high-quality prints from a local store or receive them in the mail, we will first get exposure to 3D printing through third parties.

Perhaps we will need a replacement part for a broken cot or child's buggy. A drawer handle that is no longer in production has broken, and we either have to replace every handle in the kitchen or find a way to get one matching element. A personalized key ring as a gift. Whatever it is that we want, something will eventually make most of us consider 3D printing as a solution to some need.

The office supplies company Staples has already announced that it will be rolling out 3D printing services through stores in the Netherlands and Belgium in 2013. That is how it will begin. Eventually, 3D printing will be all around us. Exactly how this will pan out, nobody knows.

We do know that we are in the first experimentation phase, as entrepreneurs test the market, searching out what customers want and will pay for through trial and error. There will be failures and bankruptcies, because that is how the capitalist economy sorts and filters the ideas that can work at scale from those that cannot. 3D printing, or some similar form of personalized, individual manufacturing, will be a substantial part of the Western world's manufacturing capability within the next twenty years.

Hopefully, traditional manufacturers will learn the lessons of the record industry. They won't seek to sue their customers. They may try to delay the onslaught of digital manufacturing in their traditional businesses by using Digital Rights Management and litigation, but in the end, it will be their competitors figuring out how to use the power of free to reach more customers that will be their biggest threat, not piracy. They will learn to adapt.

The Curve suggests three linked strategies for building a business in the digital age. Use the cheap distribution of the web to find customers; use technology to ascertain who the best customers are; let them spend money on things they really value. Manufacturers have one big advantage here: there are many people who are unlikely to want the hassle of personalized manufacturing. That means that the web is less disruptive for physical industries, in that it doesn't eliminate the existing business, but also more challenging, since manufacturers will need to adopt two totally different strategies simultaneously.

The first and most urgent order of business is to start building relationships with end users. Manufacturers might use content marketing to draw users to their websites; the ways they build relationships with their audience will become more sophisticated.

A business which makes kitchen utensils will provide all sorts of free advice on kitchen techniques. A tool manufacturer will do the same with woodworking or DIY. Toy companies will have entertaining websites (many, such as Lego, already do). They will help people cook better, or make better, or have more fun. They will use content to become more relevant to the lives of the people who buy the things they make.

Some will give away the designs of their products, knowing that few 3D printers in the world will be able to match the quality and finish of the products that they manufacture themselves. By sharing, they will start the process of connecting with their fans. They will upload digital files to sites like Thingiverse and The Pirate Bay and sell physical products on sites like Etsy to find an audience who will test out their products at their own expense. They will embed elements in their digital files that encourage users seeking a different experience to visit the manufacturer's website or to buy one of their products. They will encourage the use of 3D printers as a prototyping tool for users, knowing that quality, brand, scarcity, status and all the other tools at a marketer's disposal to create value still exist in a world of personalized manufacturing. They will use customer relationship management to put connecting with their customers at the heart of their business, not secondary to it.

Manufacturers will make less money at the cheap end of the market and much more at the expensive end. They will have to become experts in creating desire and in using technology to identify those customers who will be freeloaders for life and those who have the potential to become superfans. They will also cease to be business-to-business businesses. Every manufacturer whose products are sold at retail will need to start building one-to-one relationships with their customers. They will stop relying on a long chain of wholesalers and distributors and retailers. They will have to learn new skills.

They will have to deal with the consumerization of business.

12
WE'RE ALL RETAILERS NOW

Very few businesses are actually consumer businesses.

A consumer business is one where there is a direct relationship between business and consumer that involves money changing hands. A high street retailer is a consumer business. A coffee shop is a consumer business. A plumber who comes to your house to fix a leaky pipe is a consumer business, but a plumber subcontracted by a builder for the new extension to your house is not.

A book publisher is not a consumer business. The sales process of a book publisher involves persuading a book buyer at a high street store, or a retailer, or at Amazon to stock their books. The role of the sales department is not to persuade 10,000 people each to buy one copy of a book. It is to persuade one gatekeeper to buy 10,000 copies of that book and then manage the distribution and selling of the product to individual customers.

A music business sells to record shops. A toy maker sells to a toy shop. A game publisher sells to game shops. A musician sells to a label, a game developer to a game publisher, an author to a book publisher (often via a literary agent). These are businesses making products or services for ordinary people that have no direct connection with their own consumers, but are only linked via a long chain. The marketing departments are consumer-facing, using indirect communications like television spots, magazine advertisements and advertising hoardings on busy streets to build demand that is then indirectly satisfied by the retail trade. They use imperfect information and marketing instincts to craft campaigns they believe will lead to increased sales. It's hard to say if a campaign worked, or if the product would have sold just as well without it. It's hard to be sure which bits of a campaign were effective and which bits were wasteful. It's hard to understand what customers want when you can only talk to them in sample focus groups or understand their desires indirectly through conversations with retail gatekeepers or through high-level data – 'Oh, so this author is more popular in Boston than in Atlanta. I wonder if it's a North–South thing?'

All that is changing. The internet has ushered in a new era where any business that has a consumer-facing element needs to become properly consumer-facing. It is not enough to be a B2C marketing organization and a B2B sales organization. Anyone who markets to consumers needs to have the skills and disciplines necessary to sell to consumers as well. If they don't, they run the risk of seeing their value erode in a changing competitive environment. This is the consumerization of business and it is happening all around us. You can embrace it, and you must deal with it, but you cannot stop it.

That is not to say that I believe in total disintermediation. That all producers will have direct connections with their customers, unmediated by middlemen, a digital utopia where commerce is frictionless, where discovery is easy and where building relationships is as simple as putting a sign up that says 'I'm available'. The changing digital landscape replaces the old middlemen with new ones. The difference is that this time round there are alternatives to relying on a single retail channel. In order to make it work, not only do creators have to learn some of the roles that publishers used to fulfil, but publishers need to learn some of the roles that retailers used to fulfil.

Intermediaries are adapting. A book publisher has fewer intermediaries with which it has to negotiate when it publishes an ebook. Most platforms accept whatever a publisher loads up. Publishers supply the files, upload them, often set the price and then have to stimulate the demand. The requirements and skills for a publisher (or any former gatekeeper in a digital world) are changing.

Let's start with some basics. The heart of the Curve is that you need to use the power of free to reach the widest possible audience of your product and then use the one-to-one interactivity of the web to let your biggest fans spend lots of money on things that they truly value.

That is not to say that your audience needs to be massive or your product needs to be a lowest-common-denominator populist one. The Curve enables the niche to survive as well as the mass market. The items in trouble are those that used to be 'good enough' but not remarkable, that squeaked through the system because gatekeepers determined what got released and what was successful more than consumers.

It is not to say that you need to cut out the middleman entirely. There is still a role for specialist retailers and supermarkets and online partners in the world of The Curve. It's not to say that the gatekeepers are going away either: in the new world of digital, businesses like Google and Facebook and Amazon and Steam and Apple are new gatekeepers.

These gatekeepers are often more open than the old ones. They embrace choice and filtering rather than curation. They have abandoned the tyranny of the physical and understand that more products can be produced by more businesses for more consumers than ever before. They are nevertheless important, challenging bottlenecks that sit between creators and consumers.

Successful creators, publishers and distributors will learn when to partner with these new gatekeepers and when to circumvent them. They will learn what the new gatekeepers do so that they can choose where and how to work with them from a position of strength. In the next chapter, we'll look at a number of industries and see specific examples of how that industry can embrace the Curve. First, though, we need to return to the mix of skills that are needed in this new world.

James Woollam is the managing director of F+W Media International, the UK arm of US business F+W Media. F+W calls itself a 'community focused creator of content for hobbyists and enthusiasts'.[1] It focuses its activities on vertical communities that are formed around hobbies or interests that are easy to understand: arts and crafts, lifestyle, health, outdoors, collectibles, writing, design, genealogy, sewing, screenwriting, fiction. It offers a range of products and services to those communities. It has 225 websites, some free, some paid-for. It has a backlist of 4,000 books and publishes 600 new ones every year.

It operates forty-six magazines, twenty large-scale events and has published 3,800 ebooks. It is not just a publisher, though. It operates dozens of online stores focused on its niches. They include ShopDeer Hunting.com for the outdoors type, GardenersHub.com for gardeners, WritersStore.com for writers and filmmakers and so on.

Woollam explains, 'We've done a tremendous amount in recent years to tie together our publishing and consumer businesses. The changes we've made as publishers are extensive and far-reaching.'[2] Woollam identifies three key areas which have seen substantial changes.

For F+W, audience development, and specifically email name capture, is now a company-wide goal. It is no longer enough to create a product, to release it and to hope it sells. F+W has understood that to harness the Curve, to move customers from being 'people who have had exposure to what you do' to 'fans who will spend lots of money on things that they truly value', you need to be able to talk to them, again and again, on your own terms without needing to get permission from a gatekeeper such as a retailer or Amazon. Each new proposal, new potential partner or new project, is viewed with audience development in mind.

Audience development, or the ability to talk to customers again and understand their behaviour and preferences, in terms of both product design and purchasing patterns, is critically important, but you have to get an audience first. Woollam says F+W has invested in company-wide training on search engine optimization, or SEO. 'At least half our staff can more than competently complete keyword analysis and have an understanding of its importance. Sure, we review sales data and Nielsen [book data], but we use web analytics and keyword analysis in the content decision making process.'

SEO is the dark art of making sure that your content ranks highly in search results on the web, particularly on Google but also on Amazon and in the App Store. For much of the 1990s it was seen as having a 'secret sauce', where specialist companies could charge companies lots of money to ensure that their products appeared on the first page of Google, often by using dubious tricks such as paying for other sites to link to their clients' sites or more nefarious practices. SEO is an endless battle between Google, which wants to have the highest quality results for its users and advertisers, and SEO experts who try to game the algorithms.

My advice is not to play the game. If you create good quality content on the web, Google (and Bing and other search engines) will help others to find it. It makes sense to put yourself in the shoes of someone who might actually be searching for what you are offering when thinking about how to describe it. Putting keywords that people might actually search for in your copy is good practice. But in the end, SEO is more about making good stuff that people actually want to look at than gaming Google's algorithms.

Two quick examples can show why producing good content that people will search for is a good strategy. Many searches in Google throw up a lot of results from sites such as ehow.com and about.com which farm out cheap content creation aimed directly at optimizing for Google's algorithm. The content is often weak, and is unlikely to engage passionate fans who can be moved along the demand curve to where they will choose to spend lots of money on things they really value. Instead, this is a volume game, arbitraging getting cheap traffic from gaming Google's algorithm to gain sufficient eyeballs to build a display advertising business. It is the antithesis of the Curve.

Equally flawed is the diatribe written by John MacArthur, the publisher of American magazine *Harper's*. MacArthur is concerned that Google is making it impossible for readers to find the high-quality content that lies within *Harper's*. 'Try finding *Harper's Magazine* when you Google "magazines that publish essays" or "magazines that publish short stories" – it isn't easy,' he says.[3]

It's hard to realize that some people genuinely don't understand how a search engine works, particularly someone whose business should be about making their high-quality content easy to find for someone who is looking for it. MacArthur, presumably, believes that a user looking for a *Harper's* magazine article would search for 'magazines that publish essays' or 'magazines that publish short stories'. I could imagine typing those words into a search engine because I am a writer, amongst other things, and could imagine wanting to find a paid home for my writing. If instead I wanted to read about the countdown to economic collapse in Afghanistan, or the challenges of immigration in rural Nebraska, both topics that are covered in long-form essays in a recent edition of *Harper's*, I would search for terms relevant to those words. Articles from *Harper's* (a subscription website) would come up, as would those from *The New York Times*, *Fox News* and *The Nation*. It also ignores the fact that if a site is behind a paywall, Google's spiders often can't see the words to index them; Google can't tell people about a website if it does not know what is in there.

I visited harpers.org, the home page of the business that MacArthur runs on the web. I am no SEO expert or web developer, but I used the capability that comes with all browsers to view the underlying source code, the raw text written in HTML and CSS that is rendered by my browser to make a web page that I can read. I searched for the words 'essays' or 'short stories'. They didn't appear once on the home page. If MacArthur really thinks that people search for 'magazines that publish essays', he should at the very least put the words on his site.

(SEO is both more complex and more simple than this. It is more simple because Google *wants* to help people find relevant search results. It is winning the search engine war by providing us with the answers that we want to the questions that we search for. It is more complex because you need to do more than simply hide the keywords that people are searching for in your copy. For example, Google pays attention to the words that people use when hyperlinking to a website to tell them what *other* people think the site is about. Google also personalizes our search results based on what we have searched for before and what sites we have visited in the past. If you run two identical searches on different computers, they are likely to show different results.)

SEO is also becoming less important as more of us are finding content through other, more social means such as links or recommendations from Twitter, Facebook, Pinterest, Tumblr and so on. What it does mean is making sure that publishers are thinking as merchandisers. 'How will someone find my product?' 'What will they be looking for?' 'If they typed a query into a search engine, what keywords would I expect them to type for which [insert your product here] is the perfect solution?' That's not the dark art of SEO, that is simply putting yourself in the shoes of your customers and thinking a bit more like a consumer when building your marketing strategy, just as Marcus Sheridan did for his swimming-pool business.

The third area of change that Woollam identifies is the concept of marketing as a separate discipline.

> Marketing is a company-wide responsibility and not a department. Our marketers do great work and run specific campaigns, but an important part of their role is to conduct the wider orchestra. Our editorial and content teams, marketing and audience development work together daily. Our editors write blogs and post online, they encourage and support authors to do the same and they manage social media content.

Most of what Woollam has been focused on is

> building an audience to sell stuff we have already created, whether it's books or other products. Now, we're generating enough data and insight to actually define new products. In part we can ask our customers what they want, but more valuable is that we can see how they behave. We can review the performance of online content, search results, conversion rates and behaviour and use this to identify gaps and opportunities. We can take that data and make, or find, new products that we know we have an audience for.
>
> It's hugely exciting and has tremendous potential, but the best bit is that we've really only scratched the surface.

*

In an ideal world, we would all have a large captive audience, hanging on our every word, in a place where we could control and manage the dialogue, where only our products were for sale and where the community loved everything that we did. Sadly, we don't live in an ideal world.

At GAMESbrief, I have a blog with 20,000 monthly visitors where I can control the dialogue and the user journey. I can steer them through a sales funnel to sign up for emails (our primary goal), to buy our products (our secondary goal) and to participate in the conversation. Many of those users are fly-by users, landing on the site because they followed a link that someone tweeted, because GAMESbrief appeared high in a list of search results for a particular query or because another website quoted something we've done. My job, as a publisher, is to do everything in my power to get more users, to keep them for longer and to give them opportunities to spend lots of money on things that they really value.

Getting new users means lots of things. I need to be active on Twitter and, to a lesser extent, Facebook. (Which of the social networks is important to you depends on your audience. My audience of 'people who make games' is more active on Twitter than Facebook, LinkedIn, Tumblr or Pinterest. We are experimenting with how important YouTube is as a discovery tool for us.) I need to write guest posts on prominent blogs and websites. I need to do interviews in written, video and podcast form. I need to be visible on the web so that people who are interested in what I have to say can find me.

That is why I have, together with my colleague Rob Fahey, written an ebook for the Kindle called *Design Rules for Free-to-Play Games*. In many ways, I don't want to be on Amazon. On Amazon, I know nothing about my customers. I don't know their names or email addresses. I don't know if they have bought one of my books or all my books. I can't analyse my average revenue per user to see whether I am selling lots of books to a small number of people or if most people only buy one book from me.

Science-fiction author Cory Doctorow points out that many organizations who have to work with Amazon seem to be fighting the wrong battles. In February 2013 his young-adult novel *Homeland* was published in the US. It was a *New York Times* bestseller. Doctorow went on a whistlestop book tour of the US, covering twenty-three cities in twenty-five days. Along the way, he was asked by his internet-savvy friends, 'How many copies have you sold?' The answer he gave was that no one knows.[4]

You can get detailed answers from Bookscan if you subscribe. That gives you data from the tills of participating booksellers. But for the ebook numbers you have to wait. As Doctorow's friends said, 'You mean Amazon, Apple and Google know exactly who comes to their stores, how they find their way to your books, where they're coming in from, how many devices they use and when, and they *don't tell the publishers?*'

I've had the same experience self-publishing via Kindle. The data that Amazon shares with me about what is selling where is almost incomprehensible. Amazon varies the price, the royalty and a range of other factors and tells me what I have sold in a spreadsheet with dozens of entries for just a single book. I do at least know how many copies I have sold, via which of Amazon's six major stores, which I suppose is something.

The battle we should all be fighting with Amazon is not about co-operative marketing or pricing. It should be about getting access to the data about our products. We should be able to test different marketing copy on sales pages so we can see what works. We should be able to follow users on a journey so we can discover if making a video makes a difference, how price sensitive customers are and whether a different colour book cover changes the conversion rate. Amazon has all this data, but it isn't sharing. It controls the customer relationship, it controls the customer information, it controls the opportunities for upselling and cross-promoting. Why on earth should I be putting any effort into improving Amazon's ecosystem when I could be putting all the effort into my own tiny little ecosystem at www.gamesbrief.com?

The simple answer is because Amazon is where the customers are. If I want people to be able to find what I sell, it makes sense to be in the largest shop on earth. I need to go where my customers are, no matter the disadvantages. That doesn't mean I have to be stupid about it, though. In my head, I think of Amazon as a customer acquisition channel, not a revenue channel. It just so happens that it also generates revenue, which is a marvellous (and important) bonus. I am not in a position where I would be happy to make no money from selling products via Amazon, but I can conceive of the day when that could happen. It would work something like this:

Amazon is a recommendation engine that is highly sophisticated. It gives me the potential to reach an audience that dwarfs the audience I can find myself on my own dedicated website. I will therefore launch a number of books, both physical and digital, on Amazon and use the algorithmic recommendations, keywords and other tools available to me to help make my books appear to the kind of readers who are likely to be interested in the things that I do. I will share links on social media that drive my audience to Amazon too, because they will then share the links in turn to people who are outside my direct reach. Assuming that I have products that people want to buy at cheap enough prices, I will make some sales.

That is when it becomes up to me to do more with my books than simply let Amazon sell them. I need to use those books as a stepping stone to a direct relationship between me and the reader. Maybe I will link from the book (and particularly the ebook) to more resources on the website. Maybe I can find a way for every purchase to entitle the reader to login to an exclusive area of the website where they can chat and compare notes with other readers. Maybe I will provide them with an incentive to visit the website and give me their email address: another free ebook, access to an exclusive webinar or video series. My objective at this stage is to move the buyer of my book from being an Amazon customer to being a GAMESbrief reader to being someone I can communicate with directly. That is the necessary first step to building a relationship that will enable me to convert them into a GAMESbrief customer, then a GAMESbrief repeat customer, then a GAMESbrief superfan. I need Amazon, but that doesn't mean I have to be stupid about how I work with them.

On 27 September 2012 *The Casual Vacancy* was published world-wide by Little, Brown. The book, the first for adults from the author of the Harry Potter series, J. K. Rowling, was highly anticipated. In the UK it went straight to the top of the fiction charts, selling 124,603 copies in the first three days of its release, ten times as many as the next bestselling book, Bernard Cornwell's *1356*, which sold 12,231.[5] In the first three weeks, it sold 600,000 copies in North America.[6] By any standards, it was a phenomenal launch.

And yet there were challenges. The recommended UK retail price for the hardback edition of *The Casual Vacancy* was £20 ($30). Given the huge following that Rowling had built up through her Harry Potter novels, it seems that there was likely to be enormous pent-up demand for the book. Rowling's biggest fans might have been prepared to spend a lot more than £20 on the book. Yet, in the UK at least, £20 was not the price that many people paid. Supermarkets like Sainsbury and Tesco offered it for £10 or less. At WHSmith, you could get it for as little as £6.99, albeit in conjunction with another offer.[7] In February 2013, Amazon was selling the hardback for £8.50.

I'm sure that the book has been a success for the publishers, even with the eye-watering advances that are likely to have been paid. The US rights alone were believed to have been sold for an advance of $7 million, according to *Forbes*.[8] There was still an opportunity to make money, to make a stronger connection with fans, to weaken the stranglehold of specialist retail, supermarkets and Amazon, who don't care about Rowling's book except as a means of getting people through the door so that they can sell them other things.

To my mind, that model of selling is on the way out. Little, Brown should consider sales made at Sainsbury and WHSmith and Amazon as the start of their relationship with Rowling's fans, not the end of it. Not everyone will want to become a fan or a superfan, and that's OK. The model behind the Curve is not to treat everyone the same. It is to use the power of the web to segment people, to allow the freeloaders to experience the product for free while the superfans are given opportunities to spend money on things they truly value. Would 100,000 people have been prepared to pay £30 to get the book a week before the general release date? Possibly. Would 10,000 people have been prepared to pay £50 to get a signed, limited edition? Possibly. Would 1,000 people have been prepared to pay £300 to attend one of ten launch parties during the first month, where they could eat a fine meal in the company of one of the best-known authors in the world? Possibly. Could Little, Brown be building a database of J. K. Rowling fans so that they can talk to them again, for her next novel? Are they thinking about how to cross-promote between authors based on genre, target market, purchasing patterns and so on? Possibly.

I don't know what might have worked out differently for the launch. I am pretty sure that Rowling's first novel since Harry Potter was always going to do well. (It's the second one that will be a bit more scary for the publishers.) I do know that we are all trying to learn in a rapidly changing environment and that the winners will be the ones who have the best relationships with the fans. That might be the creators. It might be the retailers. It might be the new digital gatekeepers. It might be businesses who would traditionally have been called publishers. It is all up in the air. Those who learn the new skills and grasp the new opportunities will be the ones still standing in fifty years' time.

William Goldman is a legend in Hollywood. He is the screenwriter of *The Princess Bride*, *Marathon Man*, *Butch Cassidy and the Sundance Kid*, for which he won his first Oscar, and *All the President's Men*, for which he won his second. In 1983 he published *Adventures in the Screen Trade*, an insider's look into the workings of Hollywood. His primary axiom: nobody knows anything. To illustrate the point, Goldman related a conversation he had with the head of one of the biggest Hollywood studios in the late sixties. *Life* magazine had just published an edition with a picture on its cover of, it claimed, the biggest star in the world. Goldman asked the studio boss if he'd care to guess who was on the cover. As Goldman tells it:

'Newman,' he said.

No.

'McQueen.' Not McQueen.

A pause now. 'It can't be Poitier.'

I agreed. It wasn't.

Now a *long* pause. Then, in a burst: 'Oh shit, what's the matter with me, I'm not thinking – John Wayne.'

The Duke was not on the cover.

The situation was now getting the least bit uncomfortable. 'If it's a woman, it's either Streisand or Andrews.'

I said it was a man. And then, before things got too sticky, I gave the answer. (It was Eastwood.)

And he replied after some thought, 'They claim Eastwood? Eastwood's the biggest star?' Finally, after another pause, he nodded. 'They're right.'

The point being that if a studio giant couldn't guess the biggest star in his business, the territory is murkier than most of us would imagine.

'Nobody knows anything' is a powerful and potentially liberating axiom. In the hit-driven world of Hollywood, it is terrifying. Executives don't know if their next movie will be a massive success like *The Avengers* or an excruciating failure like *John Carter*. In a world constrained by the tyranny of the physical, executives pile on the financial risk in order to reduce the operational risk that a movie will flop. Goldman argues that with all the market research, gut instinct and experience in the world, no one in Hollywood knows which movies are going to fly and which ones will flop.

Next to my copy of *Adventures in the Screen Trade* on the bookshelf by my writing desk at home, I keep another book. In many ways, it feels like the natural companion for Goldman, even though at first glance the two seem miles apart. That book is *The Lean Startup* by Eric Ries.

Ries is a quiet, thoughtful man, an introverted character who has nevertheless become the figurehead of a movement to bring discipline and rigour into the scrappy, ill-disciplined world of startups. He was the chief technology officer of a business called IMVU, which is now a thriving community whose 10 million monthly members chat, play and hang out in an online digital world. Back in 2004, when Ries was co-founding this business, the team had a very different vision. They didn't want to build their own closed, proprietary virtual world. They wanted to combine the mass appeal of instant messaging (IM) networks with the impact and high revenue per user of a 3D virtual world. The founders believed that the best way to build scale was to build a 3D avatar system that sat on top of existing IM networks such as AOL Instant Messenger or Yahoo Instant Messenger, so they set themselves a tough deadline of six months – just 180 days – to build the system and ensure that it was compatible with half a dozen existing instant messaging systems. After an enormous number of late nights and intense pressure, they launched the product.

It flopped. Absolutely flopped. They put up a web page and asked people to register for their 'Instant Messenger add-on' product. No one understood it. No one wanted it. The depressing thing for Ries was not that he had wasted six months of his life building a product no one wanted. It was that he could have found out that no one wanted it without building the product, just by putting up the web page that asked people to sign up. When no one signed, he would have had his market research for a fraction of the money, time and effort that he spent on building the dud product.

IMVU successfully pivoted away from being an add-on to other IM networks and became its own successful virtual world. Ries took the lessons he learned from IMVU and other startups and, building on the work of Stanford professor Steve Blank, started to create a template that other startups could follow to reach success faster and more cheaply than ever before.

Before you start thinking that you don't work for a startup, think again. Here is Ries's definition of a startup:

A startup is a human institution designed to create a new product or service under conditions of extreme uncertainty.

If you work in a media business, I would say that you are operating under conditions of extreme uncertainty. If you work in manufacturing, you may soon be operating under those conditions thanks to 3D printing. All of us are seeing unprecedented change in how we communicate and do business as the web continues to shape our daily lives and business interactions. It seems to me as if almost everything in the early twenty-first century is a startup by Ries's definition.

Here's why it matters. One of the insights that Ries and Blank developed is that a corporation and a startup are very different beasts. A corporation knows what its business model is. It is the same business it was last year, and the year before that. The job of people in a corporation is not to make radical changes. It is to do what was done last year, but a bit better. It is a world of tweaks and adjustments. It is a world where a three-year plan makes sense because there is a reasonable chance that broad assumptions made about the evolution of the market and customer needs will come true. A corporation is all about execution.

A startup, on the other hand, is an organization in search of a business model. Blank defines it in more detail:

A startup is a temporary organization formed to search for a repeatable and scalable business model.[9]

A startup is operating in a world of assumptions and uncertainty. It does not know what its customers want yet. It has to go through a process of customer discovery (finding the right customers) and customer development (learning what those customers want and what they are willing to pay for). It is a place filled with uncertainty.

The most depressing thing a Lean Startup proponent can watch is a flawed plan, perfectly executed. Yet this is often what results when people trained and schooled in corporation thinking turn their attention to developing market segments. They form assumptions. They pay for expensive research and top-flight consultants to tell them what to do. They produce spreadsheets and presentations that make detailed predictions about the future. They get board-level signoff to deliver on the plan. They go off and execute against the plan, and they do it well, because that is what corporates are good at doing.

Sometimes it works, because the initial assumptions were right. More often, the initial assumptions were wrong but there was no mechanism for adapting to new data on the fly. The corporation continues to execute, pointing in the wrong direction, with no feedback loop from live customers that would have allowed it to recalibrate its objectives if only it had a process in place to listen and adapt.

For a long time, the alternative to having a plan was to have no plan at all, which was even worse. Refugees from the corporate world would refuse to plan or budget or strategize, blaming the failures to innovate that they had seen in large corporates on the flawed process for delivering projects under conditions of extreme uncertainty. This didn't work either. As President Eisenhower once said, 'Plans are useless, but planning is indispensable.'

The solution put forward by the Lean Startup movement is to focus on a new metric of success. It's not about revenues, or profits. That is what happens once you have discovered who your customers are and what they want to pay for. The metric of success in the early stages of a startup is *validated learning*. To put it another way, successful businesses operating under conditions of extreme uncertainty are those which work out how to learn faster than their competitors, and to keep learning.

There are many different ways to go about this. Have a hypothesis. Test it. If it is disproved, change your hypothesis. If not, keep going. Make a plan. Put a note in the diary for a meeting to take place six months from now to determine if the plan is working or if the organization should make a radical change (the famous – and overused – 'pivot'). If you know that you are going to have a discussion in six months' time about whether you should pivot, what data would you like to have available at the meeting to help you make an informed decision? Are you gathering that data by your activities today? If not, how can you adapt what you are doing today to answer the strategic question you expect to face in six months' time?

The Lean Startup movement provides an invaluable template for organizations whose business or operating environment is undergoing rapid change. Much like William Goldman, it involves admitting that we don't know anything, but unlike Goldman's Hollywood, where the only option is to continue to throw money at risky, hit-driven projects and hope the bets pay off, the Lean Startup approach offers an alternative. It's about learning how to learn. It's about learning how to adapt. It's about learning how to accept failure as a necessary part of doing business but at the same time using the failure as a process of learning.

Economist Tim Harford takes up the theme in his book *Adapt*. Harford has three basic rules of being adaptable: You must experiment. You must survive the failure of the experiments. You, and your organization, must learn from the experiments.

Far too many organizations fail at hurdle two, let alone hurdle three. A business initiative is launched. It struggles, probably because it is a well-executed plan built on flawed assumptions. The experiment is shut down, which is fine. The executive in charge is sidelined. The team who worked on it is re-assigned. The message is received loud and clear throughout the organization: experiments are fine, provided they are successful. Innovation dies.

It is important not only that the organization survives the failure of the experiment, but that the team members and executives behind it survive too. That means making sure the experiment is structured to deliver validated learning rather than revenues and profits *as its initial success criterion*. Using revenues and profits as criteria only makes sense if the business model is known and well understood. In many cases, new projects happen to fit known and well-understood business models. In that case, measuring success by financial metrics is sensible. Other projects are operating in an environment of extreme uncertainty where the business model is not yet known. Their success is dependent on an organization's speed of learning and efficiency at adapting. These are very different disciplines.

Supercell is a Finnish games company that is an amazing success story. It is estimated that its revenues in 2013 will top half a billion dollars from just two games, *Clash of Clans* and *Hay Day*. Yet Supercell's first game, *Gunshine*, was not a success, and the company has a strategy of embracing failure.

Ilkka Paananen is the youthful founder of Supercell. In his

mid-thirties, although looking a decade younger, Paananen is a second-time entrepreneur. His first games business was called Sumea and he sold it to mobile publisher Digital Chocolate in 2004. Based on the track record of Paananen and his team of co-founders, Supercell was able to raise $12 million from Accel Partners and London Venture Partners before they had even shipped a game.

Paananen is opposed to micro-managing. 'When you set up a company, the only thing – *the only thing* – you should care about is getting the best people,' he said. 'From that, good things will happen.'[10] He then gives those good people the flexibility to work in small teams, typically of five people or so, which he calls cells. The entire company, consisting of a number of these small teams, is the Supercell. Supercell is relaxed about projects that fail provided they fail quickly. 'This year [2012], we've killed more products than we've launched.' It is also focused on keeping the small, cell-like structure that enabled it to find the hits:

> You'll often see a gaming studio get a hit, then they'll start to grow at an astronomical rate. Then the next product they do has to be bigger in terms of the team, the headcount and the budget because they think they're better. But this model has been proven wrong multiple times. This leads to companies being risk averse and copying what has already worked. Our guiding motto is, 'Think Small, But Get Big'. We prize extreme independence and have a flat organization with little bureaucracy.

It seems to be working for Supercell. Its two games, *Hay Day* and *Clash of Clans*, are bringing in $2.5 million in revenue every day, and in February investors bought into the company for $130 million at a valuation of $770 million.[11]

The small team size ethos is reflected by many other successful technology companies. Jeff Bezos, founder of Amazon, said, 'If you can't feed a team of people with two pizzas, it's too large.'[12] (Given the size of American pizzas, that typically means a team of five to seven people, depending on their appetites.) Valve, the creators of the Steam platform that has revolutionized gaming on the PC, has a similarly flat structure. There are no team leaders and everyone is involved in the issues of business, marketing and sales. Desks are on wheels to make it easy for project teams to form. If you think something should be done, you just need to convince enough of the people with the skills you need to come and help you make it happen. It is not an environment for everyone, but it is an environment that enabled a maker of shooter games to create a platform for selling PC games and become the dominant distribution force in that market. Steve Jobs had a rule: 'I can't remember more than a hundred first names, so I only want to be around people that I know personally. So if it gets bigger than a hundred people, it will force us to go to a different organization structure where I can't work that way. The way I like to work is where I touch everything.'[13] In an organization which now employs over 70,000 people, Jobs liked to keep the people working on a single project (in this case the Mac) at fewer than a hundred.

Jobs, Bezos, Gabe Newell of Valve and Paananen have very different management styles. Some are famously controlling. Others allow the groups of talented employees that they put together or allow to form to determine what happens next. Google's approach is to allow its engineers one day a week to tinker with anything they fancy, an approach that spawned Gmail, Google News and AdSense, as well as failures like Google Wave and Google Answers. The element that combines them is their approach to keeping groups small, flexible and personal, not corporately planned and structured. It also helps if they respond to failure swiftly. Some embrace it. Jobs got angry when things failed. Eric Schmidt, former CEO of Google, said, 'We try things. Remember, we celebrate our failures. This is a company where it's absolutely okay to try something that's very hard, have it not be successful, and take the learning from that.'[14]

For Paananen, embracing failure in the hit-driven world of games is critical. It's even better if you can learn how to kill things rapidly. How to avoid the risks of executing perfectly on a flawed plan by adapting along the way. When Supercell decides to kill a project, and it killed at least three in 2012, the whole company gathers to do a post-mortem to determine what went wrong, and then the cell members involved with the failed game are each given a bottle of champagne.

'When failure is completely accepted – in fact it's celebrated – then it encourages people to take risks. When you take risks, there is more innovation. And with innovation there's better games, and eventually there are going to be hit games.'[15]

We are entering a world where business certainties are becoming uncertainties. Where revenue for traditional business models is collapsing. We are seeing physical dollars become digital dimes. We will not be able to reverse that trend. The weight of economics, of technology and changes in the social contract between creators and consumers is against us. We will nevertheless be able to make money from making stuff – both physical and digital – in the future. Those who thrive will be those who learn to be flexible, to adapt, to experiment, to succeed and to fail in the fastest, most cost-effective way. One thing that we will all have to get better at to make that work is measuring.

How do you measure success? By volume? By units sold? By product line? If so, you are trapped in old world thinking. What use is a million downloads if they were all free and hardly anyone ever looked at the thing they downloaded? Why are you thinking about products when you should be thinking about customers? Why does volume matter when it is no longer a good proxy for revenue, because we have abandoned the tyranny of the physical for the flexibility of the digital?

On Amazon's US website in May 2013, the most expensive Kindle books in the top ten were Dan Brown's *Inferno* ($14.99) and James Patterson's *12th of Never* ($11.99). There were two books at 99 cents: *Don't Say a Word* by Barbara Freethy and *Truly, Madly, Deeply* by Carly Phillips. The most expensive book costs fifteen times as much as the cheapest.

In February 2013, Amazon UK was in the midst of a price war with Sony.* The ebook version of *Life of Pi* by Yann Martel was priced at 20p. At number 20 was *Stalkers* by Peter Finch, priced at £1.99. At number 8 was *Bridget Jones: Edge of Reason* by Helen Fielding at £4.66. *Stalkers* cost ten times as much as *Life of Pi. Bridget Jones* costs twenty-three times as much. The most expensive ebook in the top hundred in the UK was Peter Brett's *The Daylight War*, which

---

* Amazon was in a price war in the UK, massively cutting the prices of certain books to maintain a competitive advantage against rival eReaders. The publishers and authors were getting the same revenue from Amazon as it sacrificed profits for market share. I believe that this position will not be sustainable: other publishers and authors will sacrifice their profits on ebooks in return for finding direct relationships with their customers, and the prices of ebooks will collapse permanently.

sold for £11.49. When pricing can vary by a factor of sixty-five times from lowest to highest, is volume really a useful measure of demand?

Anyone who works in the web world knows that 'registered users' is a useless metric. Eric Ries has a phrase for them: vanity metrics. A vanity metric can only go up. It gives the rosiest possible picture. It cannot show failure, because it only ever moves in one direction. The number of registered users is basically a measure of how old you are as a business, but says nothing about how successful you are.

The focus on registered users comes from the days when everyone paid to get access to something. When the price was fixed, volume could become a proxy for revenue. If you say, 'I sold a million copies of my album,' I could perhaps estimate that the gross revenue you generated at retail from that album was £10 million ($15 million). Lady Gaga's 1 million plays on Spotify made an estimated $167. (Not that I am suggesting these are comparable. Far from it. In the next chapter, we'll look at how Spotify fits into the Curve for an artist, but it surely isn't as the replacement for disappearing album revenue.) In a world where the price can be infinitely variable, a focus on registered user numbers, or downloads, or some other metric that can only go up is extremely misleading. Unfortunately, most journalists are caught up in the old school of thinking that the number of registrations is a proxy for revenue, while companies like publicizing the biggest numbers they possibly can.

We can see this with IMVU. The company has 50 million registered users. Of those, 10 million are active on a monthly basis.[16] For a business that is about generating revenue from the sale of virtual goods to its active community, only the active users are valuable. Moshi Monsters, the successful virtual world aimed at kids, has 80 million registered users, but doesn't break out how many of those are active on a monthly basis (although CEO Michael Acton Smith is at pains to point out that they don't focus on vanity metrics internally).[17] Bigpoint, the German browser-based games company, has 300 million registered users but no one outside the company knows how many of those are active.[18]

This can be a big problem. A company focused on registered users is a *customer acquisition* business. Its focus is to get customers through the door. It is a mentality derived from the shorthand equation that customers = revenue, a shorthand that is no longer true. I know companies with fewer than 200,000 monthly active users making high single-digit millions of dollars in revenue, while other companies with ten times those users struggle to make the same amount of revenue. Customers do not equal revenue, they are simply the prerequisites to revenue.

A company that focuses on active users (MAUs and DAUs) has two different levers it can pull to improve its metrics. It can get more customers through the door or it can make the existing customers sufficiently satisfied that they come back again. A customer acquisition company is trapped in twentieth-century thinking; a *customer retention* company has taken the first steps along the road towards making money from the Curve.

Thinking about the metrics of success in what you do, do you focus on revenue per product or average revenue per user? Are your colleagues incentivized by how well your book or album or game or tractor or overcoat or product sells, or are you incentivized by how often your customers come back and how much they spend with you? Have you got an ability to segment your users into different buckets depending on their spending habits and give them different offers, promotions, products and services depending on the type of customer they are? Do you rely on a retail partner, whether physical or digital, to do that for you, or can you do it yourself?

The Curve is not just about making money. When acting as a consultant to traditional games companies, I am often referred to as a monetization consultant, which I find strange since so much of my work revolves around helping companies shift from a product mentality to a service one. I help people move on from just worrying about how to get customers and learn how to keep them. I do think about monetization, but it is part of a strategy to engage customers, to keep them and to give them an emotional context in which spending significantly more than the average price of a physical product makes sense.

To pigeonhole the Curve as a monetization strategy is to miss the point. The Curve is a way of changing your mental picture of what you do to something different from 'creating something to sell'. Today, you build a relationship with your fans and a context within which they can spend. Then you allow them to spend amounts of money ranging from the tiny to the enormous, with technology as a tool to help you understand what they want, and to move customers along the demand curve.

Milling grain might seem like an unlikely Curve business. The business of turning grain into flour and selling that flour in supermarkets seems like a business that can't escape its physical roots. Yet King Arthur Flour, a 225-year-old milling business based in Vermont, has done just that. In 1990, the company was a small mail-order business with just five employees.[19] By 2012, the company had grown to be a nationally recognized brand with 283 employees and revenues of $97 million.[20] Along the way, it changed from being a family-owned business to being an employee-owned business. Since it became employee-owned, the company has seen remarkable growth in sales and, according to former owner Frank Sands, profitability. Its distinctive premium King Arthur Flour is now the number two brand in the US. As Sands says, 'When people KNOW that they are owners, they think and work like owners!'

King Arthur Flour has worked very hard to build a community. Its website offers thousands of detailed recipes. The blog posts are chatty and personal yet informative and helpful. King Arthur Flour's YouTube channel has 3,000 subscribers and many of its videos have tens of thousands of views. The company has an active email list and engages with its users. There is a helpline staffed with nine bakers ready to answer questions from baffled or beleaguered home bakers: 'What should dough feel like when I've finished kneading?' or 'Help, I've used baking powder instead of baking soda, what can I do?'[21]

King Arthur Flour can be found in most supermarkets in the US. The company also runs a mail-order service supplying items ranging from ingredients to pans to storage solutions. The company has published four recipe books. For the serious fans of King Arthur, the company offers masterclasses in its Vermont headquarters. You can learn how to bake gluten free cakes or make macaroons or bake bread in a wood-fired brick oven for prices ranging from free to several hundred dollars.

King Arthur Flour is not at risk from the digitization of its core product. No one is yet threatening to turn flour into easily replicable bits and bytes. Flour is a staple product and not one that naturally leaps to mind when thinking of a business where it is possible to build an emotional relationship with customers and turn them into fans. Yet that is exactly what the people who run King Arthur Flour have done. In the same way that Marcus Sheridan did at River Pools, they have created an audience by giving away high-quality information for free. They have understood how to talk to their audience and what they want through smart use of technology. They have enabled those people who love what King Arthur Flour does to spend hundreds of dollars a year with a business that, at its heart, is a miller. That is smart application of the Curve.

The company has realized that a miller can no longer just be a business-to-business if it wants to thrive. The web has encouraged the 'consumerization' of business. Your business is becoming more consumer-facing, and no matter your role in the business, you are becoming more consumer-facing too. Everyone needs to understand that they are part of the marketing organization now: sales, finance, customer service, product design, administration, everyone. To change your business from selling products to selling services is a big shift. In the next chapter, we will look at how you can make this shift, whatever you do.

13
HARNESSING THE CURVE

The Swiss town of Montreux is beautiful in January. Hugging the shores of Lake Geneva, the town nestles between the icy waters of the lake and the soaring peaks of the Alps. It has a sleepy feel, with visitors sipping sunset cocktails as the last rays disappear across the lake. It's a place where James Bond would feel very much at home.*

In 2013 I was in Montreux as the guest of MPI, the trade association for everyone involved in the events industry. Their annual peripatetic conference for European members had settled in Switzerland, and I was there to talk about how the Curve will affect their industry. I was introduced to the audience by an announcer who had the kind of voice usually associated with the movie trailer for a Hollywood blockbuster or perhaps introducing acts on *The X Factor*. A blast of jingle, a starburst of brightly coloured lights and I was on.

I wasn't sure what to expect. The Curve is about what happens to things that can be shared digitally when it becomes incredibly cheap to do that sharing. If there is one thing that is true about events, it is that they are not digital in nature. Watching a live stream of a conference is not the same as sitting in the auditorium. Chatting to someone in the live chat alongside the live stream is not the same as standing in the queue for ropy coffee† or lukewarm tea.‡ Exchanging a handshake

---

* Sean Connery's Bond, that is. Much of the town feels as if it was cutting edge in 1969.
† I'm not saying that the coffee that MPI provided was ropy.
‡ I am saying that the tea was lukewarm.

and a business card cements you in someone's mind more firmly than an email or, worse, a cold-call LinkedIn request. Events ought to be insulated from the pressures that make harnessing the Curve so urgent for people who used to sell access to content for a living. In fact, shouldn't events be beneficiaries of this transition? As people get used to having information for free, then they should value even more the new scarcities, such as one-to-one time with leaders in their field.

The problem, as always, lies in the laws of economics. The events industry is not insulated from the changes because its competitors are not insulated. Magazine publishers, desperate for new sources of revenue, see events as something which not even the most determined digital pirate can copy.* Content publishers who understand the Curve are busy trying to create events that will replace the revenue streams that are disappearing as digital dimes replace physical dollars in advertising and as the competitive environment erodes margins and the customer's willingness to pay for basic access to content. The events industry doesn't need to fear digital transition directly, but it does need to fear the competition that will move into its heartland in search of ways to make money from connecting with fans.

In a fifteen-minute 'flashpoint' and a sixty-minute 'masterclass', I took several hundred event professionals through the key concepts of the Curve. I introduced them to Robert Wadlow, Chandra Dangi and the tyranny of the physical. I showed them how everything changes – particularly the average – when you move into the digital realm. I told them about Trent Reznor's success with high value physical artefacts and how NimbleBit created a game where players were happy to spend $30 or more to make their virtual frogs grow up faster. I introduced them to the handicap principle, the bowerbird and the variable demand curve and I explained why a million South Koreans were prepared to pay a dollar for a Santa hat in a racing game. I told them that they needed to make it possible for people who love what they do to spend lots of money on things they truly value. I showed them that 'free' is a marketing opportunity while the top end of the Curve is a

---

* So do music companies, but the events I am talking about here are things like 'Business Travel Europe' or 'The Game Developers Conference', not Bon Jovi live in Hyde Park.

revenue opportunity. Then I asked them to spend ten minutes thinking of all the ways they could harness the Curve to improve their
business.

Their top answer? Charge delegates to their events extra money to
sit at a lunch table with keynote speakers. The issue with this sugges-
tion is that it only addresses one end of the Curve – the expensive
end – without tackling the issues of how to work with free and how
to move customers along the demand curve over time.

It was fantastic to have an engaged, intelligent audience run through
the issues with the Curve and as a result of that session, and many
other discussions with a wide range of smart people, I have concluded
that harnessing the Curve involves three distinct areas:

Free: How do you get customers to know about, care about and
engage with what you do?

Expensive: How do you make it possible for people who love what
you do to spend lots of money on things they truly value?

Everything in between: What products, services, skills and technology do you need to move people from one end of the Curve to the
other?

To many readers of the book, understanding the free end of the
Curve might seem like a no-brainer. Free is the enemy of your existing
way of doing things, taking things that customers in their millions
used to be happy to pay for and making them now expect to get
things of the same quality without paying for them. It seems like it is
the enemy of books and music and movies and games. The key question seems to be not 'How do I create something that I can give away
for free?' but instead 'How can I stop giving away stuff that is expensive to create and instead charge for it?' For many others, though, free
is difficult. If you run events, or sell software-as-a-service, or make
tractors, how does free help you?

The important answer to that question is that free is not an objective in its own right. It is about creating something that has value to
your customers so that they start a dialogue with you. From that dialogue can come a relationship. Having a relationship is critical to
moving people along the demand curve. A current buzzword that
reflects this thinking is 'content marketing', a phrase that, alongside
'big data' and 'responsive design', is becoming rapidly overused.

Content marketing is best understood and used as part of the process of harnessing the Curve, rather than as a technique in isolation. To anyone thinking about improving their business using the Curve, whether their business is a content business or not, understanding content marketing is important. It is also getting harder.

Five years ago, marketing agencies wanting to add a bit of spice to a client campaign might suggest making a free 'advergame'. Advergames were typically programmed in Flash, played in a web browser like Internet Explorer or Firefox and cost little to make. They were rarely any good. They weren't bad because the digital agencies who were commissioned to make them didn't understand games – although many didn't – but because the budget and timescales they had to work to made it impossible to make a good game. That was all right, though, because the game was free, while most other games that people could play – on consoles, as casual downloads or on their phones – were expensive, typically costing anywhere from $5 to $50. As you now know, that changed as games on Facebook, smartphones and browsers became high-quality, free experiences that allowed users to spend at all points on the demand curve from zero to bucketloads. Those games are reaching very high levels of quality, as seen by titles like farming simulator *Hay Day*, strategy game *Clash of Clans* or endless runner *Temple Run*. Not only are these games free to download, but their creators pay enormous sums of money to persuade users to install them. Marketing services company Fiksu estimates that the cost of acquiring a loyal user, defined as someone who opens an app three times or more, reached $1.67 in December 2012, and remained above one dollar for the whole year.[1]

With rivals paying out substantial sums to acquire customers for their free titles, and recouping that money from those users who stick around to become loyal, spending fans, what hope do advertisers have in making cheap, disposable advergames whose primary selling point is that they are free?

The simple answer is that they have none, but many of them have not realized that yet. In the context of the Curve, content marketing makes most sense as the start of the journey. It is the beginning point of building a relationship with customers that will over time mature into a paying relationship. It is no longer good enough to put something out there and expect customers to flock to it just because it is free. There is more free content out there than any of us could possibly consume. You need to create something that resonates with your intended audience and build from there.

At the other end of the Curve, you need to have something that you can sell to people who love what you do. Something that speaks to more than just its marginal cost (particularly when it is digital, with a marginal cost close to zero). You need to have products or services that are differentiated by how they make your users feel. How they work with the handicap principle. How they allow users to show their discernment or taste or wealth or knowledge or expertise. You need to give the people who love what you do the most the opportunity to spend money on something that is exclusive or braggable, or that they would want all their friends to know about.

In between, though, is the difficult part. In between you need to change the way that you think. The process of adapting to the Curve is the process of embracing new skills, new technologies and new ways of working. It is both scary and exciting at the same time. It is also crucial that you do it.

The exact technology that you need to embrace will change. It always does. What is important is that you shift the mindset from product to service, from 'How many did I sell?' to 'What is my average revenue per user?' From 'I've finished that launch, what's next?' to 'How can I take this customer who has just discovered what we do and take them on a journey to becoming a superfan?'

It will involve understanding how your product resonates emotionally with your users, how you can harness that emotion, how to offer what you can for free while reserving that which superfans will value highly at the expensive end of the Curve. It will mean changing how you view your relationships with suppliers and retailers who are now part of your entire ecosystem that exists to serve your freeloaders and your superfans and everyone between, not just the beginning and end of your business process.

How can you do that? I don't know. I can give you a bunch of examples and ideas, and I am about to do just that. But there is no fixed prescription. There is no rule book that will work for every business or organization or creator. Everything is changing.

This is a time for experimentation and adaptation. It is a time to learn how to listen to your audience, how to incorporate rapid feedback into your business thinking and to figure out how to run cost-effective experiments that will help you create things that your audience will still value and pay for.

I can help you understand the principles. I can help you understand what to test and how to do it. I can show how others have done it successfully, and why I believe their experiments worked. I can show how other people's experiments failed too, and what we can learn from that. But you need to be the ones thinking about your customers, your fans, your superfans. They're not mine, they're yours, and you know them best.

Go and give them what they want.

Let's start with some basic thoughts on how to harness the Curve. What are you going to give away for free? How do you use your existing retail and other distribution partnerships in this new world? What will your high-end products look like, and how will you sell them?

If your product can easily be shared digitally, you already know what will be at the free end of your Curve: your product. If you make music or write books or produce moving images or games, it is a given that your product will be available for free somewhere in the world, legally or illegally. When it is so trivially cheap to distribute content using peer-to-peer networks, it will happen, and there is nothing that you can do about that.

Sometimes that isn't an issue. There is no one-to-one relationship between downloads of your product and lost sales. To give just one example: clients of mine have decided to promote their paid-for game on iPhone by making it free for a day and using a promotional service such as Free App A Day to spread the word. There has been the expected spike in downloads, often tens or hundreds of times more than the game was selling before the promotion. Not all those users become players. Somewhere between half and three-quarters of those game installs have never even been opened. Those users saw that the game was free for a day, downloaded it and forgot about it. To say that each of those downloads represents a lost sale would be wrong:

the app is sitting on the devices or in the iTunes accounts, entirely legally, of thousands of people who can't even be bothered to open it. They would have been unlikely to buy it.

I anticipate being asked often why this book is not available as a free ebook. I expect that at some point it will be, either as a promotional offer or because that has become the de facto standard for ebooks. As it stands, the price of an ebook in the UK seems to vary somewhere between 20p and £20 (in the US, $1 and $15), and I expect that is where the Curve will be priced. I am in no hurry to accelerate the race to free until a) I have to and b) I have a decent business model in place to benefit from the free spread of my ideas. For now, I anticipate my website* being the free part of my Curve, while this book is part of the journey my readers will undertake as some of them move from being freeloaders to being superfans. There may be consultancy or masterclasses or speaking opportunities. There might be an online training programme or a video series or a membership club. I will experiment, learn and adapt.

The same is true for music. Music can also be easily distributed for almost no cost and many users would prefer to get all their music for free, yet Alex Day, the independent musician who is also a YouTube star, makes most of his money from selling single tracks on iTunes. He gives his music away where it is appropriate (YouTube), and charges for it where there is still a market (iTunes). Why will people still buy a product on iTunes when it is available for free on a filesharing site? There are many possible reasons. Some people don't know how to use peer-to-peer networks.† Some people like the convenience of iTunes, storing all of their music in one place across multiple devices. Some people are scared that if they download from a place they don't trust, they will become infected with viruses or Trojans or other assorted malware. Others want to pay for music because they realize that musicians need to get paid in order to keep making it, or because they are just used to paying for music and haven't lost the habit.

Some of those reasons will be with us for ever. Others are legacy

---

* www.nicholaslovell.com. Do pay me a visit.
† I'm one of them. I've never used a torrent site in my life.

benefits of the traditional system, when distribution brands were trusted (as distinct from artist brands), when it was difficult to get a high-quality copy for free and when the places that you did get them were untrustworthy. Times are changing.

Meanwhile, even if musicians are not all embracing the Curve, Apple assuredly is. As are Amazon and Steam and many other leading technology companies. This is not because they are evil or manipulative, it is because they are sound businesses which understand the Curve. iTunes has its own superfans, its own whales who spend hundreds or maybe thousands of dollars buying music on its service. iTunes lets you download a lot of stuff for free (podcasts, free tracks and so on). It allows you to spend a lot of money on many different artists, which means that its monthly average revenue per user is not capped. It has the technology to understand who its heavy users are, to communicate with them via email and the front page of their iTunes account, to move them along the Curve. Apple has embraced the Curve.

Meanwhile, the musicians whose products Apple sells to monetize the Curve have none of the advantages. They are not getting users into their own personal ecosystem. They have no idea how much money someone is spending on their music. If they have ten tracks on sale on iTunes, and they sell one copy of each in a day, they have no idea if one person bought all ten or if ten people bought a different track each. They have no understanding of their customers, or how to move them along the Curve into superfandom.

I'm not picking specifically on Apple. The same is true for Amazon, Steam and any business which owns the customer relationship. Publishers and creators have, in their desperation to bring their products to market, sleepwalked into letting distribution partners have the one-to-one relationships to their customers. Worse than that, iTunes or Amazon or Steam have no loyalty to any product. They don't care if a customer who bought an Alex Day track or an Amanda Hocking book or a game from NimbleBit buys another product from those creators: they only care whether they buy another product, full stop.

There is a solution. It is to treat these distribution partners as part of your marketing funnel. As James Woollam of F+W suggests, be very focused on audience development. Free products are a starting point at the top of your content funnel, but so are paid ones. Every customer who buys something of yours from Amazon or Barnes & Noble or Steam or iTunes or a supermarket or anywhere else is a potential superfan. You just need to build ways to nurture that relationship, to make it direct, to build one-to-one connections with those fans so that, in the future, it is you recommending what other products someone who likes your stuff might like, not a faceless algorithm that doesn't give a damn whether you, particularly you, can afford to make new stuff. Don't hate Amazon and Apple and Steam for doing what they do so well, but understand what they are doing, and use it to your advantage.

Spotify is a different beast. I love Spotify as a consumer, but as an analyst I am more concerned. In the era of the Curve, subscriptions are a difficult business model. At the low end, subscriptions are an emotional barrier to entry, stopping people from trying out a service because they are aware that at some point a paywall will come crashing down (although to be fair, Spotify's free service is entirely free, just interrupted frequently by ads). At the high end, though, is where the real danger lies. There is no mechanism for the people who love what you do to spend lots of money on things they truly value. As a Spotify subscriber, I can't imagine why I would ever pay more than my monthly £9.99 ($9.99 in the US), and I do sometimes wonder why I pay as much as that for something which is so trivially cheap to share.

That is why I believe that people who criticize Spotify for the low payouts are missing the point. Lady Gaga's $167 for a million plays of her song is not necessarily a bad deal in the era of the Curve. The Trichordist, a website focused on the Ethical Internet and the protection of Artists Rights in a Digital Age (their capitals), tried to estimate how much revenue would accrue to rights holders from a massively successful Spotify.

> If Spotify can capture what most believe is an optimistic amount of paid subscribers in the USA (30 million) that would only generate $2.5 billion in revenue for rights holders. The revenues of the record industry collapsed between 1999 when it was $14.6 billion through 2009 when it had plummeted to $6.3 billion leaving a loss of $8.3 billion since that time. Maybe we're missing something. If streaming is the

future how does $2.5 billion in revenue from a massively successful Spotify replace the loss of $8.3 billion in annual earnings?[2]

My answer is that it can't and it won't. Those revenues have gone away for ever. The trivially cheap cost of distributing recorded music over the web and the disappearance of the album as the primary music product, together with a challenging competitive environment and a set of consumers who have grown up rarely expecting to have to pay for music, means that the sales of recorded music will never reach the $14.6 billion reported in 1999. It's gone away. For every major record label and artist bemoaning how much easier it was in the old days, there are new artists coming along looking for new ways to give away their music, connect with fans, charge for some things and not others and make it possible for those who love what they do to spend lots of money on things they truly value.

Spotify's weakness as a business is, to my mind, that it is a volume game. Price is fixed and the only measure of success is volume. In an era when one-to-one communications and granular price discrimination have become easy, a one-price-fits-all model seems archaic. That is not to say that Spotify won't succeed, but simply that it is leaving lots of money on the table while also having to compete with free. It is popular with the record labels not because it is the best way to deal with the challenges of the digital era, but because it is the easiest to understand. It is easy because it doesn't move away from the fixed-price, increase-revenue-by-increasing-volume model that is familiar and comforting.

Artists should take the advice of cellist Zoe Keating, who said, 'Spotify is awesome as a listening platform. Artists should view it as a discovery service rather than as a source of income.'[3] If it can be both, so much the better.

If the basic prescription of how to harness the Curve is simple – have something free (preferably) or very cheap to start your relationship with customers, use technology to deepen that relationship, to understand your customers and to communicate with them on a one-to-one basis, and then offer those who become superfans the opportunity to spend lots of money on things they truly value – the detail is more tricky. Every industry is different and every product or service within that industry will have a different emotional relationship with its customers. In the remainder of this chapter, I will try to set out some ways in which you can harness the Curve for a variety of businesses.

If you want insight and ideas at the expensive end of the Curve, you could profitably spend some time researching and backing some Kickstarter, Indiegogo or other crowdfunding sites. Crowdfunding is not the be-all and end-all, and it doesn't start with free (unless you count the entertainment value of watching projects fund or fail to fund), but it does include using technology to build direct relationships with fans and it is chock-full of inventive, extraordinary high-end rewards for the superfans.

Remember that anything can be made more valuable in a number of ways. Live is better than recorded. Limited editions are more valuable than the standard edition. Something signed is more valuable than something unsigned.

When science-fiction writer Cory Doctorow set out to find a way to make the limited edition of his short-story collection *With a Little Help* stand out as a special edition, not only did he go for high-quality printing and binding, he wrapped every copy in a burlap sack that had previously been used to transport coffee beans from Java. Every one of the purchasers of the $275 limited edition would get the aroma of fresh coffee bursting out of the packaging as they unwrapped the parcel that the postman delivered. That sort of thought is not always that expensive, but it makes the experience much more special in the eyes of the superfan. (Doctorow self-published *With a Little Help* and documented the process in detail online.[4] As at 28 March 2012, he had generated income of $45,182.65, expenses of $26,882.02 and a profit of $18,300.62. Not a huge amount of money but not bad for a short-story collection that no publisher would touch.)

The heart of my advice is that there is no fixed blueprint. Follow the basic rules but use your understanding of your audience and your creativity to give them something they will really value. Be flexible. Be creative. Be remarkable. Make people want to show the limited editions to their friends, to share and brag and boast about the things that they choose to spend lots of money on.

Make them happy to be superfans.

MUSIC

Give your music away for free. Build a community relationship with customers using your website, YouTube, Twitter, Facebook and any other channel that gives you access to your customers. Encourage your fans to share your music legally by making it available on YouTube, Spotify and other online services. Make it possible to buy your music legally in as much of the world as you can. Create bespoke physical artefacts (albums, T-shirts, hand-crafted this and artisan that) that discerning fans will value as an expression of who they are. Use events (Kickstarter campaigns, music tours, releases of art books that inspired you, anything) to create a moment in time that your fans can get behind and support. Tour, by all means, but create the bespoke high-end elements that some people will pay for. If you want to get $10,000 out of a single person, be inventive. Amanda Palmer allowed Kickstarter pledgers to pay her $10,000 to paint them clothed or nude. No one knew if it would work, and Palmer made it a limited edition of just ten pledges, but managed to sell only two. But she would never have known if she hadn't experimented, and her campaign would have been $20,000 poorer.

BOOKS

Books are an impossible category to simplify, because they encompass so many different ideas. If you write **non-fiction** aimed at business audiences, like *The Curve* or what Seth Godin does, have a website that gives away high-quality thoughts, ideas and content for free. Encourage people to sign up for your email lists with free ebooks or similar content. Offer books in physical form that people can pay for. Make the hardbacks an artefact so that people who own them will want to display them in their living room, not hide them away in a study. Manage the ebook pricing carefully as it trends to zero, but don't be the last to become free if it means you no longer have a wide audience. Create other products and services that fans of your work can access – video courses, online seminars, physical seminars, consultancies, speaking gigs. Make sure that your time is (generally) expensive while that which can be shared at low marginal cost is easy to share so that you spread the word, build a bigger audience and make it easier to charge a premium for your high-end offerings.

Fiction is harder, particularly for first-time authors. In fact, I think it's possible that self-publishing will be the route through which many, if not all, of the fiction writers of the future will be discovered. Their works will be available at little or no cost on Amazon and elsewhere. Instead of the gatekeeper being the literary agent and commissioning editor, it will be the hordes of readers and users on the open web. Good-quality content will catch the eye of someone – a community manager, a well-connected Twitterer, or even a traditional agent or editor – and the ebook will become a physical book. The publisher will no longer be at the heart of getting the product discovered, it will be about taking a product that is already discovered and making it more global, more professional, more profitable.

For established authors, the principles of 'owning the shelf' will apply. A successful fiction writer aspires to have an entire shelf of a bookstore devoted to them. It's why the covers of books by Terry Pratchett, Tom Clancy or J. K. Rowling are so distinctive. You can tell at a glance that the books in the popular series from these authors are connected without reading the author's name or the title of the book. The same happens with much genre fiction, with historical series and many more. This will only get worse. Publishers will give away books in the series in order to attract new readers, much like Michael Hicks and many other self-published authors do. The first book in the series might be permanently free to entice readers in. Other books might be offered for free on a regular basis, meaning a savvy reader might be able to get the entire *oeuvre* for nothing. At the same time, publishers will offer collector's editions, signed editions, limited editions. There will be dinners with the author and annual get-togethers. Depending on the nature of the book, there might be tours and events. A crime writer specializing in Glasgow might have weekend 'Discover Glasgow' tours complete with sightseeing, a talk and dinner with the author. Publishers will need to be inventive to create new experiences and events which work with the content of the book, the nature of the author and the desires of the superfans.

To readers filled with dread, worrying that writing will be secondary to showmanship, that the author will become a mere entertainer, that fiction will be dumbed down by this focus on performance, I say, 'Yes, that is a risk.' But it is a risk that is worth taking, I believe, because there is no alternative. The idea that we can keep things as they are is a pipe dream that will fade under the twin pressures of economics and technology. We must adapt.

I also think that the form of the novel will change. In the model I outlined above, it might make more sense for the first 'book' to be 30,000 words, not 90,000. The traditional length of the novel might be abbreviated because there is no longer any pressing need for a book that is 250 or so pages long. The ebook will thrive and so will the hardback, but the paperback will come under pressure. It will neither be the cheapest version of the book nor the most desirable, trapped in the middle of the Curve. This development will pose a particular challenge for genre writers reliant on holiday reading, the disposable chick-lit, crime novel or thriller that is purchased, read on the beach and then discarded. Those are the authors who will need to focus on building a base of committed fans to protect them from the disappearance of the casual reader who will, if they read them at all, get them for free on their Kindle.

Children's books provide yet another challenge. In many ways, they are the most insulated from the digital changes. The middle-class parents and grandparents who purchase the books obsess about minimizing screen time and are delighted when the child spends time with a physical book rather than an iPad, a television or a games console. They will continue to buy physical books to encourage reading, touching, learning and so on. At the same time, children will be embracing touch screens and the content they display. Touch screens are brilliant for children, particularly young ones, and I expect every primary-school child to have a touch screen device within my lifetime. Anyone who creates children's books and the formats that will emerge from them will need to stop thinking about the books as individual products and instead to start thinking about the child as a reader and a fan. How do you help the reader discover all that your content world has to offer, and how do you make parents comfortable with spending money on your products?

Puffin recently released seventeen book apps based on the adventures of Lynley Dodd's Hairy Maclary (a troublesome mongrel and his canine friends).[5] I think that their approach was a mistake. I would have released one app containing one or preferably several Hairy Maclary stories for free. Children and parents would get to know and love the stories in a high-quality app which they could enjoy together. Eventually parent or child (probably parent) would get bored with reading the same story over and over again and feel comfortable spending £2.99 ($4.50) on buying a single additional story as an upgrade. And then another one. And another. Puffin would have one app ranked very highly in the App Store, rather than seventeen apps spread throughout it. They would have better data on repeat visits, on usage, on whether they were selling all seventeen apps to a small number of people or some of the apps to lots more. They would be building a connection with the families, possibly even a community, instead of selling seventeen products.

Oxford University Press has gone partway down this road with their series *Read with Biff, Chip and Kipper*. This product has two price points in the App Store: free or £149.99 ($219.99). (My jaw did drop when I saw that figure.) The free version contains a few pages selected from different books designed to help readers of different ages and abilities learn how to read on their own. Once users have had a taste of the experience, they can upgrade within the app by buying some of the books at £3.99 ($5.99) or all of them at once for £149.99. However, OUP are failing at the free end because they don't give users a good experience. They make it clear that they are getting just a taster of the full experience, partial stories that jump around. OUP has got over the hardest hurdle faced by the producer of any app: getting a user to download and use it. However, they then say to their customer, 'Sorry, you can't have the full version, because you are an evil freeloader. Until you pay up, you can only have this partial, poor experience.' Some parents will pay because they are familiar with the brand from the physical books but others will conclude that they have not yet experienced the digital version sufficiently, they still don't know if their children will like it, and besides, there are lots of great free apps available on the App Store.

The approaches taken by both OUP and Puffin are redolent of

old-school thinking, when the aim was to sell products rather than attract users, and when you couldn't give away something for free because then you wouldn't have anything to sell. Both are taking steps in the right direction, but they are still trying to protect the best of the old world while failing to embrace the best of the new. I am delighted that Puffin and OUP are experimenting, because we all learn and improve from experimentation. My most fervent hope is that they learn from the experiment.

LAW AND ACCOUNTANCY

If ever there was an industry that was ripe for disruption, it is the business of law. Much of the bread-and-butter work of lawyers could be given away for free. Standard wills, employment contracts, non-disclosure agreements, freelance agreements and many more contracts could be offered for free simply for the price of registering. Companies such as Legal Zoom and Clerky already exist offering these services at rates that are much lower than a practising lawyer would charge. A law firm might start a relationship with potential clients through offering these contracts, with no legal advice as to their relevance to the client's situation. Over time, that relationship could expand to include bespoke contracts, training, litigation and specific advice on difficult areas of law. Lawyers could choose to give up their fees for the same, dull, repetitive contracts which can easily be shared across the web and instead focus on the value-added end of being a lawyer, giving situation-specific advice on negotiation, legal alternatives and so on.

The same is true of accountancy. I already pay Free Agent, an online book-keeping service, about £300 ($450) a year, a fraction of the amount I would need to pay a book-keeper or accountant to run my accounts. Free Agent does not have an upsell path beyond the subscription, but it is not hard to imagine a professional accounting firm offering book-keeping services entirely for free over the web, and then applying a modest charge for preparing statutory accounts, dealing with tax affairs and helping the client save money in its financial dealings.

Of course, both law and to a lesser extent accountancy are amongst the last 'guilds' left in the commercial world, self-regulated and with a vested interest in protecting the status quo for the benefit of insiders, not users of the guild's services. It will be fascinating to see how the legal and accounting industries respond to the challenges of the digital era and the Curve in the twenty-first century.

EVENTS

As discussed above, combine high-end, bespoke events with content marketing or magazine publishing. Use the power of free to keep and engage the community who are interested in your events during the long periods of time when your events are not happening. Use the communications ability of the web to allow delegates to pick and choose from a smorgasbord of offers by letting them, for example, pay extra to sit at the table of a high-profile speaker during the gala dinner.

MOVIES AND TELEVISION

The movie and television industries have an interesting challenge. On the one hand, they have more stars and free press coverage than almost any other field. On the other, the stars have their own strategies for success, which may or may not tie into the success of the movie or the television series being promoted. Production companies will have to strengthen the ties between the audience and the core brand, rather than between the audience and the stars.

Movies are either free (pirated DVDs and downloads) or have a middling price (the price of a cinema ticket or a legal DVD). Some executives think that the movie industry is already exploiting a Curve strategy through 'windowing', the process by which movies are released to movie theatres, to pay-per-view, to DVD, to pay television and eventually to free-to-air. By now, I hope you realize that is not a true Curve strategy because it is a volume game: the most committed fan is not spending a hundred times more than a casual viewer. Movies do, of course, exploit many ancillary rights: books, merchandise, and so on, particularly when they are franchise movies or aimed at children.

Longer term we will see movie makers experiment with more direct relationships with fans. The first wave of experimentation (which is already starting) will be independent filmmakers using crowdfunding sites like Kickstarter to get movies made. They will sell the right to be in the film, to attend the premiere, to affect the plot, to get a credit on IMDB and anything else they can think of. Hollywood will take longer to experiment, because they are still about the volume game, and the big are getting bigger. Perhaps Hollywood will never embrace the Curve, and the Curve will be a funding model for independent movies only, not blockbusters.

Television is changing rapidly too. Power is shifting from those who control the means of distribution (broadcasters) to those who control the means of production (production companies). I would be much happier being a production company like Shine, Endemol or Fremantle than I would being a terrestrial broadcaster which has only one geographic region to serve. (Most broadcasters are also production companies, which insulates them from some of this risk, but this shift of power remains a real threat.)

As film critic Roger Lloyd said, television is becoming as much about self-expression as music is.[6] I expect sales of boxed sets, particularly those that are high-end artefacts, to be valuable. I expect independent television makers to experiment with crowdfunding, with fans participating in production and with having live events involving stars from the show to make more money.

We are already seeing stage musicals springing up based on old movies such as *The Bodyguard*. This is a fascinating way of extracting $50 or more from an audience that would barely pay $5 for the DVD.

Movies and television will be slow to adapt. The advantages of the theatre experience for movies and the broadcaster oligopoly for television will mean that these industries will maintain their old ways of doing business for a long time.* I also expect them to spearhead the

---

* While television is fragmenting into hundreds of channels, the majority of power still rests with the handful of major broadcast networks in each territory. This is an oligopoly that still controls a vast proportion of the production budgets for content and attracts much of the advertising revenue. This may change one day, but for now they are one of the best ways for advertisers to reach a mass market.

demands for legislative change to stem piracy. My hopes rest on independent film makers turning to the web as both a funding source and a distribution channel, to show us all how audiovisual entertainment can adapt to the twenty-first century.

THE PREMIER LEAGUE

Of all the industries that ought to benefit from the Curve, football should head the list. It has a social context, oodles of free marketing in the endless coverage it receives on television, in newspapers and on social media and it has fans prepared to spend lots of money on supporting the teams they love. Football has an offering at every stage of the Curve. Fans can watch the matches cheaply in a pub or at a friend's house. They can subscribe to cable or satellite to access matches whenever they want. They can go to games and buy season tickets. Attending all nineteen away matches played by Manchester United in 2012/13 would have cost £840 ($1,300) in admission tickets alone. Fans can buy team strips and memorabilia. (I was surprised to learn that a unique scarf can be bought at every Premier League match, complete with fixture details and the date.) Tickets for the FA Cup Final sell at up to £10,000 ($15,000). Serious fans can expect to spend £100,000 on supporting their team over their lifetime.[7]

The ultimate status symbol is not to buy a season ticket or attend every match: it is to become a Premier League owner, with tycoons such as Roman Abramovich, Malcolm Glazer and Tony Fernandes, paying tens or hundreds of millions of pounds for the privilege.

Yet there is a problem, so far as the Curve is concerned. Despite the costs, Premier League football is as popular as it has ever been. BT and Sky paid £3 billion for the rights to broadcast matches over three years from 2013/14.[8] Rights to the Premier League are so attractive to subscription broadcasters because for many fans they are must-have programming that helps keep subscription rates high and churn low. As the threat of piracy increases for these matches, a Curve strategy would suggest accepting the freeloaders while allowing the fans to spend lots of money on things they truly value. The challenge for football is that it may already have done all it can to let the fans spend lots of money. It is possible that if technological and legislative measures fail to halt the spread of piracy, football will be unable to grow its revenues by embracing its fans, simply because it has already done it so well.

Since the commercialization of football has largely enriched the players beyond all measure at the expense of their fans, perhaps that isn't a bad thing after all.

CHARITY

Harnessing the Curve for charity presents an interesting challenge. On the one hand, charities already have a strategy for allowing people to donate anything from a few pence up to the large sums given by the most generous benefactors and patrons. A Curve strategy would focus on building an online presence that made a real connection with potential donors. A good starting point for a small charity would be to ask, 'If someone were to land on our site, what question might they be asking?' and make sure it is answered. They should then work to encourage visitors to sign up to something such that the charity could talk to them again, perhaps via Twitter, Facebook, YouTube or, ideally, email. (Note that offering the people the chance to sign up to your newsletter is often a turn off. Do you actually want to receive dozens of regular newsletters? Do you?) A better strategy is to offer something that a user might actually want there and then: some information on autism for an autism charity, an introduction to opera for an opera charity, insight into the challenges facing the environment for an ecological charity. It is all about building a long-term relationship with potential donors through giving them for free something that costs you nothing to duplicate after the initial effort of creation.

The greatest challenge concerning donations lies in managing the high end of the Curve. Some people want to be very open about the amount they donate to charity while others prefer to be discreet. As we saw in the Humble Bundle, where users are able to pay as much or as little as they like, it can be beneficial to show potential donors how much other people donate on average, to give them reasons to pay more than the average and to present an anchor price point to give people some guidance on how much to donate.

In many ways, harnessing the Curve for a charity is about taking what charities have always done – talked to supporters, asked for money – and doing it in a structured way.

MANUFACTURERS AND SERVICE PROVIDERS

Suppliers of services and physical goods should aim to be a repository of useful information for their target markets. Home Depot uses YouTube videos to draw customers into its physical shops and e-commerce site. King Arthur Flour offers free online recipes and advice to would-be bakers, which not only strengthens the brand value of their premium flour but also enables them to sell products and services such as baking masterclasses to their biggest fans. Marcus Sheridan of River Pools has become a leading and trusted source of information on the ups and downs of fibreglass swimming pools and as a result has generated significant revenue growth even during a prolonged recession. The key is to offer free content, information or experiences that resonate with your target market and turn them from being passers-by to people who are engaged with your brand for the long haul.

NEWSPAPERS

Finding a Curve strategy for the newspaper business is hard, but not impossible. An understanding of the Curve shows why a hard paywall strategy is so challenging: the Curve aims to have a large audience so that you can find those customers who love what you do enough to pay more. A hard paywall is more like a traditional, pre-digital business where you are either a customer or not, with little middle ground.

The industry is watching experiments like those of Andrew Sullivan with interest. Sullivan is a British journalist and blogger who now lives in the US and blogs about US politics, culture and society at The Dish, which was, until recently, commercially tied to the Daily Beast.

In early 2013, Sullivan announced that he was breaking from the

Daily Beast. He wants to see whether he can fund the annual running cost of a news and analysis site from donations and subscriptions, but without advertisements. The business model is evolving rapidly as Sullivan learns more about his audience. Sullivan has tightened the 'meter'. Users used to be able to read seven stories in full for free every thirty days. That has changed to five stories every sixty days, a porous paywall that is designed to showcase the best of Sullivan's content to casual readers arriving from a social media link or search referral while making those who visit more often pay for access. He initially planned to charge $19.99 for access, but the night before he put the experiment live, he decided to leave the amount customers needed to pay blank but with a minimum of $19.99, so customers could pay more if they wished to. By March 2013, The Dish had made $660,000 from 25,000 subscribers. Leaving that box blank has earned The Dish $100,000, estimates Sullivan.[9]

Sullivan's experiment is not yet a proven success. He hasn't reached his target of $900,000 at the time of writing (May 2013) and even if he hits it, that figure is still only paying for a small team. However, with the exception of leaving the amount-to-pay box blank, it is not a Curve strategy. Sullivan's paywall is all about limiting access. I think it would be helpful if he could experiment with different models to allow readers to fund him in different ways, while making sure that it is easy for fly-by readers to discover his work. Sullivan's strategy is fascinating but may need to be adapted in two areas: making it easier for new readers to get access to his writing to start the process of becoming superfans, and giving superfans a clear opportunity to spend lots of money to support Sullivan in a way that they value.

Last year I was talking with the digital director of the *New Statesman*, a left-leaning British periodical with an illustrious history. Like many media businesses, it is wrestling with how to adapt to an online world. I proposed the following thought experiment as a potential business model:

'Your audience doesn't want just to read the news. They want the *New Statesman* to help change the world. How about we let them be part of it. Start an "upstanding journalism" scheme. Take a leaf out of the crowdfunding book. Make it possible for people to contribute to a fund that directly goes to fund investigative journalism. It might dig into the expenses of elected officials. It might seek out stories of whistleblowers who have been intimidated or cover-ups perpetrated by the powerful. It will live by William Randolph Hearst's dictum that the news is what people don't want you to print, and everything else is just advertising.

'Your readers could contribute at different levels. For £20 they could be a supporter, with a badge alongside their comments on the website. For £100, they could be a concerned citizen, with exclusive access to premium content and a T-shirt showcasing their support. At high tiers, they might become patrons who fund individual salaries or instigators who can help identify areas to research. If you play this right, you might get high-profile individuals paying tens of thousands of pounds to support you.'

This thought experiment takes the idea that what some people would value is helping support the investigation of the rich, powerful or corrupt and turns it into something that people can pay for. It used to be that people subsidized this public good through buying a newspaper in order to read the sports results and television listings. That model is no longer working, and this seems to me to be a worthwhile experiment.

It is also a *cheap* experiment. You could test the viability of this experiment simply by building a web page explaining what you wanted to do and asking people to pay for you to do it. If no one pays, it turns out that this model is not going to work. You may have to adapt your business to become an events business, or even a dating business. (In the UK, both the *Daily Telegraph* and the *Guardian* have successful dating services.) As magazines are becoming more events driven, so I suspect will newspapers, offering wine tastings with their wine critics, evening audiences with foreign reporters and anything else they can think of.

What I do believe is that newspapers need to be accessible to a wide readership (which limits the effectiveness of paywalls) while also allowing those avid readers of news and supporters of journalism to pay more than the casual reader (which is also a limitation of paywalls). Newspapers need to solve that conundrum. A porous paywall is a good start, but the real success will come when they stop thinking of their customers as either subscribers or evil pirates and embrace a continuum from paying nothing to paying enormous sums.

COACHES AND TRAINERS

Anyone who teaches anything can be a beneficiary of the Curve. Yoga teachers. Martial artists. People who offer classes in pottery or wood-working or speaking Mandarin or singing opera. Personal trainers. Nutritionists. Anyone who services clients with their particular needs. The basic strategy is to use a website to offer high-quality advice in your area of expertise. You might offer blog posts on relaxation techniques. You might post YouTube videos showing how to throw a pot or cut a dovetail joint. You might publish a healthy-eating menu for a whole week, complete with the shopping list containing every ingredient your customer would need to buy, or a plan for learning guitar chords in six weeks. You are obviously going to have some competition: if every single coach, trainer and instructor in the world had a website, there would be a lot of free content available. There will be more famous trainers than you in the world. Won't everyone gravitate to the biggest and best? If, say, Eric Clapton put up a series of 'Learn to Play the Guitar with Slowhand', why would anyone watch yours?

The answer is that you are not competing with the biggest and most famous people on the planet. You can't. You are offering something different – a local, personal, one-to-one service. You may have to use traditional marketing techniques to acquire customers in the first place. Advertisements in the local gym or community centre. Targeted campaigns with Google AdWords. Leaflets and flyers. The objective of those marketing campaigns is to drive people to your website. The objective of the website is to start the process of connecting with fans.

Your core product will remain what it always was: one-to-one teaching or classes teaching groups in your specialist area. You will now have a website as a way of building a direct connection with those people outside your classes, and of giving potential custom-ers the confidence that you know what you are talking about. Over time you may develop a suite of products: free advice on the website; a cheap ebook; an expensive self-published physical book; an online course made up of videos, written materials and feedback ses-sions. These can range in price from the very cheap to the very expensive. The most expensive should be that which is most scarce: your time.

RESTAURANTS

Restaurants can follow the same pattern. Use the website to start building a relationship with customers. If you make Thai food, talk about it. If you care about provenance, talk about it and help people understand why it matters and help them source their own food better. A restaurant already benefits from the marketing value of its physical location, so an online presence is about building a relationship with those of your customers who have the potential to become regulars. You can set up regular events on the quieter parts of the week by offering themed nights or special events.

By using the direct relationship you have with customers through the web, you can determine what works and what doesn't – without even running the event. For example, post on your website that if thirty people book for dinner at your restaurant on a Tuesday night, there will be a poetry reading. Belly dancing. A talk from a master cheesemonger. A demonstration on how to prepare a gurnard. If thirty people don't book, don't hold the event. You've lost nothing and learned something about your customers. At the high end you can offer customers gala evenings with a premium entrance price and exclusive dishes. For your very best customers, you could offer to send one of your chefs round to their house to cook dinner.

The joy of the web is that you can test many of your ideas on a website without having to put them into practice if the demand is not there. Be inventive and be courageous.

ART

Artists create artefacts that naturally sit at the high end of the Curve. They are bespoke, personal, scarce and have a value that is anchored in how much someone is prepared to pay more than in the amount it cost to make.

An artist, whether that be a painter, a photographer, a sculptor or any of the myriad forms of art maker, needs to achieve three things through a Curve strategy. They need to sell their creations, they need to allow people to buy something at prices ranging from low to high, and they need to build awareness of their work both to drive sales but also to push up the prices of their top-end artefacts.

So an artist should have a website. It should not only be a sales website. It should be the starting point for a user to move from someone who has only just discovered an artist to a true fan. Perhaps there is a mailing list that offers occasional small pieces of art to brighten someone's day. Or by signing up, users get a wallpaper background for their PC desktop or mobile screen that captures some of the artist's talent or spirit. There might be cheap products – postcards, Christmas cards, thank-you cards – and medium products like prints or small originals.

More value might be added by the tricks that artists are already familiar with: Numbered editions. Original signatures. Dedications. Personal elements.

An artist might then use the website to take on commissions or, more scalably, to sell the works already created. A Curve strategy would allow an artist to make more money from visitors who are still on their journey towards superfandom while also potentially increasing the amount an artist can charge for high-end products through increased awareness, reputation and a closer connection with their biggest fans.

TRANSPORT

Budget airlines are already harnessing the Curve. Airlines such as Ryanair, easyJet, Jet Blue and SouthWest offer flights for a very low price, sometimes even for free.* They charge extra for each bag you check into the hold. They charge extra to check in at the airport rather than online. They charge extra to board first, to pick your seat before other passengers or for more legroom. They charge for inflight meals,

* Except for airport charges. And taxes. And fuel surcharges.

for inflight drinks, and threaten, probably for the publicity, to charge for access to the inflight toilets. Customers who are very price sensitive can get very cheap flights. For those who want to travel on that route but are not price sensitive, the upgrades for extra legroom, speedy boarding, airport check-in and a cup of airline coffee are worth it. The airline uses the promise of cheap flights to attract customers but now has sophisticated ways of satisfying the differing demands of different customers.

RETAIL

Retailers ought to start with an advantage. They already have customers. They have CRM systems to help them know more about their customers. They can satisfy high spenders simply by letting them buy lots of things from them. Yet in my experience most retailers are focused on selling products, not satisfying users. Their databases and analyses rest on whether products are shifting and how many units they have sold. The Curve suggests thinking of their audience in a different way. In an online world with unlimited shelf space and alternative retailers just a search away, retailers need to focus on relationships.

Naked Wines is an online wine merchant that champions independent winesellers. Of course, you can just buy wine from them. The website also offers a community and discussion groups for novices and experts alike. More committed wine buyers can become a Naked Angel, committing to giving Naked Wines at least £20 ($30) every month which accumulates until they choose to spend it. This commitment gives Naked Wines the financial security to, for example, buy the entire output of a vineyard, helping secure a great price for everyone. They offer tastings and T-shirts and other events. A superfan of Naked Wines can spend hundreds of pounds a year and feel like they belong to a community that is, at its heart, a business that sells wine.

Retailers that will thrive in the digital world will be more than just a place where a transaction happens. They will understand their customers. They will work out how to offer them things that they want. Like the budget airlines, they will offer low prices to those who are price sensitive but for those who are prepared to pay for the exclusive, for the premium, for the personalized or for an experience, the option will be there.

FASHION

Fashion might be like art, or it might be like retail. The more bespoke the product, the more the Curve strategy of a fashion business might resemble the strategy of an artist. Otherwise, it will probably look more like a retailer. The challenge for fashion businesses, making clothes that can be purchased on the high street, in department stores or via their own website, is when to be happy making revenue because another retailer closes the sale with the buyer and when to fight tooth and nail to build a one-to-one relationship with that person.

Let's try a thought experiment. Imagine that the key performance indicator (KPI) at a fashion house was not 'How many frocks did I sell?' but 'What is my average revenue per user?'

I could imagine a strategy where high street retailers are a sales outlet but also a customer acquisition outlet. The fashion house aims to build one-to-one relationships with the best customers, say 10 per cent of them. Those are the ones who love the brand, not just an occasional frock. They will be receptive to email marketing, to offers, to buying something every month or something several times. Some will buy everything in the new collection each time.

Venture capitalist Nic Brisbourne says that for top fashion boutiques, online or offline, 10 per cent of their customers make up the majority of their revenues.[10] That suggests that fashion boutiques are already businesses that manage a user journey from casual purchaser to superfan. By finding a way to offer something at the free end of the Curve, and getting better at using technology to help users make that journey, fashion businesses will be able to thrive by building meaningful relationships with the customers who love what they do.

For every business or creator, the three questions are the same: What can I give away for free that I can make once and give away as many times as I like for no extra cost? How do I make sure that when people like my free stuff, I can talk to them again? How can I offer those people a range of different products or services at a range of different price points, so that those who only want to spend a little with me can do so, as well as those who want to spend an enormous amount?

If you can answer all three of those questions, you have cracked the Curve.

The challenges facing businesses in the twenty-first century are legion. The solution is not to use the lobbying power of the incumbents to persuade governments to prop up ailing business models. It is to adapt to the changes through a process of structured experimentation and learning. It is to embrace free as an opportunity while building dialogues and relationships with end users that resonate on an emotional level.

It is a scary time to be in business, and a wonderful one. There has never been a better time to be in the business of delighting your customers.

Epilogue: The Curve Redux

It has taken me a while to formulate the theory of the Curve.

I've been a believer in the power of free since I took a business called GameShadow from being a subscription service to a free service in 2007. I've been a believer in the transformative nature of the web since I was an investment banker and entrepreneur during the dotcom boom and beyond. I have experimented with content marketing, high-end consultancy and products in between at GAMESbrief for five years. I have worked with clients taking their traditional single-player games and watched, overjoyed, as they transformed them into highly profitable free-to-play games that allow users a great experience for free while letting those who love the game spend lots of money on their primary hobby.

I am not convinced that all products have to be free, but I am convinced that all products have to compete with free. Free is going to become the default price point for anything that can be shared digitally, not just content but, with the advent of 3D printing, physical goods as well. At the same time, people who sell stuff that can't be shared digitally – tractors, say, or breakfast cereal – will have to embrace new marketing techniques that build real connections with those users. The smartest ones will use these content marketing strategies to build one-to-one relationships with their customers, to learn what they value and eventually to sell high-level products to their biggest fans.

Everyone, in every organization, will begin to be part of the marketing process. In an age when a minor transgression in customer service can be instantly shared across social networks, every interaction with a customer or potential customer becomes a marketing transaction. At the same time, we are moving away from the era of the mass market to the era of mass customization. We are becoming freed from the tyranny of the physical and the only thing constraining us is habit: the habits of a lifetime and the habits of many lifetimes before us.

It is an exciting time. We can learn faster than ever before, using new techniques such as validated learning to test our theories, to prove or disprove them, to learn from them and to develop. We can use the power of free to reach wider audiences than ever before and we can use the one-to-one communication of the web to connect with superfans and allow them to spend lots of money on things they truly value.

One final plea: don't take anything in this book as the only way. I can tell you the principles and explain to you why I believe they work. I can show you examples of what has worked and give you ideas, thoughts and suggestions on how to apply it to your own business, sector or area of expertise. But you are more expert on your business or sector than I am, and there are many more of you than there are of me. Take *The Curve* as your starting point, and be brave. Experiment, but survive the experiment. Learn and adapt. Share your results. Share them within your organization and, if you wish, with me. I'd love to hear from you at www.nicholaslovell.com.

Above all, embrace this challenge. Find new ways of doing cool stuff and your fans will love you. Whether you are free, expensive or everywhere in between, experiment, learn and adapt. That's what will enable you to keep doing what you want to do. There's nothing holding you back.

Go on, give it a go.

Acknowledgements

Many authors and writers have inspired me, and acted as the starting point for the ideas that became *The Curve*. Chris Anderson's *The Long Tail* and *Free* showed how the web changes business in fundamental ways, while *Makers* showed how manufacturing changes when web-style disruptions come to physical items. Seth Godin, in *Tribes*, *Purple Cow* and many other works, shows how important it is to be remarkable and connect with your audience. Michael Masnick of TechDirt identified the formula of success for artists in a digital age as CwF+RtB (Connect with Fans plus Reason to Buy), while Kevin Kelly first espoused the 1,000 True Fans concept. Nassim Taleb, Tim Harford and Eric Ries all write about how to function in a world of extreme uncertainty and have transformed the way I perceive the world. Psychologists Dan Ariely, Elliot Aronson, Robert Cialdini, Sheeny Iyengar, Geoffrey Miller and Carol Tavris have helped me understand how humans make decisions, establish value and build relationships with brands, artists and suppliers. Richard Rumelt, Joe Pine and James Gilmore have all helped me understand how business and strategy go hand in hand, and where to look for value. Without their research and thought, *The Curve* could never have come to fruition.

Many people have helped me over twenty years of my career, five years at GAMESbrief and more recently as I wrote *The Curve*. If I left you out of this list, I apologize. If you think I should have thanked you, I probably should have done. Thank you.

In 2011 I asked a dozen people to help me figure out a central metaphor for a book I had in mind. Individuals from venture capital and law, television and games, magazines and the web came together in the offices of law firm Osborne Clarke, where I set out the very preliminary thoughts on what would become the Curve. We spent hours in that room and failed to come up with the metaphor. We did spend a long time discussing the kernel of the idea that would become the Curve, though, and that day convinced me that there was something to this idea in my head. Thank you to Nic Brisbourne, Paul Gardner, Justin Gayner, Dan Griliopoulos, Kevin Heery, Tadhg Kelly, Patrick O'Luanaigh, James Wallis and Gill Whitehead.

Thank you to venture capitalist Mark Evans of Balderton Capital. A catch-up meeting over a cup of coffee in 2009 planted the seed that grew into *The Curve*. It wasn't obvious at the time, but a passing comment on how encyclopedias showed how value was being redistributed between content creators, publishers and consumers, started a process that transformed my world view.

Numerous people agreed to be interviewed for *The Curve*. My thanks to David Barnard, Brandon Curiel, Alex Day, Eric Hautemont, Sharna Jackson, Ian Marsh, Simon Read, Torsten Reil, Benji Rogers, Alice Taylor, Chris Thorpe and Victoria Vox. Thanks also to all the people I spoke to about *The Curve* for helping me to experiment with different ways of expressing the core ideas.

Many friends and business colleagues agreed to review the manuscript. Others helped me with particular points I was struggling with. More provided ideas or insight on questions or issues that were niggling me. I am particularly grateful to Barnaby Willitts-King, Chris Hunt, Rebecca Cassidy, Justin Gayner and Ben Sipe.

The team at GAMESbrief (Zoya Street, Rob Fahey, Heather Cotton, Elizabeth Cunningham, Jay Margalus) handled my absence to write *The Curve* with aplomb. My clients were equally accommodating about extended absences to write.

I am grateful to everyone, and there are very many of you, who have helped me in business over the last twenty years. Thank you for helping me to think, for challenging me when I have sounded glib or when my arguments were not thought through. Thank you for employing me, and for working with me. Thank you to my readers at GAMESbrief for caring about the business of games enough to read what I write, to challenge it and to improve it. Thank you in particular to everyone who has offered guest writing on the site. It is improved for having a multitude of voices.

Thanks, for many reasons, to Michael Acton Smith, Jon Bernstein, Ben Board, Dan Buckley, Jennifer and Jonathan Chadwick, Charles Chapman, Tom Chatfield, Steve Chippington, Fintan Coyle, Richard Cumbley, Stuart Dredge, Robert Dudley, Chris Etches, Stephen Francis, Nick Gibson, Simon Goldrick, Tony Gowland, Wil Harris, Leonie Hirst, John Holmes, Dan House, Jon Howell, Eric Huang, Ian Livingstone, Brett Lock, Stephen Lovegrove, Juan Mateos-Garcia, Pete Morrish, Joe Murray, Ilkka Paananen, Griff Parry, Andy Payne, Simon Protheroe, Jas Purewal, Anna Rafferty, Chris Ruen, Andrew Smith, Daegal Tsang, George Walkley, Alex Waterston, Tim Whiting and Richard Williamson.

I would like to thank my agent, Jon Elek, without whom the book would never have got this far. My editors at Portfolio, Joel Rickett and Niki Papadopoulos, were a pleasure to work with, despite their excellent detailed comments meaning that I had substantial rewriting to do. Thanks also to my copy-editor Trevor Horwood and to the production team and designers at Portfolio who turned my ideas into the volume you see before you.

Thank you to you for reading. If you want to help me improve these ideas, and share your own, do visit www.nicholaslovell.com and become part of the conversation.

Thank you to my parents for an education which taught me that I can do most things I want to, if only I put my mind to it.

Finally, I'd like to thank Catherine, Alasdair and Lucy. This book was written in a short space of time around a busy consulting schedule. Thank you for letting me write in the play room. And thank you for giving me the time to finish it. I love you all.

Notes

PREFACE

1 www.theage.com.au/news/web/steal-music-nails-frontman-tells-fans/2007/09/18/1189881482912.html

2 For more on Reznor's background, read Jonathan Gold's *Rolling Stone* interview from 1994. www.rollingstone.com/music/news/love-it-to-death-19940908

3 http://en.wikipedia.org/wiki/Trent_Reznor

4 www.nndb.com/people/534/000025459/

5 www.people.com/people/archive/article/0,,20105007,00.html

6 http://trent-reznor.narod.ru/1994_article19-original.html; original by Jonathan Fine, in *Option Magazine*, July/August 1994.

7 www.allmusic.com/artist/nine-inch-nails-p5033/biography

8 www.music2dot0.com/archives/36

9 http://leisureblogs.chicagotribune.com/turn_it_up/2008/03/reznors-one-wee.html

1. THE CURVE

1 http://money.cnn.com/2010/02/02/news/companies/napster_music_industry/

2 Henry Ford, *My Life and Work* (NuVision, 2007), p. 35; http://books.google.co.uk/books?id=bUbdMRx43JgC

3 James Gilmore and Joseph Pine, *Authenticity* (Harvard Business School Press, 2007), pp. 5–6.

4 www.ew.com/ew/article/0,,20532978_2,00.html

5 www.viragobooks.net/bookclub/josephine-harts-introduction-to-damage/

6 www.independent.ie/lifestyle/the-life-and-death-of-josephine-hart-2672754.html

7 www.guardian.co.uk/media/2007/mar/11/pressandpublishing.books
8 www.absolutewrite.com/novels/alexandra_cooper.htm
9 www.guardian.co.uk/books/2012/jan/12/amanda-hocking-self-publishing
10 http://slushpilehell.tumblr.com/post/13513202171
11 www.amazon.com/Last-Man-Who-Knew-Everything/dp/0452288053
12 http://youtube-global.blogspot.co.uk/2013/05/heres-to-eight-great-years.html
13 www.nytimes.com/2013/02/28/business/smallbusiness/increasing-sales-by-answering-customers-questions.html?pagewanted=all&_r=0

2. SCARCITY AND ABUNDANCE

1 https://twitter.com/ladygaga/status/266036323394142209
2 https://twitter.com/ladygaga/status/266197568667676672
3 www.readwriteweb.com/archives/top_10_youtube_videos_of_all_time.php
4 www.techdirt.com/articles/20100524/0032549541.shtml
5 www.ifpi.org/content/section_resources/dmr2011.html
6 www.ifpi.org/content/library/DMR2012.pdf; www.ifpi.org/content/library/dmr2010.pdf; http://en.wikipedia.org/wiki/List_of_best-selling_singles
7 www.forbes.com/sites/zackomalleygreenburg/2011/01/12/why-lady-gaga-will-earn-100-million-in-2011/
8 Advertising is generally sold on a CPM basis. CPM (bizarrely, it stands for cost per thousand) is an advertising metric for how much an advertiser will pay or a media owner will charge for 1,000 impressions of an advertisement. The CPM can vary from over $100 for a highly targeted website or publication to only a few cents for those annoying ads for teeth whitening or suspicious-looking security products; http://techcrunch.com/2012/08/15/online-video-ads-all-up-in-your-grill/
9 http://torrentfreak.com/lady-gaga-earns-slightly-more-from-spotify-than-piracy-091121/. The figure of $167 was originally publicized by Swedish newspaper *Espressen* and reported on TorrentFreak. Spotify hit back at these accusations, arguing that this figure was misleadingly low for many reasons, such as that it was in the early days of Spotify, when the rates paid to artists were still being determined, that it was related to only some of the income Lady Gaga received from Spotify and was for a single territory (Sweden) for a short period of time. www.telegraph.co.uk/technology/7590782/Spotify-rejects-claims-that-it-rips-off-artists.html
10 www.smh.com.au/technology/technology-news/from-lady-gaga-to-the-future-of-social-media-20121105-28sv7.html

11 www.forbes.com/sites/victoriabarret/2012/11/13/dropbox-hits-100-million-users-says-drew-houston/

12 http://assets.panda.org/downloads/bottled_water.pdf; www.bottledwater.org/content/us-consumption-bottled-water-shows-significant-growth-increasing-41-percent-2011

13 Gunnar Knapp, Cathy A. Roheim and James L. Anderson, *The Great Salmon Run: Competition Between Wild and Farmed Salmon* (TRAFFIC North America/World Wildlife Fund, 2007); www.traffic.org/species-reports/traffic_species_fish25.pdf

14 Chris Anderson, *Free* (Random House Business Books, 2009), p. 50.

15 Ibid., p. 46.

16 Ibid., p. 180.

3. COMPETITION, ECONOMICS AND A MAN CALLED BERTRAND

1 www.youtube.com/watch?v=ftf4riVJyqw

2 http://commons.wikimedia.org/wiki/File:IPhone_sales_per_quarter.svg#Data_and_references

3 www.slideshare.net/kleinerperkins/2012-kpcb-internet-trends-yearend-update

4 http://cnettv.cnet.com/jobs-unveils-iphone-app-store/9742-1_53-32454.html

5 http://finance.yahoo.com/news/LIVE-APPLE-EARNINGS-siliconalley-917229125.html?x=0

6 Anderson, *Free*, p. 172.

7 http://uk.ign.com/articles/2012/07/18/the-ridiculous-launch-of-the-iphone-app-store

8 Ibid.

9 Ibid.

10 www.appchatter.com/2010/12/over-70-ea-games-on-sale-for-0-99/

11 http://authormichaelhicks.com/free-novel/

12 www.forbes.com/sites/karstenstrauss/2013/04/18/the-2-4-million-per-day-company-supercell/

4. EVERYTHING, JUST FOR YOU

1 www.ingentaconnect.com/content/maney/aaa/2008/00000005/00000002/art00003

2 http://depts.washington.edu/chinaciv/miltech/crossbow.htm

3 This and subsequent quotes are from Ford, *My Life and Work*, pp. 52–3.
4 www.wiley.com/legacy/products/subject/business/forbes/ford.html
5 http://people.duke.edu/~mccann/cpg/cg-chg.htm
6 http://media.ford.com/article_display.cfm?article_id=28558
7 www.starbucks.co.uk/menu/beverage-list/espresso-beverages
8 Sheena Iyengar, *The Art of Choosing* (Abacus, 2011), pp. 183–7.
9 Ibid., pp. 210–11.
10 http://iam.peteashton.com/keep-calm-rape-tshirt-amazon/
11 www.solidgoldbomb.com/pages/our-apology
12 www.kk.org/thetechnium/archives/2008/03/1000_true_fans.php
13 www.guardian.co.uk/commentisfree/2010/dec/20/christmas-show-one-nation-television?INTCMP=SRCH. The ratings figure is now disputed. ITV claims that it was 21 million while the *Guinness Book of Records* quotes 28 million.
14 http://en.wikipedia.org/wiki/100_Greatest_British_Television_Programmes
15 www.guardian.co.uk/media/2012/dec/12/most-viewed-tv-programmes-in-2012
16 Roger Lloyd, 'Is TV the New Rock?', *Los Angeles Times*, 30 December 2012.
17 www.techradar.com/news/mobile-computing/tablets/more-people-are-now-watching-iplayer-on-tablets-than-phones-1145613
18 http://jadensocial.com/gangnam-style-the-social-media-impact-of-a-viral-video/
19 www.guardian.co.uk/music/2012/nov/18/gangnam-style-psy?INTCMP=ILCNETTXT3487; interview with Jonathan Ross: www.youtube.com/watch?v=LPMG-Qvl-7E
20 http://ir.take2games.com/phoenix.zhtml?c=86428&p=irol-newsArticle&ID=1141120&highlight=
21 http://investor.activision.com/releasedetail.cfm?ReleaseID=425018
22 http://investor.activision.com/releasedetail.cfm?ReleaseID=531581
23 http://investor.activision.com/releasedetail.cfm?ReleaseID=624766
24 www.gamesbrief.com/2010/11/media-conglomerates-turn-their-backs-on-consoles/
25 Not all the stores were shut. A buyer was found for the rump of the business, which still operates: www.bbc.co.uk/news/business-17512143
26 http://articles.latimes.com/2009/mar/05/business/fi-cotown-thq5
27 www.latimes.com/entertainment/envelope/cotown/la-et-ct-thq-bankruptcy-20121219,0,156382.story
28 www.gamasutra.com/view/news/181343/Even_November_cant_save_US_game_retail_now.php

5. THE TYRANNY OF THE PHYSICAL

1 Nassim Nicholas Taleb, *The Black Swan* (Penguin, 2008), p. 231.
2 www.ons.gov.uk/ons/dcp171776_303450.pdf
3 www.telegraph.co.uk/finance/9233605/Sunday-Times-Rich-List-2012-Wealth-of-richest-grows-to-record-levels.html
4 www.census.gov/people/wealth/files/Wealth%20Highlights%202011.pdf
5 Bigpoint's most recent reported revenues were €200 million ($280 million) in 2010, but I don't have the detailed breakdown of their profitability before then. www.gamesbrief.com/2011/06/bigpoints-revenue-growth/
6 http://articles.latimes.com/2009/nov/18/business/fi-ct-duty18
7 http://blogs.independent.co.uk/2011/12/20/an-unsigned-act-for-the-christmas-number-1/
8 Interview with Alex Day, January 2013.
9 www.musicweek.com/news/read/chart-analysis-weekly-digital-album-sales-finally-break-million-mark/047677
10 www.officialcharts.com/chart-news/the-full-festive-2011-albums-and-singles-round-up/
11 www.nielsenbookscan.co.uk/uploads/press/NielsenBook_BookProduction Figures3_Jan2010.pdf
12 www.bowker.com/assets/downloads/products/isbn_output_2002-2011.pdf
13 www.bowker.com/en-US/aboutus/press_room/2012/pr_10242012.shtml
14 www.examiner.com/article/30-famous-authors-whose-works-were-rejected-repeatedly-and-sometimes-rudely-by-publishers
15 www.guardian.co.uk/politics/2010/aug/16/tony-blair-royal-british-legion
16 http://hypebot.com/hypebot/2012/11/offering-fans-a-consumer-experience-why-artists-should-sell-to-fans-and-let-labels-sell-to-consumers.html (A highly recommended read.)
17 www.nme.com/news/radiohead/66647

6. WHAT'S IT WORTH?

1 www.wired.com/gamelife/2012/11/meet-the-whales/all/
2 www.liverpoolfc.com/news/announcements/fa-cup-final-ticket-news
3 www.dailymail.co.uk/sport/football/article-2139428/FA-Cup-final-tickets-sold-black-market-10k.html
4 www.washingtonpost.com/wp-dyn/content/article/2007/04/04/AR2007 040401721.html?hpid=topnews

5 One busker blogged that perhaps Bell's problem is that he is a stage performer, not a busker. 'A busker is someone who can turn any place into a
stage . . . As a busker one needs to interact with those around, break walls
of personal space, and lure people into a collective and spontaneous
group experience on the street, in the moment, with you.' That is valid,
but doesn't alter the way in which the context matters. (www.subway
musicblog.com/busking/is-joshua-bell-a-good-busker/)

6 Dan Ariely, *Predictably Irrational* (HarperCollins, 2009), p. 24.

7 Ibid., pp. 31–6.

8 www.guardian.co.uk/music/2008/oct/16/radiohead-album-sales

9 http://paidcontent.org/2007/11/06/419-data-on-radiohead-experiment-
38-percent-of-downloaders-choose-to-pay/

10 http://news.cnet.com/8301-10784_3-9814155-7.html; www.wired.com/
listening_post/2007/12/thom-yorke-disc/

11 www.humblebundle.com/#contribute

12 www.gourmet.com/magazine/2000s/2004/08/shattered_myths

13 www.riedel.com/fileadmin/page_content/flip/sguide_en/files/assets/basic-
html/page13.html

14 http://scienceblogs.com/cortex/2007/11/02/the-subjectivity-of-wine/

15 www.gamesbrief.com/2011/11/bigpoint-sells-2000-spaceship-drones-for-
1000-euros-each-in-just-four-days/

7. FREELOADERS

1 www.pocketgamer.biz/r/PG.Biz/PapayaMobile+news/news.asp?c=42792

2 www.avc.com/a_vc/2006/03/my_favorite_bus.html

3 www.forbes.com/sites/jeffbercovici/2013/01/02/tumblr-david-karps-800-
million-art-project/

4 Ariely, *Predictably Irrational*, pp. 51–4.

5 http://appcubby.com/blog/the-sparrow-opportunity/

8. GAWKERS

1 www.guardian.co.uk/books/2009/aug/08/spent-geoffrey-miller-book-review

2 http://guynameddave.com/about-the-100-thing-challenge/

3 www.cjr.org/cover_story/steams_of_consciousness.php

4 Nick Wingfield, 'Virtual Products, Real Profits', *Wall Street Journal*,
9 September 2011.

5 www.nytimes.com/2010/09/07/business/media/07adco.html?_r=2&

6 www.nytimes.com/2009/11/07/technology/internet/07virtual.html?_r=1&

7 www.insidesocialgames.com/2010/12/24/cityville-passes-farmville-and-farmville-gets-a-chinese-language-version/

8 www.bbc.co.uk/news/entertainment-arts-20905931

9 I suspect that the figure is lower, since the 1 billion user statistic is for the number of users who logged into Facebook in the previous month, while the number of friend connections is a lifetime figure.

10 http://thesocietypages.org/cyborgology/2011/02/24/digital-dualism-versus-augmented-reality/

11 Jurgenson calls this 'mild augmented reality': http://thesocietypages.org/cyborgology/2012/10/29/strong-and-mild-digital-dualism/

12 www.businessweek.com/stories/2005-06-22/dude-wheres-my-digital-car

13 *Asahi Shimbun*, 'Nettojou no bunshinkyara "abataa": kisekaesakan', 'Dressing up: "avatar" online alter-egos', 23 February 2006, accessed via http://blog.hangame.co.jp/tapo/article/3441351/

9. SUPERFANS

1 http://blog.priceonomics.com/post/48216173465/the-business-of-phish

2 www.pollstarpro.com/files/charts2012/2012YearEndTop200NorthAmerican Tours.pdf

3 http://fallenlondon.storynexus.com/

4 www.kk.org/thetechnium/archives/2008/03/1000_true_fans.php

5 www.utsandiego.com/news/2011/sep/25/no-app-for-gratitude-ipads-will-have-to-do/

6 www.pocketgamer.biz/r/PG.Biz/NimbleBit+news/news.asp?c=37414

7 www.pocketgamer.biz/r/PG.Biz/NimbleBit+news/news.asp?c=23448

8 www.pocketgamer.biz/r/PG.Biz/NimbleBit+news/news.asp?c=26369

9 http://148apps.biz/app-store-metrics/?mpage=appcount

10 www.gamesbrief.com/2010/09/whales-infest-the-iphone-pocket-frog-proves-that-29-99-works/

11 www.tuaw.com/2010/09/20/NimbleBit-over-half-a-million-playing-pocket-frogs-3-4-buyi/

12 I estimated that *Tiny Tower* was on track to make $3 million in the first year. The company has told me that this is a conservative estimate. www.gamesbrief.com/2011/07/ios-tiny-tower-on-track-to-make-3-million-in-its-first-year/

13 www.abc.net.au/lateline/content/2012/s3592166.htm

10. THE POWER OF THE CROWD

1 www.doublefine.com/news/comments/twenty_years_only_a_few_tears/

2 www.scummbar.com/resources/articles/index.php?newssniffer=readarticle& article=1033

3 Ibid.

4 www.videogamesblogger.com/2007/11/06/grim-fandango-2-and-other-sequels-tim-schafer-would-love-to-make-but-he-prefers-to-create-new-games-like-brutal-legend.htm

5 www.kickstarter.com/projects/doublefine/double-fine-adventure

6 The Double Fine Kickstarter page can be found at www.kickstarter.com/projects/doublefine/double-fine-adventure

7 The number of pledges and revenue generated per tier in Figures 3 and 4 are lower than those reported as the total number of backers and amount raised by Kickstarter. There are two reasons: firstly, some backers choose to back a campaign but don't opt for any reward, which means they don't show up in any of the pledge tiers; secondly, backers can pledge any amount and opt for a reward tier that is below that amount – so, for example, someone could pledge $200 but select the $100 reward.

8 www.indiegogo.com/blog/2012/07/indiegogo-insight-perk-pricing-practices. html

9 http://investors.wmg.com/phoenix.zhtml?c=182480&p=irol-newsArticle_pf&ID=942828&highlight=

10 www.indiegogo.com/projects/ashens-and-the-quest-for-the-game-child

11 www.kickstarter.com/projects/freddiew/video-game-high-school

12 www.kickstarter.com/projects/freddiew/video-game-high-school-season-two

13 www.guardian.co.uk/music/appsblog/2013/feb/08/bjork-cancels-biophilia-kickstarter

11. MAKE-IT-YOURSELF

1 http://blog.jaggeree.com/post/42862389672/joining-the-dots-to-here-button-badges-from-my-youth

2 www.thesun.co.uk/sol/homepage/news/3995627/Boffins-spot-God-particle. html

3 www.forbes.com/sites/andygreenberg/2013/05/08/3d-printed-guns-blueprints-downloaded-100000-times-in-two-days-with-some-help-from-kim-dotcom/

4 Disclosure: I am an advisor to and have a small equity stake in Makielab.

5 www.youtube.com/watch?v=ZVUoMfTnZ8Y

6 www.tci-network.org/media/asset_publics/resources/000/000/980/
original/PLE_1_Enright.pdf

7 http://designbeyondtime.wordpress.com/design-icons/

8 http://sb.mybigcommerce.com/products/Juicy-Salif-Gold-Limited-Edition.
html

12. WE'RE ALL RETAILERS NOW

1 http://fwmedia.co.uk/about/

2 www.jameswoollam.com/vertical-publishing-and-the-search-for-the-holy-
grail/

3 http://harpers.org/blog/2013/01/googles-media-barons/

4 www.thebookseller.com/blogs/tangible-assets.html

5 www.telegraph.co.uk/culture/books/booknews/9584404/JK-Rowling-Casual-
Vacancy-tops-fiction-charts.html

6 http://blogs.wsj.com/speakeasy/2012/10/19/after-strong-start-j-k-rowlings-
the-casual-vacancy-falls-on-charts/

7 http://forums.moneysavingexpert.com/showthread.php?t=4201265

8 www.forbes.com/sites/jeffbercovici/2012/09/27/critics-not-charmed-by-j-k-
rowlings-casual-vacancy-will-readers-care/

9 http://steveblank.com/2010/01/25/whats-a-startup-first-principles/

10 http://techcrunch.com/2012/11/21/supercell/

11 www.forbes.com/sites/karstenstrauss/2013/04/17/is-this-the-fastest-growing-
game-company-ever/

12 www.fastcompany.com/50106/inside-mind-jeff-bezos

13 http://kinnon.tv/2010/10/steve-jobs-on-the-perfect-group-size.html

14 http://techcrunch.com/2010/08/04/google-wave-eric-schmidt/

15 http://pandodaily.com/2012/11/27/supercell-is-accels-fastest-growing-company-
ever-and-it-has-a-ball-pit/

16 www.imvu.com/about/faq.php

17 www.telegraph.co.uk/technology/news/8559744/Moshi-Monsters-hits-50-
million-members.html

18 www.develop-online.net/news/42713/Bigpoint-passes-300-million-registered-
users

19 www.veoc.org/kingarthurflour

20 www.bcorporation.net/blog/king-arthur-flour-a-company-built-to-last#.
UYpP5MphDo8

21 www.7dvt.com/2013when-kitchen-calamities-strike-king-arthur-flours-baking-
hotline-comes-rescue

13. HARNESSING THE CURVE

1 www.fiksu.com/resources/fiksu-indexes#loyal-index
2 http://thetrichordist.com/2013/02/08/music-streaming-math-will-it-all-add-up/
3 https://docs.google.com/spreadsheet/ccc?key=0AkasqHkVRM1OdEJFUnhyNFFkZjVSUWxhWGl1dE9lQXc#gid=3
4 http://craphound.com/walh/
5 www.theappside.com/2012/10/24/hairy-maclary-comes-to-ipad-with-17-book-apps-at-once/
6 Roger Lloyd, 'Is TV the New Rock?', *Los Angeles Times*, 30 December 2012.
7 www.guardian.co.uk/football/2006/sep/14/sport.comment1
8 www.guardian.co.uk/media/2012/jun/13/premier-league-tv-rights-3-billion-sky-bt
9 www.businessinsider.com/inside-andrew-sullivans-attempt-to-turn-the-digital-media-business-model-on-its-head-2013-4
10 www.theequitykicker.com/2013/05/23/building-businesses-around-passionate-communities-of-users/

Bibliography

Chris Anderson, *Free* (Random House Business Books, 2009)

—, *The Long Tail* (Random House Business Books, 2007)

—, *Makers* (Random House Business Books, 2012)

Dan Ariely, *Predictably Irrational* (HarperCollins, 2009)

Nicholas Carr, *The Shallows* (Atlantic Books, 2011)

Clay Christensen, *The Innovator's Dilemma* (Harvard Business School Press, 1997)

Robert Cialdini, *Influence: The Psychology of Persuasion* (First Collins Business Essentials, 2007)

Henry Ford, *Autobiography* (BN Publishing, 2009)

James Gilmore and Joseph Pine, *Authenticity* (Harvard Business School Press, 2007)

—, *The Experience Economy* (Harvard Business School Press, 1999)

Seth Godin, *Purple Cow* (Penguin, 2005)

—, *Tribes* (Piatkus, 2012)

William Goldman, *Adventures in the Screen Trade* (Abacus, 2001)

Tim Harford, *Adapt* (Little, Brown, 2011)

Sheena Iyengar, *The Art of Choosing* (Abacus, 2012)

Andrew Keen, *The Cult of the Amateur* (Nicholas Brealey, 2010)

Gunnar Knapp, Cathy A. Roheim and James L. Anderson, *The Great Salmon Run: Competition Between Wild and Farmed Salmon* (TRAFFIC North America/World Wildlife Fund, 2007); available at www.traffic.org/species-reports/traffic_species_fish25.pdf

Robert Levine, *Free Ride* (The Bodley Head, 2011)

Geoffrey Miller, *The Mating Mind* (Vintage 2001)

—, *Spent* (Penguin, 2010)

Evgeny Morozov, *The Net Delusion* (Penguin, 2012)

David A. Price, *The Pixar Touch* (Vintage Books, 2009)

Parke Puterbaugh, *Phish, The Biography* (Da Capo Press, 2010)

Eric Ries, *The Lean Startup* (Portfolio Penguin, 2011)

Chris Ruen, *Freeloading* (OR Books, 2012)

Clay Shirky, *Here Comes Everybody* (Penguin, 2009)

Nassim Nicholas Taleb, *The Black Swan* (Penguin, 2008)

Carol Tavris and Elliot Aronson, *Mistakes Were Made (But Not By Me)* (Pinter and Martin, 2008)

Mark Twain, *The Adventures of Tom Sawyer* [1876] (Kindle edition)

Thorstein Veblen, *The Theory of the Leisure Class* [1899] (Kindle edition)

Tim Wu, *The Master Switch* (Alfred Knopf, 2010)

Index

Page numbers of diagrams, etc., are given in italics.

about.com 170
Abramovich, Roman 207
abundance 22–3, 26–37, 46,
    78, 80, 159
Accel Partners 182
accountancy 204
Activision 62–3
Acton Smith, Michael 185
Adapt (Harford) 181
Adventures in the Screen Trade
    118, 177
airlines
  easyJet 214
  Jet Blue 214
  Ryanair 214
  South West Airlines 214
Alessi 7, 160–62
Amazon
  digital publishing 19, 21, 47–8,
      71, 108
  embracing the Curve 201
  filtering systems of 78
  lack of customer information
      173–6
  not a truly digital business
      124–5

recommendation engine of 57–8
and SEO 169
and UK price war 184
Amnesiac (Radiohead) 97
anchoring 95–8
Anderson, Chris 45, 69, 118, 157
Android (operating system)
    39–40, 108
Anheuser Busch 14
App Cubby 110–11, 136
App Store
  charts of 77, 80
  children's books 203
  concept of 40–43, 45, 46–9
  and freeloaders 108
  and games 77
  Pocket Frogs 132
  productivity apps 110
  and SEO 169
Apple 17, 38–43, 45, 47–8, 74, 111,
    132, 196–7
ArcelorMittal 67
Ariely, Dan 94–7, 99, 109–10, 115
ARPU (average revenue per user) 107
art 216
Ashen, Stuart 146–7

Assael, James 95
Authenticity (Gilmore/Pine) 56
avatars 122, 126
Aweber 33

Bachmann 153
'Bad Romance' (Lady Gaga) 27
Bala Lake Railway 152
Barnard, David 110–11
Basecamp 106
BBC 32, 59–60, 76
Bell, Joshua 94
Bertrand, Joseph 43–5
Bertrand competition model 43–5,
    47–9, 70, 126–7
Bezos, Jeff 182–3
Biggest Loser, The (TV programme)
    147
Bigpoint 63, 68, 102, 185
Biophilia (iOS app) 148
BitTorrent xi, 80, 156
Björk 84, 148–9
Blair, Tony 83
Blank, Steve 178–9
Bodyguard, The (theatre
    production) 206
Book of Heroes (game) 108
books 120, 172–4, 200–205
    children's 202
Bookscan 173
Bordeaux wine 99–100
bowerbirds 113
boxed sets 60–61, 206
Braben, David 145
Braff, Zach 147
Brisbourne, Nic 216
Britain's Got Talent (TV programme)
    59, 61
Brochet, Frédéric 100–101
Broken (Nine Inch Nails) x

Broken Sword (game) 145
BT 207
Burgundy Grand Cru wine 99–100
BuzzFeed 118

Call of Duty series (games) 62–3, 140
Captain O. M. Watts (chandlery) 104
Carter, Troy 29
Casual Vacancy, The (Rowling) 175
Cecil, Charles 145
Chaconne (Bach) 94
Channelflip 74, 147
charity 208–9
China 51
Christensen, Clay 16, 161
Chronicles of Syntax 148
Cialdini, Robert 115–16
Clancy, Tom 201
Clapton, Eric 212
Clash of Clans (game) 49, 89, 107,
    129, 133, 181–2, 192
Clerky 204
coaches 212
coffee 2, 11–13, 56, 110
Coleridge, Samuel Taylor 22
commodities 11, 115, 159
competition
    Bertrand model 43–5, 47–9,
        70, 126–7
    Cournot model 43–5
    and piracy xii, 1–2, 5, 7, 9–10,
        112, 150–51, 153, 156,
        160–63, 207–8
ComScore 97
containerization 35
Cournot, Antoine 43–5
Cournot competition model 43–5
Cowell, Simon 76
CRM systems 215
crossbows 51–2

crowd, the 137–50, 199, 206, 210
crowdfunding 84, 89, 136, 141,
    145–8, 199, 206, 210
    see also Indiegogo; Kickstarter
CSR Racing (game) 49, 135
curation 23, 77, 80, 168
Curve, the 4–5, 9, 107–8, 197,
    206–8
customer acquisition business 185
customer retention company 186
Customer Relationship
    Management (CRM) 4, 164
    systems 215

Daily Beast 209–10
Daily Telegraph (newspaper) 211
Damage (Hart) 17, 20, 22
Dangi, Chandra Bahadur 65–6, 190
DarkOrbit (game) 2, 68–9,
    102–3, 134
Darwin, Charles 13–14, 114
DataStream 31
DAUs 108, 186
Davis, Justin 46–7
Day, Alex 1, 72, 75–6, 79, 85,
    147–50, 195–6
Defense Distributed 154
Dell 56, 58
Design Rules for Free-to-Play
    Games (Fahey/Lovell) 173
Digital Chocolate 182
digital dualism 123–5
digital holism 125
digital manufacturing 10, 151,
    154–5, 157–8, 163
digital publishing 71
Digital Rights Management 7, 163
Digital Surveys 152
Dinorwic Quarry Slate wagon 153
Dish, The 209–10

'disruptive innovation'
    (Christensen) 16
Doctorow, Cory 173, 199
Dodd, Lynley 203
Double Fine Adventure (book/game)
    141–2, 142–3, 144–5, 150
Draeger's grocery store 56
drones 102
Dropbox 32–3

easyJet 214
ebooks 47–9, 108, 112, 169, 184,
    195, 200
Echo Bazaar (game) 129
ehow.com 170
Eidos 125
Eisenhower, President 180
Electronic Arts 45, 47, 108, 146
elephants 65–6
Elite (videogame) 145
Ellis, John 128
Environment Protection Agency 91
Etsy 106, 164
Experience Economy, The
    (Gilmore/Pine) 56
externality 33n, 110
Extremistan 67–9, 107

FA Cup Final 90, 207
F+W Media 168–9, 196
Facebook
    billion active users 121–4
    Björk 149
    and Farmville 122
    'Gangnam Style' 61–2
    getting new users 173
    Lady Gaga 29
    Victoria Vox 87
Fahey, Rob 173
Failbetter Games 129

Farmerama (game) 68
Farmville (game) 63, 119–20, 122–3
fashion 18, 216
Fernandes, Tony 207
Fifty Shades trilogy (James)
    63, 80, 109
Fighting Fantasy (Livingstone) 125
filesharing 1
filtering 77
fixed-action patterns 116
Flexiscale Company 153
flowers 122
Food and Drug Administration
    (FDA) 91
food production 35
Fooled by Randomness (Taleb) 65
football 90, 207–8
Forbes magazine 28, 32, 68,
    107, 175
Ford, Henry 6, 36, 52–4, 159
'Forever Yours' (Alex Day) 72–4
Fox, David 137–8
free
  App Store *see* App Store
  Ariely experiment 94–7, 99,
    109–10, 115
  freeloaders 104–13, 127, 165,
    176, 193, 195, 207
  games 10, 15, 41, 46, 63–4, 77,
    84–5, 102 105–7, 131–3, 135,
    192, 218
  power of it ix–xii, 2–5, 7–8, 25,
    27, 32–3, 41–3
  worth 87–103
Free Agent 204
'free-tard' 48
freemium model 33, 106
Fuller, Simon 76
fused deposition modelling
    (FDM) 155

GAME 63
Gameforge 63
games 45–9, 63–4, 68–9, 77, 84–5,
    104–7, 112, 117, 131–5, 173–5
GAMESbrief 85, 174
GameShadow 218
'Gangnam Style' (Psy) 61–2, 109
gatekeepers
  and Apple 41
  erosion of role of 158, 201
  and games 140–41
  and marketing 57, 150
  retail 166–9
  role of 20–23, 57, 72, 75–9, 81,
    83, 84, 86
Gates, Bill 68, 162
Gaussian distribution 65–8
gawkers 112, 113–27
Gayner, Justin 147
Gelblum, Ehud 40
Ghosts I–IV (Nine Inch Nails) xi–xii,
    4–6, 136, 162
Gilbert, Ron 140–42
Gilmore, James 56
Glazer, Malcolm 207
Goldman, William 118, 176–8,
    180–81
Google 17, 22, 28–9, 31, 39, 47, 74,
    169–71, 181–3, 212
Google AdWords 212
Grand Theft Auto IV (game) 62
Guardian (newspaper) 30, 211
Gunshine (game) 181

Hail to the Thief (Radiohead) 97
Hairy Maclary (Dodd) 203
handicap principle (Zahavi) 14,
    114, 117, 120, 190, 193
hard paywalls 211
Harford, Tim 181

Harper's (magazine) 170–71
harpers.org 171
Hart, Josephine 17, 19–20
Hauser, Fred 157–8
Hay Day (game) 49, 107,
    181–2, 192
Hay Literary Festival 18
Hearst, William Randolph 211
Hershey's Kisses chocolates 109–10
Hicks, Michael R. 47–8, 201
Hocking, Amanda 19–21, 79,
    147, 196
Homeland (Doctorow) 173
Hornby 153
How to Publish a Game (Lovell) 21, 81
Huberty, Katy 40
Hubertz, Heiko 102
Huddle 106
Hulman, Tony 152
Humble Bundle 98–9, 208

IAPs 111, 132, 134–5
IBM 17
Iger, Bob 63
IMDB 206
IMVU 178, 185
In Rainbows (Radiohead) 97
indie games 63
Indiegogo 145, 147, 199
*Influence: The Psychology of
    Persuasion* (Cialdini) 115
injection-moulding 157
Innovator's Dilemma (Christensen)
    16, 40, 161
Interscope Records x–xi, 26, 146
Interstate Highway System 55
iOS 39
iPads 39–40, 42
iPhones 39–42, 45–8, 83, 105, 111,
    130–32, 148, 194

iPlayer (BBC) 60
iPods 38–40, 47, 60
iTunes 28, 30, 40, 47, 60, 72, 195–7
Iyengar, Sheena 56–7, 77

Jaboulet Côtes du Rhône Parallèle
    45 (1998) wine 96
Jaboulet Hermitage La Chappelle
    (1996) wine 96
Jackson, Sharna 129
Jagex 63
Jam experiment (Iyengar) 56–7, 77
James, E. L. 76, 80
Jet Blue 214
Jillette, Penn *see* Penn and Teller
Jobs, Steve 38–42, 45–6, 183
Juicy Salif (lemon squeezer) 160–62
Jurgenson, Nathan 123–5

KartRider (game) 126–7
Keating, Zoe 198
Kelly, Kevin 58, 129–31, 134
Kennedy, Alexis 129
Kickstarter 3, 89, 141–2, 145–6,
    148, 150, 199, 200, 206
Kindle 19, 47–8, 82, 108, 118,
    130, 149, 184, 202
King Arthur Flour 187–8, 209
Kleiner Perkins Caufield Byers 40
Kongregate 63
Koster, Bart ix–x

Lady Gaga 26–30, 27, 185, 197
law 204–5
Lean Startup movement 180
Lean Startup, The (Ries) 178
Lee (gamer) 89–90
Legal Zoom 204
Liberator (handgun) 154–5
Lindt truffles 109–10

Liverpool Football Club 90
Livingstone, Ian 125–6
Lloyd, Roger 60, 206
London Venture Partners 182
Lucas, George 137
LucasArts 140, 146
Lucasfilm 138–9

MacArthur, John 170–71
McCann, John M. 54–5
magazine publishers 190
Majesco 146
Makerbot Replicator 2 (3D printer) 155, 160–61
Makers (Anderson) 157
Makielab 155–6
Maling, battle of 51
marginal cost 45, 47, 49, 70, 126–7, 193, 201
marketing
  advertising 105–7
  agencies 6–7
  building demand 82
  discipline of 1
  freeloaders 108
  gatekeepers 57, 149
  mass *see* mass marketing
  sales 1
  as a separate discipline 172
Marsh, Ian and David 131
mass marketing
  concept xii, 3, 5–7
  end of dominance of 10, 50, 55–7, 61, 64, 219
  erosion of gatekeeper 84
  and true fans 129
Masterchef (TV programme) 147
Matrix, The 123
Mattel 155, 157
MAUs 108, 186

mean (arithmetical) 65–7
measurement 184–6
median (arithmetical) 66–9, 71
Mediocristan 65–8, 72, 105, 107
Meeker, Mary 39–40
Merlin (TV programme) 147
metrics *see* measurement
microbrew beer 14
Microsoft 17, 21, 39–40, 68, 162
Miller, Claire Cain 119
Miller, Geoffrey 14, 114–17, 121
milling 187
Mittal, Lakshmi 67
mode (arithmetical) 66–8, 135
Model T Ford 53–4, 159
monetization 186
Montreux 189
Moore's Law 155
Morecambe and Wise Show, The (TV programme) 58–9, 61
Morgan Grenfell 30–31
Morgan Stanley 40
Moshi Monsters 185
movie industry 205
MP3 players 61
Murdoch, Elizabeth 147
MySpace 87

Naked Wines 215
National Resources Defense Council 91
natural selection 13
NaturalMotion 49, 135
Netflix 58, 60
New Star Soccer (game) 134–5
New Statesman (periodical) 210
Newell, Gabe 183
newspapers 55, 119, 152, 207, 209–11
Nexon 126

NimbleBit 131–4, 190, 196
Nine Inch Nails ix–xi, 4–6, 85, 90
Nintendo DS 45
NPD market research 63

obesity 35
Official Charts Company 72–3
Olsen, Elisabeth 119
On the Origin of Species
    (Darwin) 13
*1,227 QI Facts To Blow Your
    Socks Off* (Lloyd/
    Mitchinson) 108
Oxford University Press 203

Paananen, Ilkka 181–3
Palmer, Amanda 84, 144–6,
    149–50, 200
Papaya 106
Pareto principle 69
pay-what-you-want strategy 98
paymium business model 111
PC games 117, 183
Pearl King 95
Penn and Teller 90–94, 98
Penn & Teller: Bullshit
    (TV programme) 91
Penrhyn Quarry 152–3
Peretti, Jonah 118
Phish 23, 128
Pine, Joseph 56, 220
piracy xii, 1–2, 5, 7, 9–10, 112,
    150–51, 153, 156, 160–63,
    207–8
Pirate Bay, The xi, 156, 164
PlayStation 2, 32, 63
PledgeMusic 85, 89
Pocket Frogs (game) 131–4, *133*
'Poker Face' (Lady Gaga) 27–8
Portfolio 81–3

Pratchett, Terry 201
Predictably Irrational (Ariely) 95
Prelec, Drazen 96
Pretty Hate Machine (Nine Inch
    Nails) ix–x
Psy 61–2
publishing 18–22, 71, 76, 79, 82,
    146–7, 150, 169, 173, 201, 205
Puffin Books 203–4

Q-play 126
Qin Shi Huang, Emperor 51–2
Quantcast 107
QuarkXPress 20
Quiz Quiz see Q-play

Radiohead 97–8, 128
Rainmaster (automatic sprinkler
    system) 157–8
Read, Simon 134–5
Recherches (Cournot) 43
recycling 33
registered users 185
Reil, Torsten 135
restaurants 92, 213
retail 215–16
Reznor, Trent ix–xii, 4–6, 85, 90,
    136, 146, 162, 190
Riedel (wine-glass makers) 99–101
Ries, Eric 178, 185
risk 70–72, 76, 78–9, 82–4, 140–41,
    177, 181–3
River Pools and Spas 24–5, 188, 209
Roadrunner Records 144, 146
Rogers, Benji 85
Rowling, J. K. 185–6, 201
Ryanair 214

Saatchi, Maurice 17
salmon fishing 34

Sands, Frank 187
Santa hats 126–7
scarcity 5, 14, 22, 26–37, 46, 58, 80, 164
Schafer, Tim 137–42, 145–6, 149
Schmidt, Eric 183
Schumpeter, Joseph 16
Scoops (game) 131
Sculpteo 152
Seafight (game) 68
Secret of Monkey Island, The (game) 139–40
Sega 45
self-publishing 147, 173, 201
SEO (search engine optimization) 169–71
sexual selection 13–14, 114–15, 121
Sheridan, Marcus 24–5, 171, 188, 209
Shine Group 74, 147, 181, 206
Simon, Herbert 36
Sky 207
slush piles 17–20, 79
Smashwords 47, 71, 82
soap operas 55
social networking 121
soccer *see* football
Solid Gold Bomb 58
Sony 2, 48, 108, 184
SouthWest Airlines 214
Spotify 2, 28–30, 80, 185, 197–8, 200
Staples 163
Starbucks 12–13, 56
Starck, Philippe 160–61
startups 46, 178
status symbols 102–3, 115, 117–18, 120–21, 162, 164
Steam 63, 119, 141–2, 168, 182, 196–7

Stone, Brad 119
Stratasys Dimension SST (3D printer) 155
'Stupid, Stupid' (Alex Day) 75
subscription businesses 107
Sullivan, Andrew 209–10
Sumea 182
Supercell 49, 89, 107, 181–3
superfans xii 2, 8, 75, 90, 128–36, 156, 165, 193–6, 198–201, 210, 219

Take-Two Interactive 62
Talbot, Martin 73
Taleb, Nassim Nicholas 65–6, 118
Tatchell, Terri 19
Taylor, Alice 155–6
television 55, 59–61, 205–7
free-to-air 105, 205
Teller *see* Penn and Teller
Theatre Is Evil (Amanda Palmer) 144
Theory of the Leisure Class, The (Veblen) 115
Thingiverse 153, 158–60, 164
Thorpe, Chris 152–4
THQ 63
3D printing 7, 10, 36, 49, 152–5, 157–64, 178–9, 218
time-shifting 60–61, 109
Timer (app) 111
Tiny Tower (game) 134
trainers *see* coaches
transport 55, 199, 214–15
Trichordist 197
'True Fans' 10, 29, 129–31, 134
see also superfans
Tumblr 77, 106–8, 173
TVT x, 146

Twain, Mark 101–2
Twitter
  Björk 149
  getting new users 173
  Lady Gaga 26–7
  Victoria Vox 87
  'water-cooler' usage 124
tyranny of the physical
  constrained by 177
  definition/understanding of 65–86
  ending of xii, 3, 64, 131, 158,
    168, 184, 219

Ultimate bundle (IAP) 111
Universal Music x, 146

validated learning 180–81, 219
value
  ascribing 94–8
  Bertrand model 44
  changing world 167, 169–70,
    172, 176, 191–2, 194,
    199–200, 207, 218–20
  created by context 97–8
  the crowd 143–6, 150
  customization 56, 58
  and freeloaders 106–12
  gawkers 115–26
  hard to pin down 86
  nebulous concept 90
  perception of 115
  publishers 81–2
  and scarcity/abundance 30–31,
    35–6
  social/emotional bond 159
  understanding/status of 1–21, 25
Valve 182–3
vanity metrics 185
variable pricing xii, 33, 107
Veblen, Thorstein 115–16, 120

Venan Entertainment 107–8
Victor, Ed 17–18
Video Game High School (web TV
  series) 148
vinyl LPs xii, 120, 144–5
virtual goods 49, 63, 119–23,
  126–7, 135, 185
Vox, Victoria 87–9, 91, 129,
  136, 148

Wadlow, Robert Pershing 65–6, 190
Warring States Period 51
water
  bottled 33, 91–4, 104
  'L'Eau du Robinet' 92
Wilkin & Sons 56
Williams, David 51–2
Wilson, Cody 154
Wilson, Eric 91
Wilson, Fred 106
Windows operating system 39
wine
  Bordeaux 99–100
  Burgundy Grand Cru 99–100
  Jaboulet Côtes du Rhône Parallèle
    45 (1998) 96
  Jaboulet Hermitage La Chappelle
    (1996) 96
Wingfield, Nick 118
Winifred (steam engine) 152–4
Winston, Harry 95
Wish I Was Here (film) 147
With a Little Help (Doctorow) 199
Wong, Freddie 148
Woollam, James 168–9, 172, 196
word-of-mouth 108–9
World Vision 72

X Factor, The 64, 72, 189
Xbox 63, 71, 119

Year Zero (Nine Inch Nails) x–xi
Yique, battle of 51
Young, Thomas 22
YouTube
  Alex Day 2, 72, 149, 195
  Ashens 146
  Freddie Wong 148
  'Gangnam Style' 61–2, 109

  importance as a discovery
    tool 173
  Lady Gaga 26–30

Zahavi, Amotz 14, 113–14
Zhao Zing 51
Zwerdling, Daniel 99, 101
Zynga Inc. 106, 118–19, 122–3